THE
PERFECTION
OF
SOLITUDE

Andrew Jotischky

THE PERFECTION OF SOLITUDE

Hermits and Monks
in the
Crusader States

The Pennsylvania State University Press
University Park, Pennsylvania

Library of Congress Cataloging-in-Publication Data

Jotischky, Andrew, 1965–
    The perfection of solitude : hermits and monks in the Crusader
States / Andrew Jotischky.
        p.   cm.
    Includes bibliographical references and index.
    ISBN 0-271-01346-X (alk. paper)
    1. Monasticism and religious orders—Palestine—History—Middle
Ages, 600–1500.   2. Monasticism and religious orders—Syria—
History—Middle Ages, 600–1500. 3. Monasticism and religious life—
History—Middle Ages, 600–1500.   4. Carmelites—History.
I. Title.
BX2690.J68   1995
271′.0095694′0902—dc20   94-12641
                                                          CIP

Published by The Pennsylvania State University Press,
University Park, PA 16802-1003

It is the policy of The Pennsylvania State University Press to use acid-free paper for
the first printing of all clothbound books. Publications on uncoated stock satisfy the
minimum requirements of American National Standard for Information Sciences—
Permanence of Paper for Printed Library Materials, ANSI Z39.48–1984.

For Caroline

Contents

List of Illustrations

Maps

Figures

Preface

One of the most prominent ecclesiastical figures of the thirteenth century, Jacques de Vitry, arrived to take up his appointment as bishop of Acre in the Latin kingdom of Jerusalem in November 1216. He was scandalized by what he found: the condition and standards of the local church fell far below his expectations. He had, perhaps, expected too much of the Frankish settlers in the Holy Land. His generation seemed to contrast poorly with the heroes who had captured Jerusalem in 1099 and had founded a Christian protectorate over the holy places. Describing this original settlement, Jacques wrote warmly of a "garden of delights" abounding in monasteries, churches, and the grottoes of hermits. The church in the Latin East, however, encountered serious problems in tending and nurturing this garden. The monastic culture that emerged between 1099 and 1291—the subject of this book—was a hybrid plant growing in alien soil. It was a combination of elements of traditional Benedictine monasticism and the "unofficial" reform monasticism spreading throughout the West at the time of the First Crusade. In addition, it became subject to the influences of indigenous Greek and Eastern Orthodox monastic traditions at the very time that relations between the Latin and Greek churches in Rome and Constantinople were declining to their lowest point. This book examines the character of the Latin Church in the crusader states by studying individuals drawn to the monastic or eremitical life in places regarded as holy by association with biblical narrative or Christian tradition.

I have attempted to bridge two worlds: the Western Middle Ages of the twelfth and thirteenth centuries, and the Latin society established in the Near East in the wake of the First Crusade. In describing this Latin society, I refer to the "crusader states" or to the "Latin East." In both cases, this means the kingdom of Jerusalem, the County of Tripoli, the Principality of

Antioch, and, until 1144, the County of Edessa. The institutions of the crusader states have been subjected to increasingly sophisticated analysis in recent years. We now know a great deal about the crown and the feudal hierarchy in the kingdom of Jerusalem in theory and practice,[1] about the origins of crusader law, and about the military resources of the kingdom and the status of the Muslims and Jews under crusader rule.[2] Archaeological research has advanced our understanding of the Frankish settlement of the hinterland of the kingdom, and the architecture, sculpture, and interior decoration of crusader churches is becoming ever clearer.[3]

Relatively little has been done, however, to amplify Bernard Hamilton's work on the institutional church.[4] In particular, the monastic culture of the Latin East has been illuminated only by narrow shafts of light. For the most part, we rely still on the cartularies of a few great abbeys, published in the late nineteenth century. By contrast, the various forms of monastic life in the West, where there is a wealth of surviving evidence from the eleventh to the thirteenth centuries, have been consistently in the forefront of scholarly research. Hermits, with whom the history of monasticism may be said to have begun, are ever popular subjects of study. The conclusions reached by historians who, like Henrietta Leyser, have shown the importance of eremitical inspirations for the burgeoning monastic reform movement of the period circa 1050–1200 have not yet been applied to the Latin East.[5] By using recently discovered evidence from the kingdom of Jerusalem that seems to complement the direction of research into Western monasticism, this book allows the results of recent scholarship on Western monasticism to be put to the test for a different but dependent society—the crusader

1. E.g., J. Prawer, *Crusader Institutions* (Oxford, 1980); S. Tibble, *Monarchy and Lordships in the Latin Kingdom of Jerusalem, 1099–1291* (Oxford, 1989).

2. Prawer, *Crusader Institutions*; C. Marshall, *Crusader Warfare, 1187–1291* (Cambridge, 1992); Prawer, *The History of the Jews in the Latin Kingdom of Jerusalem* (Oxford, 1988); B. Z. Kedar, "The Subjected Muslims of the Frankish Levant," in J. M. Powell, ed., *Muslims Under Latin Rule* (Princeton, 1990), 135–75.

3. Among many such works, see D. Pringle, *The Churches of the Crusader Kingdom of Jerusalem: A Corpus*, vol. 1 (Cambridge, 1992); and J. Folda, ed., *Crusader Art in the Twelfth Century* (Jerusalem, 1982). All these topics have been the subject of detailed studies in the published papers of the Society for the Study of the Crusades and the Latin East: P. W. Edbury, ed., *Crusade and Settlement* (Cardiff, 1985); B. Z. Kedar, ed., *The Horns of Hattin* (Jerusalem, 1992).

4. B. Hamilton, *The Latin Church in the Crusader States: The Secular Church* (London, 1980). See also H. E. Mayer, *Bistümer, Klöster, und Stifte in Königsreich Jerusalem*, Schriften der MGH 26 (Stuttgart, 1977).

5. H. Leyser, *Hermits and the New Monasticism* (New York, 1984).

states. It will enhance still further our knowledge of crusader society and of the institutional history of the Latin East. Monasticism in its various forms was the most important expression of the Christian life in the period covered by this book, and the Holy Land was the focus of the military and spiritual aspirations of Christians. The time to study both phenomena together is long overdue.

This book starts with a paradox. People were drawn to the monastic life (in its broadest sense) in the Latin East because of the spiritual benefits of living in the Holy Land. However, two leading monastic reformers in the West, Bernard of Clairvaux and Peter the Venerable, tried to minimize the importance of such benefits. They regarded monastic involvement in the Holy Land with suspicion because it undercut the value of the monastic life in general, which, with its emphasis on the cloister as the representation of Paradise, obviated the need for special holy places. The physical sites of the Holy Land threatened the whole theory of monasticism. The main subjects of this book represent a universal majority culture acting in opposition to, or in ignorance of, the main currents of thought expressed by some of the leading ecclesiastical thinkers of the day.

The hermits and monks discussed in Chapter 1 are ghostly figures glimpsed in the surviving fragments of a work by a twelfth-century Latin bishop in Syria, Gerard of Nazareth. Enough of their lives can be reconstructed to make comparisons with representatives of eremitical monasticism in the West. We are thus able to see the characteristic features of the reform monasticism of the West as it developed between around 1050 and 1130 and was transported to the East. The hermits described in the twelfth century by Gerard of Nazareth were succeeded by a community that, by the 1220s, had come to be known as the hermits of Mount Carmel. The origins of the eremitical foundations that became the Order of Mount Carmel, when examined in detail, provide us with a case study for the reception and development of monastic traditions in the Latin East. The fate of the Order founded from the scattered communities on Mount Carmel was to move away from its eremitical origins to become, by the middle of the thirteenth century, an order of mendicant friars. In thus conforming to the new directions in the spiritual life of the church, the Carmelites become for the historian a paradigm of Latin monasticism not just in the crusader states but also in Europe as a whole.

An added tension is present in the lives of Frankish hermits in the East. These pioneers found they were tapping the same reserves of spiritual power as the indigenous monks, and in some cases even settling at the same holy places. Were the Franks, after all, conforming to Western practices, or did they borrow new elements from Eastern traditions and incorporate them into the communities they founded? The revival of Orthodox monasticism is examined here both in terms of the restoration of Byzantine monasteries in the twelfth century and in terms of the continuing presence of early Christian monastic practices in traditional eremitical sites in the Holy Land. We shall see that despite opportunities for extensive contact with Orthodox monks, which are best exemplified by the mixed communities of hermits on Mount Carmel, Latin foundations were never fully integrated into the traditions of the indigenous monasticism of the Holy Land. By the end of Latin rule in the East, in 1291, all the reforming communities of the twelfth century had been either abandoned or absorbed into international orders. The autonomy enjoyed by Orthodox foundations or individual Orthodox hermits flowered only briefly in Latin monasteries.

A book that began as a doctoral dissertation has by definition undergone a series of metamorphoses and incurred a number of debts in each. I trust that those whom space does not permit me to thank by name, especially the graduate colleagues at Yale University from whose conversation and example I benefited at an early stage of research, will forgive the omission. This work could never have been begun without the clear direction and warm enthusiasm of John Boswell, nor would it have been completed without his continuing support. The care and encouragement for her students of Ingeborg Glier is well known to those fortunate to have known her as Director of Medieval Studies at Yale. An earlier, all-encompassing debt is due to Hugh Mead, who introduced me to the medieval church before I had any idea where such introductions might lead. I hope he will take pride in this product of his fine and sensitive teaching. I have been touched by the interest shown in my work by a number of scholars: I would like to thank especially Christopher Brooke, Giles Constable, Bernard Hamilton, and Benjamin Kedar for their suggestions and comments on the text at various stages of writing. Peter J. Potter of Penn State Press has been a supportive and skillful editor whose insights have been invaluable. The staff of the Sterling Memorial Library at Yale, the Bodleian Library, the Cambridge University Library, the British Library, the John Rylands University Library of Manchester, and the British School of Archaeology in Jerusalem have been helpful and generous with their time throughout the research and writing of this book. The Woodrow Wilson National Fellowship Foundation kindly awarded me a Charlotte E. Newcombe Dissertation Fellowship for the year 1990–1991, and the generosity of the Seven Pillars of Wisdom

Trust enabled me to see and study firsthand most of the sites described, and to illustrate the book with photographs. Thanks are also due to the photographers at the History of Art Department of the University of Manchester, Peter Burton and Michael Pollard, for their expertise, and to Andrew Fairhurst, for his help with the maps.

Not all the support given to historians is financial or scholarly. I would like to thank Jeffrey Denton and the Department of History at the University of Manchester for the warmth of their welcome; Paul Binski, Paul Fisher, Toby Macklin, Christopher Marsh, and Katie Marsh, Victoria Mora, Harry Mount, David Phillips, Athene Reiss, Andrew Wareham, and Patrick Zutshi for their judgment in knowing when to provide academic guidance and when to distract me from what might have become an eremitical existence. The greatest debts are the most intimate. My brothers and sister have put up with the demands of an obsessive medievalist over the years with patience and good humor. My parents have been a constant source of support of every kind, and their unwavering faith in me has been inspirational. Finally, the dedication to Caroline Hull reflects a debt, scholarly and personal, so profound as to amount to a share in authorship.

Abbreviations

AASS	*Acta Sanctorum Bollandiana.* Ed. Société des Bollandistes. 3d ed. 62 vols. Brussels, 1863–1948.
CCSL	*Corpus Christianorum, Series Latina.* Turnhout: Brepols, 1953–.
CCCM	*Corpus Christianorum, Continuatio Medievalis.* Turnhout: Brepols, 1966–.
MGH	*Monumenta Germaniae historica inde ab anno Christi quingentesimo usque ad annum millesimum et quingentesimum auspiciis societatis aperiendis fontibus rerum germanicarum medii aevi,* ed. G. H. Pertz et al. Hanover, 1826–.
MGH SS	*MGH Scriptores.*
PAM	Palestine Archaeological Museum. Archives of the Department of Antiquities of Palestine. 1914–48.
PG	*Patrologiae cursus completus. Series graeco-latina.* Ed. J.-P. Migne. 161 vols. Paris, 1857–66.
PL	*Patrologiae cursus completus. Series latina.* Ed. J.-P. Migne. 221 vols. Paris, 1844–64.
PO	*Patrologia Orientalis.* Ed. R. Graffin and F. Nau. Paris: Firmin Didot, 1907–.
PPTS	*Palestine Pilgrims Texts Society Library.* 13 vols. London, 1890–97.
RHC	*Recueil des historiens des croisades.* Ed. Academie des Inscriptions et Belles-Lettres. 16 vols. Paris, 1841–1906.

RHC Arm.	*RHC. Documents Arméniens.* 2 vols.
RHC Lois	*RHC. Les Assises de Jérusalem.* 2 vols.
RHC Occ.	*RHC. Historiens Occidentaux.* 5 vols.
William of Tyre	*Willelmi Tyrensis Archiepiscopi Chronicon.* Ed. R.B.C. Huygens. *CCCM* 63 (1986).

Introduction: Monks and Jerusalem

The medieval church was perpetually wary of clergy on the move. The Council of Chalcedon's legislation against itinerant clergy performing religious duties outside their dioceses, repeated periodically in legal compilations, found more eloquent expression in Benedict's distrust of wandering monks—the detestable "sarabaites" who lived in small, self-regulating groups wherever they pleased, with no superior to guide them—and, even worse, of the "gyrovagues," who drifted from one monastery to the next, feeding their gross appetites.[1] In eleventh- and twelfth-century Europe, Benedict would have found outside their monasteries or hermitages not

---

1. J. D. Mansi, *Sacrorum conciliorum . . . nova collectio* (Venice, 1759), 7:394–95; *Sancti Benedicti regula monachorum: Textus ad fidem cod. Sangall. 914*, vol. 1, ed. P. Schmitz (Brussels, 1949), 7–8.

only vagabond monks conforming to his picture of "gyrovagues" and "sarabaites," but also perfectly respectable monks from important monasteries, among them the abbots Richard of Saint Vannes, Gervin of Saint Riquier, Thierry of Saint Evroul, Ulric of Cluny, Leonius of Saint Bertin, and Poppon of Stavelot. Between the 1020s and the 1080s these all made pilgrimages to the Holy Sepulcher and escaped official censure.

In 1124, however, a proposed monastic pilgrimage to Jerusalem caused a crisis in the new Cistercian Order. The Chapter-General discussed at length the case of Arnold, abbot of Morimond, who had set off for Jerusalem with some of his monks, and concluded with a strict condemnation of the errant abbot.[2] The controversy can be followed more closely in the correspondence of Bernard of Clairvaux, who took a characteristically outspoken stance. In December 1124 Bernard wrote to Arnold, begging him to consider the "great ruin" he would cause by carrying out his proposed pilgrimage. He accused the abbot of deserting his flock. Who would now resist the assault of the hungry wolf who thrived on tribulation and discord in the cloister?[3] By leaving for Jerusalem without permission, Arnold was disobeying the statutes of the Order; he should have consulted his own brethren and his fellow abbots, especially the abbot of Cîteaux. As it was, he was threatening the principle of unity enshrined in the *Carta caritatis*.

As if this were not enough, Arnold was making matters worse by taking his own monks with him, and thereby corrupting them. This, to Bernard, was inexcusable no matter how one looked at it. Had he taken experienced and mature monks, he would have been guilty of leaving the abbey perilously exposed, but the young and vulnerable monks he had persuaded to accompany him were not yet ready for such a journey, and by taking them he was endangering their vows.

Bernard was not content to let the matter rest by chastising Arnold himself. He mobilized support for his position by asking the pope to intervene, warning him somewhat dramatically that Arnold's pilgrimage might lead to the destruction of the Order.[4] At the same time, he described

---

2. J.-M. Canivez, ed., *Statuta capitulorum generalium ordinis Cisterciensis, 1116–1786*, 2 vols. (Louvain, 1933–41), 1:4–5.

3. *S. Bernardi opera*, ed. J. Leclercq, H. Rochais, and C. H. Talbot, 8 vols. (Rome, 1957–), 7:24–27, Ep. 4. ". . . Non metuis magnam ruente te mox procul dubio ruinam secuturam?"

4. Ibid., 8:305, Ep. 359. "Qua in re si quem ei, quod absit, assensum praebueritis, ipse perpendite quantae possit nostro Ordini esse destructionis occasio, cum exemplo huius, quicumque abbas pastorali se sentiet sarcina gravatum, mox illam abiciat, utpote quam se licite posse abicere arbitretur."

Arnold's behavior in a letter to Bruno of Cologne as "a grave scandal for the whole Order," comparing Arnold to a secular lord because he had made such a decision without proper consultation.[5] Again, he spoke of the danger of "seducing" his companions—Evrardus and Adam, monks of Morimond, and Conrad of Welf, a hermit—by taking them along. In December 1124 Bernard wrote to the monk Adam, reminding him of his oath to remain in the cloister.[6]

Arnold of Morimond died before reaching Jerusalem, perhaps averting the worst of the crisis. Soon after his death, Bernard wrote a second letter to Adam, long and paternal in tone, appealing to him to return before he tore apart the unity of the Order and broke the "bonds of peace." Now that Arnold was dead, he argued, Adam had no filial obligation to continue the pilgrimage.[7] Here Bernard showed his sensitivity to the young monk's conflict of loyalties, but he maintained that he had erred in following a human command—Arnold's—rather than a divine command. It was no use his seeking a license or dispensation to continue (as Adam seems to have proposed). Where would such a license come from? How could something illegal be licensed?[8] It might seem noble to follow a command blindly—as, for example, Saint Anthony had done—but one should first consider whether the command came from God. Would Adam, Bernard taunts, plunge a sword into his own throat if ordered?[9] The letter ends with an exposition on the virtue of stability, and the insistence that this be a permanent and inviolable rule for all monks.[10]

The case of Arnold of Morimond is a salutary reminder of the suspicions under which all pilgrimages, and sometimes pilgrims themselves, could be held. More important, however, is that it exposes the different expectations and standards required of monks as opposed to those living in the world, and the difficult role played by Jerusalem in the spiritual lives of "Regular" clergy (i.e., clergy who lived according to a specific Rule, as opposed to ordinary clergy). Pilgrimages could be helpful to lay people, if undertaken in a spirit of piety and penance rather than mere adventure, but for monks, they were unnecessary and served only to distract them from their proper vocation.

In a letter to Marquis Rainier, the eleventh-century monastic reformer

5. Ibid., 7:30, Ep. 6.
6. Ibid., 7:28, Ep. 6.
7. Ibid., 7:31–32, Ep. 7.
8. Ibid., 7:36–37, Ep. 7.
9. Ibid., 7:40, Ep. 7.
10. Ibid., 7:42–43, Ep. 7.

Peter Damian enumerated the advantages of the pilgrimage for a man of the world, not least of which was the possibility of obtaining a miraculous cure. Rainier's pilgrimage would be a spiritual exile, in the accomplishment of which he would find a true home.[11] But monks, canons, and anyone who lived according to a specific Rule were prohibited from making the pilgrimage. They had found their home when they entered the cloister and took their vows of stability. Any kind of travel, other than a journey on the monastery's business, was an infringement of the vow of stability. This was only the most obvious facet of a still deeper problem. To make the pilgrimage to the earthly Jerusalem was to deny, or to fail to comprehend, that the cloister was as close as the monk could come to the heavenly Jerusalem. Arnold of Morimond incurred Bernard's wrath because, in choosing the earthly Jerusalem above the heavenly, he exposed a horrifying lack of understanding of the nature of the monastic vocation.

I have chosen to introduce this book with the example of the luckless Arnold because pilgrimage to Jerusalem and monastic or eremitical settlement in the Holy Land are branches of the same tree. The earliest pilgrims were trying to provide tangible and fixed points of reference for their faith. By seeing for themselves the places described in the Old and New Testaments, by traveling on the same roads as the Children of Israel or the apostles, they could endow the narrative of their religious heritage with visual memories. More profound, from the fourth century onward pilgrims began to express their sensual or emotional experience of such journeys in terms of devotion to places or pieces of land where events had happened: the place where God gave the Law to Moses; the places where Jesus called Peter and Andrew or performed miracles of healing; and, most important of all, the places of Jesus' birth and crucifixion.[12] Men and women who chose the cloister or wilderness in the Holy Land, whether they were native to the East or not, were simply making such a pilgrimage permanent.

The development of the idea of a holy or sacred place is a subject both too broad and too deep for this study, but it forms the intellectual background. The material assembled here shelters under the umbrella of what

11. Peter Damian, *Epistolae* 7.17, *PL* 144:456. "And thus the upset of travel will result in peace, and wandering from your country a home."

12. On medieval pilgrimage in general, see J. Sumption, *Pilgrimage: An Image of Medieval Religion* (London, 1975). On the early Christian pilgrims, see E. D. Hunt, *Holy Land Pilgrimage in the Later Roman Empire, 312–460* (Oxford, 1982); and M. B. Campbell, *The Witness and the Other World* (Ithaca, 1988), 15–47.

the historical geographer J. K. Wright called "geopiety."[13] Attachment to the places where Jesus and the apostles lived became one of the most tangible features of medieval Christianity. It is tempting to see this phenomenon as an example of the model of religious anthropology erected by David Hume in his essay *The Natural History of Religion*. There was, Hume argued, a natural flux and reflux in the human mind from the principles of "idolatry" to "theism" and back again.[14] Devotion to "holy places," the cult of relics of the saints to which such devotion is inextricably linked, and the belief in miracles are all features of what Hume characterized as Christian idolatry. Disapproval of pilgrimages to the Holy Land expressed by, for example, Saint Jerome in the fourth century, appears at first sight to conform to such a model, in which the intellectual few, understanding the essential principles of religious faith, stand opposed to the masses for whom religion must be visibly operative: Newman's "religion of the multitude . . . tinctured with fanaticism and corruption."[15]

The reality is more complex. Jerome himself emigrated to the Holy Land and lived in a cave in Bethlehem, from where he fostered by correspondence a succession of pilgrimages by educated and noble Roman ladies.[16] If the idea of a specific place being holy by virtue of past associations, and thus conferring some degree of spiritual benefit on those who traveled there in order to stand on "holy ground," found easy purchase on the faith of the uneducated masses, it is nevertheless from the highly articulate accounts of the pilgrimages of educated men and women of late antiquity and the Middle Ages that our knowledge of such strands of "popular religion" is derived. Monks, the most educated of all medieval people, knew perfectly well that the sight of Calvary or the Grotto of the Nativity was no guarantee of spiritual perfection, yet they continued to make pilgrimages to Jerusalem. Even today the streets of the Old City are thronged at Easter time with groups of parish priests from all over the world leading parties of pilgrims to pray at the holy sites. The intellectuals and the masses cannot, in the Middle Ages at least, be so easily separated.

13. J. K. Wright, "Notes on Early American Geopiety," in his *Human Nature in Geography* (Cambridge, Mass., 1966), 250–85. This subject is treated more fully in my final chapter, below.

14. David Hume, "The Natural History of Religion VIII," in *Essays: Moral, Political, and Literary*, vol. 2 (London, 1875), 334.

15. J. H. Newman, *Difficulties of Anglicans*, vol. 2 (London, 1891), 80–81.

16. On this topic, see esp. Hunt, *Holy Land Pilgrimage*, 86–87, 91–92, 155–79.

Neither within the Cistercian Order nor in the church as a whole could monastic pilgrimages be stopped altogether. The sequel to the Morimond affair was, from Bernard of Clairvaux's point of view, even worse. In 1127, only three years after the trouble caused by Arnold of Morimond, Bernard tried to dissuade Stephen, abbot of the Benedictine house of Saint John in Chartres, from making a pilgrimage to Jerusalem, using the same arguments he had used against Arnold. He likened the abbot's flock to a spouse and quoted Paul's first letter to the Corinthians: "Art thou bound to a wife? Seek not to be loosed."[17] Bernard's reprimand fell on deaf ears. Stephen not only made his pilgrimage but was elected patriarch of Jerusalem in 1128 and never returned to Europe.

This book deals with some of Stephen's humbler contemporaries who, like him, made the pilgrimage to Jerusalem and found the compulsion to settle in the Holy Land greater than the familiar attractions of home. Many were laypeople who made pilgrimages or journeyed to the Latin East as crusaders and decided to settle as monks or hermits in established monasteries or to found hermitages of their own. For them, the Holy Land was a living relic, and the Latin kingdom a powerful expression of God's direction of human affairs. Many—such as Bernard of Blois, founder of a reformed community near Antioch; Elias of Narbonne, an eremitical leader who became an unhappy abbot; the monks who founded the reformed house of Palmaria in Galilee, where Elias was to end his career; or the hermits of Mount Carmel—believed they were breaking away from the established modes of Benedictine monasticism.

These examples are valuable because they enable us to fit the crusader states into the full context of monastic culture in the West. We can compare the ideals and careers of these pilgrims with those of such well-known Western hermits and founders as Peter Damian, Stephen of Grandmont, Robert of Arbrissel, Robert of Molesme, Stephen Harding, Stephen of Obazine, and Bruno the founder of La Chartreuse.[18] Essentially, they were all trying to achieve the same ends: to found monastic communities that could claim the integrity they celebrated in the earliest Christian monks. If

17. *S. Bernardi opera*, 7:214–15, Ep. 72, quoting 1 Cor. 7:27.
18. See, in general, H. Leyser, *Hermits and the New Monasticism* (New York, 1984). Our knowledge of these crusader figures is more fragmentary. For more detailed specific studies, see J. Leclercq, *Saint Pierre Damien: Ermite et homme d'église* (Rome, 1960); B. Bligny, *Saint Bruno* (Rennes, 1984); J. Becquet, "Les institutions de l'ordre de Grandmont au moyen âge," *Revue Mabillon* 42 (1952), 31–42; and B. Lackner, *The Eleventh-Century Background of Cîteaux* (Washington, D.C., 1972).

the theory of holy places underlies the actions of the hermits in this book, a more direct approach to their careers can be taken by comparing their attempts to found reformed communities with carefully chosen Western examples.[19] In the first chapter, I discuss the points of contrast and similarity between crusader and Western hermits and the conditions they faced, and try, within the limits of the evidence, to compare their rates of success.

The institutional church in the Latin East was centered above all on shrines and holy places that were part of a common Christian culture.[20] The hermits and monks in whom I am primarily interested must be seen in the context of the great monastic foundations of the Latin East, such as the Benedictine abbey of Notre-Dame de Josaphat, Saint Mary Latin, and the Templum Domini. The lives of irregular monks can be appreciated only if seen in contrast to the more established monastic society of their day. Some aspects of the character of the monastic church (but not a comprehensive survey of monasteries) are considered in Chapter 2. The settlement of hermits and ascetics throughout the Holy Land, both in groups and as solitaries, may be seen as another layer of religious life. Of necessity they cultivated unoccupied land, thus developing new holy places, such as Mount Carmel, or reviving early Christian sites, such as Mount Quarantana, the Mount of Temptation. Few hermits of the crusader states are known by name, so it is impossible to assess their impact or role quantitatively. We shall never know, for example, whether the proportion of hermits to conventual monks in the Latin East outweighed that in the West. This may make an appraisal of the eremitical character of the church in the Latin East difficult and elusive, but it does not make the individual hermits unworthy of study.

The hermits and monks of the Latin East appear radical both in their return to the purest forms of monastic life and in their choice of a "frontier" society, the kingdom on the edge of Christendom. This, however, was a settled frontier. Hermits inserted themselves into an established monastic landscape, literally and figuratively. Palestine and Syria had been the most fertile provinces of the Roman Empire for eremitical monasticism. Many of the Orthodox monasteries founded in the fifth and sixth centuries were either still operative or under restoration in the twelfth century, and solitary

19. Stephen of Obazine is used in Chapter 1 because he is a less well known Western hermit and his career provides obvious contrasts to the crusader examples.

20. See B. Hamilton, "Re-building Zion: The Holy Places of Jerusalem in the Twelfth Century," in D. Baker, ed., *Renaissance and Renewal in Church History* (Oxford, 1977), 105–16.

hermits from the Eastern churches were a constant if elusive presence. There was nothing original or new about the choices made by the monks in this book. On the contrary, these monks were imitators. Through their precise and literal imitation of Elijah or Moses or Jesus, they distinguished themselves from their contemporaries in the West. Orthodox monks had been doing the same—and living on the same sites that were "discovered" by Frankish hermits—for centuries. The third chapter is devoted to these "original" cultivators of the Levantine holy landscape, and particularly to the status of the Orthodox Church in the twelfth century. The mechanics of monastic and eremitical settlement in the Levant must be seen in the relationship between the native monastic traditions—whose tangible points of reference were the Greek Orthodox monasteries themselves—and the newcomers, both Franks born in the crusader states after the first generation of settlement, and those who emigrated there during the twelfth and thirteenth centuries.

This book owes its genesis to the reading of a specific text: the surviving fragments of a treatise by a twelfth-century Latin bishop in Syria, Gerard of Nazareth, on Franks who had become monks or hermits in the crusader states.[21] Gerard's hermits need more than a purely physical landscape. Throughout this study, I have tried to reconstruct if not their lives at least the influences that inspired them: the kind of eremitically inspired reform monasticism in western Europe in which Gerard was interested, and the salient features of the Orthodox monasticism with which Franks came into contact in the East. There are no simple answers to the questions posed here. Sometimes direct comparisons can be made between Frankish eremitism in the Latin East and forms of life developed in the West; equally, some features of Frankish eremitical and monastic practice clearly owed a great deal to Orthodox customs. More often, for lack of evidence, we can only infer.

One group of Western hermits, however, emerged as a distinctive Order within the church, the only contemplative Order to be created in the crusader states. The origins of these hermits (and later friars) of Mount Carmel allow us to see in microcosm the themes engaged in this book: the spiritual power of a holy place, the difficult and perhaps reluctant process of

---

21. B. Z. Kedar, "Gerard of Nazareth, a Neglected Twelfth-Century Writer of the Latin East: A Contribution to the Intellectual History of the Crusader States," *Dumbarton Oaks Papers* 37 (1983), 55–77. Kedar's article includes an edition of the surviving fragments of Gerard's text.

establishing a monastic foundation, and the relationship between Latin and Greek hermits on a cult site. The sources through which we must view the origins and development of the Carmelite Order introduce yet another theme: the creation of historical tradition by a Religious Order.[22] Frankish hermits always had a more fragile hold on the landscape of the Holy Land than their Orthodox counterparts, because they enjoyed no continuous history of occupation of specific sites. The Carmelite Order represents an attempt, however flawed, to plant such roots in the consciousness of the Western Church.

The monks and hermits of the Latin East provide illumination on the impact of crusading on Western society from an unexpected quarter. They also bring a wealth of comparative examples to the study of hermits and reform monasticism in the West. In short, figures like Bernard of Blois, Elias of Narbonne, William of Maraval, Gabriel the Stylite, Godric of Finchale, and the putative early Carmelite hermits "Berthold" and "Cyril of Constantinople" are consummately medieval characters and fascinating individuals in their own right.

I used the case of Arnold of Morimond as a starting-point for examining the phenomenon of monastic and eremitical set‧ement in the Holy Land because it suggests a paradox. At the same time that Bernard of Clairvaux was deploring monastic pilgrimages and monastic settlement in the East, the Holy Land itself abounded "with many Regular clergy, religious people, hermits, monks, canons, nuns, cloistered virgins dedicated to God, and chaste holy widows."[23] Celebrating the flourishing of the Latin Church in Outremer in the first generation of the Frankish settlement, Jacques de Vitry described how,

> from all parts of the world, all tribes and tongues, and from every people under heaven, drawn by the sweet odor of the holy places, pilgrims devoted to God and Religious of all Orders rushed to the Holy Land. The ancient churches were repaired and new ones built; monasteries were constructed in the same places with the donations of barons and the alms of the faithful.[24]

22. For an approach to this huge topic, see my forthcoming "Gerard of Nazareth, John Bale, and the Origins of the Carmelite Order" (*Journal of Ecclesiastical History*, 1995).

23. Jacques de Vitry, *Historia Hierosolymitana* 52, in J. Bongars, ed., *Gesta Dei per Francos* (Hanau, 1611), 1076–77.

24. Ibid., 50 (Bongars, 1074–75).

Jacques was writing in the 1220s, a time when nostalgia for the heady days of the kingdom of Jerusalem was understandable. By contrast, in his own day he could find little trace of the passion of the early settlers. It was perhaps too easy to assume that the establishment of monasteries and the repair of churches in the newly conquered territories was a logical corollary of the conquest itself. The crusade was, in the view of many contemporaries, designed to establish in perpetuity a Christian protectorate over the holy places of Christendom. The difficulties the institutional church encountered in the Latin East cannot entirely be explained by military failure at the hand of the infidel. The monastic culture that emerged in the two centuries after the First Crusade was prey to internal schism as well as to external threats, of the same kind that plagued Western monasteries and gave rise to new Orders and unauthorized foundations. The Crusader Church, in addition, had to compete with the established monastic traditions of the indigenous Orthodox Church.

Bernard of Clairvaux's opposition to the Morimond pilgrimage, showing that the monastic enterprise in the East was not always viewed with enthusiasm in the West, gives an indication of why it was so difficult to live up to the standards of the first crusaders. Before crossing to Outremer with Jacques de Vitry's pilgrims, monks, and hermits, it is necessary to ask why monastic pilgrimage and monastic settlement in the Holy Land aroused such doubts.

In 1147 Bernard had to write a general letter to all Cistercian abbots, reminding them not to permit their monks to go to the Holy Land and recommending that monks who violated the prohibition should be excommunicated. This was enshrined in the statutes of the Order at the Chapter-General of 1157.[25] Strictures against monks going on pilgrimages had been common since the late eleventh century, and the Cistercian statute probably reflects their failure to dissuade would-be pilgrims.

Anselm of Canterbury told a monk who had proposed making the pilgrimage to Jerusalem: "This is contradictory to your vow, in which you promised stability in the presence of God in the monastery in which you accepted the habit of a monk, and it runs contrary to apostolic obedience."[26] As Peter Damian had made clear, monks who felt the need to

25. S. Bernardi opera, 8:511–12, Ep. 544; Canivez, Statuta, 1:53.

26. S. Anselmi Cantuarensis Archiepiscopi opera omnia, 6 vols., ed. F. S. Schmitt (Stuttgart, 1968), 5:355, Ep. 410. "Est enim contra professionem tuam, qua promisisti stabilitatem coram deo in monasterio, in quo habitum monachi accepisti, et est contra apostolici obedientiam."

make pilgrimages did not realize that by so doing they were breaking their vows. But if abbots were critical of monastic pilgrimages, greater censure was reserved for monks who wanted to participate in the crusade. Anselm had to use his authority as regent of England to prevent the abbot of Cerne from embarking on the expedition of 1096. The abbot had apparently bought a ship and equipped it with thirty knights, but, worse than this, he was encouraging his monks to accompany him "in perditionem." In response, Anselm had the threat of anathema for would-be crusading monks circulated throughout the dioceses of England.[27]

Monks, of course, were never intended participants in the crusade, yet it is difficult to see how new religious communities could have been founded in the aftermath of the Frankish conquest, or shrines staffed by the requisite chapters, if Regular clergy were prohibited from going to the Holy Land. Such monastic leaders as Bernard or Peter the Venerable could hardly have expected the monasteries to be filled by recruits from the laity alone. It is notable that no Cistercian house was founded in the Holy Land until 1157, four years after Bernard's death, and that the Cluniac influence in Outremer became significant only after the first two generations of the Frankish settlement. Paradoxically, the first Cistercian house in the Holy Land, Belmont, was founded the same year the prohibition on monastic pilgrimages was made into a statute of the Order. From the end of the twelfth century, however, the Cistercian Order continued to play an active role in supporting the crusade movement by prayers and organized financial contributions from Cistercian houses. In 1203, 1207, 1214, 1278, and 1279 special measures were taken to punish delay in paying the subsidy, and in 1279 an abbot was deposed for neglecting this duty.[28] Cistercians were instrumental in the planning and early stages of the Fourth Crusade, until the abbot of Vaux-de-Cernay denounced the attack on Zara.

The attitude of Bernard himself toward crusading and the Latin kingdom of Jerusalem was ambivalent. Bernard is celebrated as the most eloquent preacher of the Second Crusade, and the propagandist of the Order of the Temple. In 1153 he replied to a letter from his uncle, Andrew, Master of the Temple, from whom he had heard recently of the dangers threatening the kingdom. Bernard sent his compliments to the Templars and the

---

27. Ibid., 4:85–86, Ep. 195. Anselm seems also to have been concerned about the abbot of Cerne for behaving like a youth, consorting with women, and bringing his office into disrepute. There were also other matters of complaint that Anselm refused to divulge.

28. Canivez, *Statuta*, 1:290, 340, 424; 2:178, 186.

Hospitallers—and also to "the hermits, and all holy men"—and blamed the present troubles of the kingdom on its rulers. His advice, however, seems remote and lofty. Their labors, he said, like all earthly efforts, will fail because their eyes are on the earthly Jerusalem, not the heavenly Jerusalem. The Templars, Bernard reminds his uncle, should be fighting for the salvation of souls, not for earthly success.[29]

With the bitter experience of the failure of the Second Crusade, Bernard's tone is understandably resigned. Yet this ambivalence was a feature of his preaching of the crusade itself. Writing in 1147 on the occasion of the expedition against the pagan Wends, he reminded crusaders of the true objectives of their vow: neither military glory nor financial reward, but the salvation of souls—both the souls of the Wends, by conversion, and their own souls, by participation in the crusade.[30] A little earlier he had encouraged Vladislav, duke of Bohemia, to avenge the honor of Jesus by crusading in the Holy Land.[31] Bernard's emphasis is not on the defense of the holy places, or even on the absolute military defeat of the infidel, but on the necessary spiritual benefits of the crusade for the participants. The Holy Land's primary function seems to be to provide opportunities for salvation for the laity: for Regular clergy it was redundant.

In May or June 1150, Bernard wrote a gentle rebuke to Peter the Venerable, abbot of Cluny, after Peter had excused himself from attending the Council of Chartres held in April to discuss future crusading plans. He begged Peter not to miss further such councils, stressing the importance of the affair and the dire threat to the kingdom of Jerusalem.[32] Peter, like Bernard, displayed a troubled ambiguity in his attitude to the temporal affairs of the Latin kingdom.[33] He appeared to be genuinely concerned

29. *S. Bernardi opera*, 8:203, Ep. 288. See also ibid., 8:65, Ep. 206, a letter to Queen Melisende in which Bernard commends to her a kinsman who wants to join the Temple; and ibid., 7:393, Ep. 175, a letter of 1130–31 asking the patriarch of Jerusalem to keep a paternal eye on the Templars.

30. Ibid., 8:432, Ep. 457.

31. Ibid., 8:434, Ep. 548.

32. Ibid., 8:483, Ep. 521; Peter the Venerable, *Letters*, ed. G. Constable, 2 vols. (Cambridge, Mass., 1967), 1:396–98, Ep. 164, for Peter's letter explaining his nonattendance.

33. In the discussion that follows, it is not my intention to suggest that the sometimes comparable views of Bernard and Peter on the kingdom of Jerusalem or the holy places should be allowed to obscure their differences on other matters of monastic conduct, or even that the views expressed in their letters should stand as representative of Cistercians and Cluniacs in general. For a specific example of the debate between these Orders in the twelfth century, see Idung of Prüfening's dialogue in J. O'Sullivan, ed., *Cistercians and Cluniacs*, Cistercian Fathers

about its fate—for example, writing to John Comnenus, the Byzantine emperor, urging zeal in its defense, or expressing his regret to Suger of Saint Denis on the death of Raymond of Antioch (in June 1149) and the subsequent threat to the city posed by Nur ad-Din.[34] Yet, while Bernard was preaching the crusade in 1146, Peter wrote to ask Louis VII why he was taking the trouble to go to Jerusalem to fight Muslims when there were so many Jews to be converted in France.[35] After Theobald, abbot of Saint Columba at Sens, had taken the cross at Vézelay, Peter wrote a letter of cautious advice that falls distinctly short of endorsement. He admitted the usefulness to one's faith of the physical presence of the holy places, given the impossibility of the bodily presence of Christ in this life. The crusader, however, must embark on the journey with heart and mind purged of all except the hope of salvation.[36] He must not desire military glory; indeed, the result of the expedition in military terms is less relevant than the welfare of the individual soul. Military success, so far as the monk is concerned, is contrary to the purpose of his Order.

Both Bernard and Peter thus stressed different priorities when addressing monastic as opposed to lay audiences. Bernard's championing of the Templars, and his preaching of the Second Crusade, underline his view of the armed pilgrimage to Jerusalem as appropriate for laypeople. His correspondence with Queen Melisende, moreover, shows a continuing interest in the affairs of the kingdom.[37] In a letter to William, patriarch of Jerusalem (1138–45), however, there is a subtle edge. Bernard honored the patriarch for being, of all bishops in the world, responsible for the most holy place, "which nurtured the living grass and brought forth fruit according to its own kind."[38] Jerusalem is holy, he says, the same way the ground where Moses trod barefoot before the burning bush is holy, but to an even greater

Series 33 (Kalamazoo, Mich., 1977), 3–141; and A. Wilmart, "Une riposte de l'ancien monachisme au manifest de saint Bernard," *Revue Bénédictine* 46 (1934), 296–344.

34. Peter the Venerable, *Letters*, 1:208–9, Ep. 85; 1:389–40, Ep. 166.

35. Ibid., 1:322–30, Ep. 130.

36. Ibid., 1:358–59, Ep. 144. "Cavendum est, ne de spoliis forte vicendorum hostium spes lucri subintret, et servum dei postposita commissarum animarum cura, huc illucque non iam devotio, sed avaritia vagari compellat." See also *Lettres des premiers chartreux*, ed. and trans. "un chartreux" (Paris, 1962), 154–61, for the letter of Prior Guiges I to Hugh de Payen emphasizing the greater value of spiritual warfare than bodily.

37. *S. Bernardi opera*, 8:65, Ep. 206; 8:205–6, Ep. 289; 8:297, Ep. 254; 8:299, Ep. 255.

38. Ibid., 8:365, Ep. 393. "Quae germinavit herbam virentem et facientem fructum secundum speciem suam."

degree. Those who would step with confidence in such a place must themselves be genuinely holy.[39]

The idea of the sacred quality of the Holy Land also preoccupied Peter the Venerable. He flattered the bishop of Bethlehem by alluding to the great glory of living in the Holy Land, but almost took back the compliment by hinting that the real prize for Christians was the celestial Jerusalem.[40] Writing to the monks of Mount Tabor, Peter quoted God's commandment "Be holy, as I am holy." These words, he remarked, had special relevance for monks who lived in the Holy Land: they must, to be worthy of their profession, live up to the holiness of the land itself.

> This is said with particular meaning to you, whom not only the Christian faith, not only monastic devotion, but also the fact of dwelling in that holy place must make more ready to exhibit every goodness, to return thanks and to be happier [than others] in constant perseverance of these things.[41]

The Holy Land deserves to be revered above all others because from that place Christ's word spread throughout the world. This, however, brings with it a special responsibility for the monks who live there, for where the word was first heard it must sound most clear. The monks of the Holy Land have the responsibility to continue saying the liturgy on behalf of those whose physical location is less fortunate and who might thus be the more excused for stinting their worship of God. Moreover, as Peter points out, there is no guarantee that changing location will change one's heart. Monks must strive to lead holy lives rather than relying on the spiritual charge of the place itself to make them holy. As always, Peter reminds them of the greater glory of the promised heavenly city. Even in the Holy Land Christ can be glorified only "spiritually," not "corporeally." He can be seen in the virtues of others, but in the New Jerusalem he will be seen and worshiped face-to-face.

Peter was prepared to admit the usefulness of the holy sites for the

---

39. Ibid., 8:365–66, Ep. 393.

40. Peter, *Letters*, 1:106, Ep. 31.

41. Ibid., 1:215–16, Ep. 80, quoting Leviticus 11:44. ". . . vobis tamen quodammodo specialius dicitur, quos non tantum christiana professio, non tantum monastica devotio, sed et ipsius ut dixi sancti loci inhabitatio, ad omne opus bonum promptiores exhibere, devotiones reddere, et in his constanter perdurantes beatiores facere debet." (All biblical references are to the Vulgate in the Douay-Reims translation.)

Christian faith, but such aids to devotion were superfluous for the monk, who was already leading the best possible Christian life by virtue of his profession. Thus Peter wrote to a knight, Hugh Catula, to dissuade him from making the pilgrimage to Jerusalem and arguing that he should instead enter the cloister at Cluny:

> It is better to serve God in perpetual humility and poverty, than to complete the journey to Jerusalem in pride and luxury. If it is a good thing to visit Jerusalem, where the feet of the Lord stood, it is by far better to long for heaven, where he will be seen face-to-face.[42]

Similarly, Bernard was prepared to upset Templar sensibilities in favor of his own Order. In an unusual case, a Templar who wanted to become a Cistercian was rejected by the monastery where he sought admission, for fear of the Templars. The monks took him inst' ad to a Benedictine abbey, but the Templars regarded the whole affair as illegal and tried to get him back. Bernard wrote to the pope, protesting the Templars' efforts to retrieve their knight.[43] In Bernard's mind, the cloister, wherever it might be, was above the defense of the Holy Sepulcher.

The settlement of monks in the Holy Land was seen as detracting from the fundamental vocation of monasticism. Implicit in the monastic ideal was the rejection of special places, or spiritual benefits accruing from being in a certain location rather than any other. The cloister in France or Italy, because it represented Paradise, surpassed the holiest of sites in the earthly Jerusalem. This is stated explicitly by Bernard in a letter circa 1129, explaining to Alexander, bishop of Lincoln, that his clerk Philip, who had set out for Jerusalem on pilgrimage, had stopped at Clairvaux and would go no farther:

> He crossed, in this narrow sea, a great and spacious expanse, and, sailing with the wind, reached the hoped-for shore, and stood at last at the gate of salvation. His feet now stand in the forecourt of

42. Ibid., 1:152, Ep. 51. "Maius est vero deo perpetuo in humilitate et paupertate servire, quam cum superbia et luxu Ihrosolimitanum iter conficere. Unde si bonum est Ihrusalem ubi steterunt pedes domini visitare, longe melius est, caelo ubi ipse facie ad faciem conspicitur, inhiare." See also G. Constable, "The Vision of Gunthelm, and Other *Visiones* Attributed to Peter the Venerable," *Revue Bénédictine* 66 (1956), 92–114.

43. *S. Bernardi opera*, 8:170–71, Ep. 261.

> Jerusalem. . . . But, if you want to know, that Jerusalem is Clairvaux.[44]

Bernard asked Bishop Alexander to free Philip from his prebend so that he could profess at Clairvaux.

The idea of referring to the monastery as "Paradise" also appears elsewhere. Anselm wrote a congratulatory letter to Turold, a monk of Bec, on his decision to leave the world: "Divine mercy has directed you to paradise, and by receiving you into the cloistered life of a monk has introduced you to paradise in this life."[45] Peter the Venerable tried to attract Hatto, bishop of Trier, to retirement in Cluny by comparing the monastery to paradise:

> Before the paradise of desire, a paradise of love awaits you at Cluny; there is the tree of life, there joyful conveniences, and glittering things beautified with aromas and incense, whose sight will delight you, whose smell will please you and whose taste will satisfy you.[46]

The explicit identification of the cloister as paradise on earth can be seen as an attempt to defuse the spiritual charge of the holy places, but the evidence of pilgrimage literature from the twelfth and thirteenth centuries shows that the attempt was unsuccessful. Probably the majority of those whose accounts survive were clerics, some of them monks or Regular canons, who had obviously made the pilgrimage in defiance of opinion. Moreover, pilgrims from both western Europe and the Byzantine world knew that they would find attached to all the major shrines—the Holy Sepulcher, the tomb of the Virgin, the Grotto of the Nativity, Mount Tabor, and so on—monasteries with possessions throughout Outremer and Europe, sustained and enriched by laypeople for whom their ministry in the land of Jesus and the apostles was a powerful point of contact with the heavenly Jerusalem.

---

44. Ibid., 7:157–58, Ep. 64. "Transfretavit in brevi hoc mare magnum et spatiosum, et, prospere navigans, attigit iam litus optatum atque ad portum tandem salutis applicavit. Stantes sunt iam pedes eius in atriis Ierusalem. . . . Et si vultis scire, Claravallis est."

45. S. Anselmi opera, 5:363–64, Ep. 418. "In vitam paradisi vos direxit divina clementia, immo in quendam paradisum huius vitae vos introduxit, cum vos in claustralem conversationem monachi propositi respiciat."

46. Peter, Letters, 1:227, Ep. 86. "Expectat te in Cluniaco tua ante paradysum voluptatis paradysus caritatis, ubi lignum vitae, ubi amenitas iocunda, ubi aureolae aromatum consitae a pigmentariis, quorum aspectu iocundaberis, odore oblectaberis, gustu satiaberis."

1

Gerard of Nazareth and Western Hermits of the Crusader States

Jacques de Vitry's enthusiasm for the Latin Church in the first flush of the Frankish settlement embraced not only members of Regular communities but also those who chose to live as hermits or anchorites. Hermits were to be found throughout Frankish Palestine and Syria, especially on the Black Mountain just outside Antioch; on Mount Carmel; in the Judaean desert to the south and east of Jerusalem, and in the Jordan Valley around Jericho.[1] The most important concentration in the thirteenth century was the one on Mount Carmel, which was given a Rule by the patriarch of Jerusalem Albert of Vercelli (1205–14) and in 1226 was recognized as a religious order by the pope. Frankish Syria experienced the effects of monastic reform ideas no less than Western society, but most of the evidence for pre-Carmelite eremitical settlements or for individual hermits is incidental and patchy.

1. Jacques de Vitry, *Historia Hierosolymitana* 52 (Bongars, 1075).

For this reason, the surviving fragments of the *De conversatione servorum Dei*, a collection of brief lives of contemporary Frankish hermits by the twelfth-century bishop Gerard of Nazareth, are particularly important. The *De conversatione* provides evidence for reception of the reforming ideals current in Western monasticism since the 1050s in a "frontier territory," and throws new light on the nature of the Latin Church in the crusader states.

In 1983, Benjamin Kedar rescued Gerard of Nazareth's work from the obscurity of a sixteenth-century compendium of church history.[2] Matthias Flacius Illyricus and his collaborators, the "Centuriators" of Magdeburg, published their seven-volume history of the church as material for Protestant attacks on medieval Catholicism[3] and in so doing, preserved for posterity some medieval works of which no manuscripts survive. The only other known fragment of Gerard's *De conversatione* has been found in three Carmelite treatises of the fourteenth century: Philip Ribot's *De institutione et peculiaribus gestis religiosorum Carmelitarum*, Bernard Ollerius's *Informatio circa ordinem, institutionem et confirmationem Ordinis Fratrum Beatae Virginis Mariae de Monte Carmelo*, and John of Hildesheim's *Dyalogus inter directorem et detractorum de ordine Carmelitarum*. The Centuriators compiled thematically, with the result that Gerard's treatise is split between five chapters of the *Duodecima centuria* and interspersed with extracts of his closely related *Vita abbatis Eliae*, a theological treatise entitled *De una Magdalena contra Graecos*, and a tract on the same subject written to counter criticism, *Contra Salam presbyterum*.[4]

---

2. See Kedar, "Gerard of Nazareth," 55–77. The conception of this book would have been impossible without Kedar's pioneering work.

3. Matthais Flacius Illyricus et al., *Ecclesiasticae historiae, integram ecclesiae Christi ideam . . . secunda singulas centurias perspicuo ordine complectens*, 7 vols. (Basel, 1562–74); the volume containing Gerard's works is vol. 6, *Duodecima centuria*.

4. Kedar published the relevant extracts from the *Duodecima centuria* and Gerard's other works ("Gerard of Nazareth," 71–77). No manuscript of any of Gerard's works has yet been found, although the Centuriators must have had access to the *De conversatione* in some form. The English bibliographer and antiquary John Bale had, by 1533, included Gerard and many of his hermits in his biographical account of the Carmelite Order (Oxford, Bodleian Library Selden Supra MS 41, fol. 148v). Disparities in the material from Gerard included in Bale's manuscript and the Centuriators' text indicate that they knew different manuscript versions of the *De conversatione*. It seems likely, therefore, that at least two versions of some, if not all, of Gerard's works survived until the 1560s. Gerard's works were known among Carmelites at least in England and Germany. Besides the extract from his preface to the *De conversatione* quoted by Ribot, Ollerius, and John of Hildesheim, there is a reference to his *Contra Salam presbyterum* in the *Defensorium* of the Carmelite John Hornby, written in 1374, Oxford, Bodleian Library MS E museo 86, fol. 202r. The transmission of Carmelite historical materials is a subject I hope to treat in proper detail in a separate study.

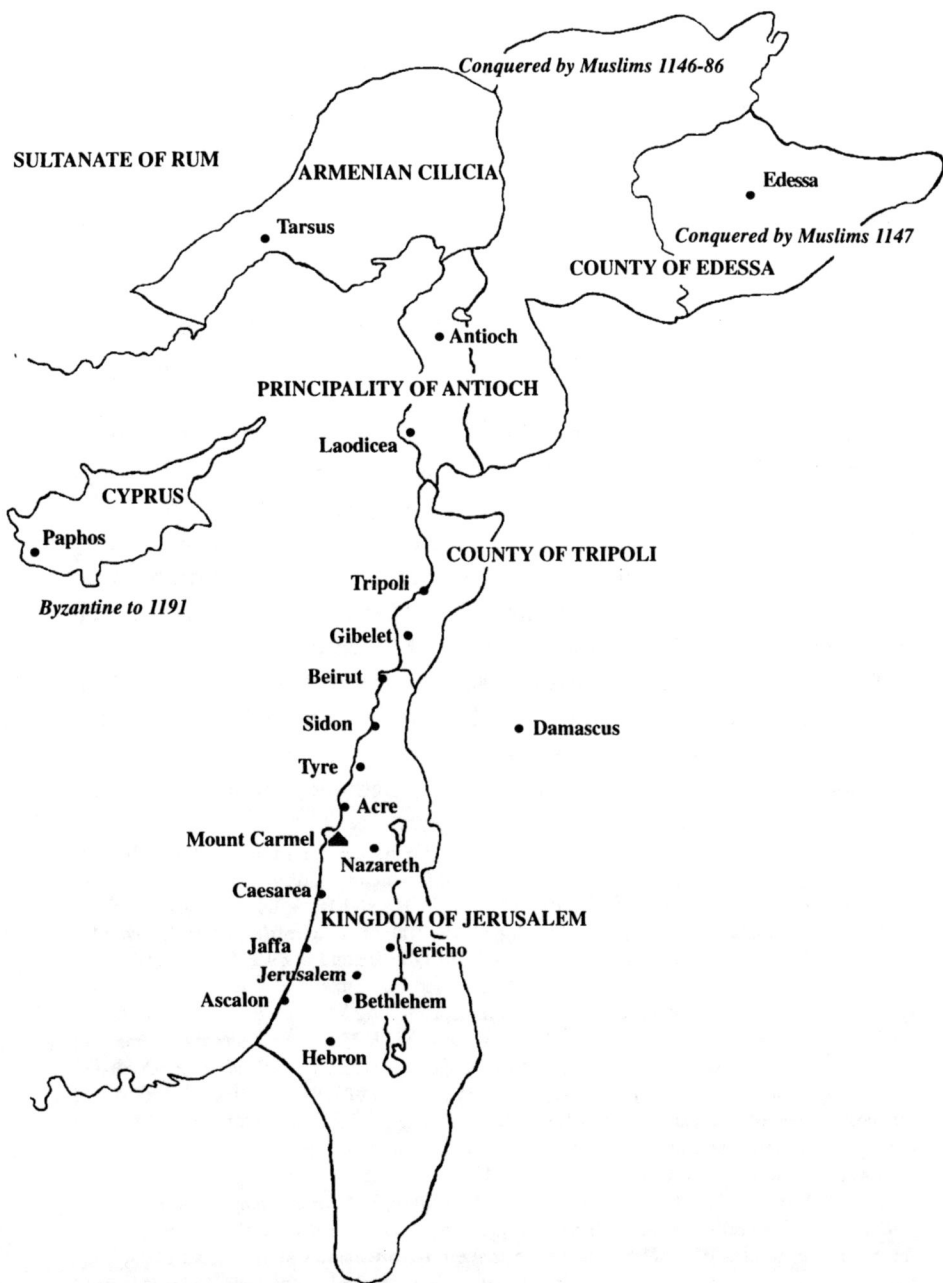

SULTANATE OF RUM

ARMENIAN CILICIA

Conquered by Muslims 1146-86

Tarsus

Edessa

Conquered by Muslims 1147

COUNTY OF EDESSA

Antioch

PRINCIPALITY OF ANTIOCH

Laodicea

CYPRUS

Paphos

COUNTY OF TRIPOLI

Byzantine to 1191

Tripoli

Gibelet

Beirut

Sidon

Damascus

Tyre

Acre

Mount Carmel

Nazareth

Caesarea

KINGDOM OF JERUSALEM

Jaffa

Jericho

Jerusalem

Ascalon

Bethlehem

Hebron

lap 1. The Crusader States

The thematic method of the Centuriators means that only the portions of Gerard's work that they wanted to preserve have survived. The selective nature of the compilation is underlined by the recent discovery of three more of Gerard's hermits in another sixteenth-century manuscript containing, inter alia, John Bale's *Cronica seu fascicula temporum ordinis Carmelitarum*. This manuscript is a notebook in Bale's own hand, to which he added at different dates. The *Cronica* can be dated to 1527–33, with later additions up to 1540, but it is not complete.[5]

Bale's *Cronica* is a biographical history of the Carmelite Order and of figures associated with the genesis of the Order. An entry for Gerard of Nazareth is included, followed by a list of twenty-three hermits that corresponds closely but not exactly to the 21 names in the *Duodecima centuria*.[6] The relationship between the historical work of Bale and the Centuriators belongs, properly, to a study of Carmelite historiography and therefore lies outside the scope of this work. Bale's inclusion of Gerard at least thirty years before the Centuriators, however, provides independent testimony for the *De conversatione* and for our knowledge of Gerard's other works, even if it does little to add to the extracts made by the Centuriators.

The question of the trustworthiness of the Centuriators' representation of Gerard's work inevitably arises. Although they were Protestants, the Centuriators' method is not polemical. They were trying to compile a reference work, not a refutation of medieval Catholic practices.[7] Matthias

5. Bale's *Cronica* occurs in an Oxford manuscript (Oxford, Bodleian Selden Supra MS 41, fols. 107r–196r). Bale, born in 1495, was a professed Carmelite monk at the Norwich convent and was educated at the Cambridge studium between 1514 and 1529. By 1536 he had left the Order and become a Protestant, and in 1540 he fled to the Low Countries, where he lived for eight years. In 1552 he was appointed Bishop of Ossory in Ireland but was forced to flee after only a year in office. Between 1553 and 1560 he lived in Switzerland and Germany, corresponding with Protestant theologians and historians, including Matthias Flacius and his fellow Centuriators. For a full study of Bale's life and works, see H. McCusker, *John Bale: Dramatist and Antiquary* (Bryn Mawr, Pa., 1942), and L. Fairfield, *John Bale: Mythmaker for the English Reformation* (West Lafayette, Ind., 1976). For the question of Bale's reading of Gerard, see Jotischky, "Gerard of Nazareth, John Bale, and the Origins of the Carmelite Order." For the dating of Bale's manuscript works, see Fairfield, *John Bale*, 157–64.

6. Oxford, Bodleian Library Selden Supra MS 41, fol. 148v.

7. P. Polman, "Flacius Illyricus, historien de l'église," *Revue d'histoire ecclésiastique* 27 (1931), 62: "The authors' polemical purpose is often relegated to second place; one confronts the fevered eagerness of scholars anxious to make their discoveries known at all costs, . . . one encounters many documents that hardly serve the polemical intent." As Kedar ("Gerard of Nazareth," 59) shows, the Centuriators sometimes used Gerard purely for corroborative evidence, as, for example, in establishing the date of the death of Ralph of Domfront (*Duodecima centuria*, 1373). Kedar compared the Centuriators' account of the treatment of

Flacius himself explained his techniques in the *Consultatio de conscribenda accurata historia ecclesia*, published in 1554. His emphasis was on representing doctrine and its historical context, which were to be accompanied by brief biographical sketches.[8] The biographies of Gerard's hermits were therefore included, in abridged form, to amplify the Centuriators' general account of twelfth-century monasticism. John Bale's *Cronica* dates from the period before his conversion to Protestantism, so the question of critical representation does not occur. Even after his conversion, however, Bale found it difficult to turn his back on the assumptions that had informed his understanding of church history. His *Anglorum Heliades* (1536), based largely on notes he had made in the 1520s, shows little sign of having been adapted to take account of his conversion. As late as 1539, the only indication of his dissatisfaction with the Carmelite version of the past is his rejection of the vows of celibacy.[9]

Gerard's work, so far as it can be reconstructed from the *Duodecima centuria*, not only is favorable toward eremitism as a valuable form of monastic life, but also argues for great tolerance by the church in the Latin East in the control of unregulated monasticism. Historians of Western monasticism have long acknowledged the contribution hermits made to the reform movements of the eleventh and twelfth centuries. Variously expressed as provoking a "crisis"[10] and as occupying "the very highest rung of the ladder of perfection," hermits and the ideals of solitude could be found at the center of scores of new foundations, from Camaldoli in the early eleventh century, to the Cistercian house of Radmore in the diocese of

---

Patriarch Aimery of Antioch at the hands of Reynald de Châtillon with that of William of Tyre and found the Centuriators' an accurate and painstaking abridgment, with the sections relating to ecclesiastical practice copied verbatim from William.

8. Kedar, "Gerard of Nazareth," 59.

9. Fairfield, *John Bale*, 50–51: "The new wine of Bale's radical theology had not yet burst these old wineskins of convention." For an example of Bale's continued reliance on Catholic conventions, see his *Anglorum Heliades*, London, British Library Harleian MS 3838, fols. 4r–5r, 15r.

10. Jean Leclercq, "La crise du monachisme aux XIe et XIIe siècles," *Bullettino dell' Istituto storico Italiano per il medio evo* 70 (1958), 19–41; N. F. Cantor, "The Crisis of Western Monasticism, 1050–1130," *American Historical Review* 66 (1960), 47–67, for an extreme view; Derek Baker, "Crossroads and Crises in the Religious Life of the Late Eleventh Century," in D. Baker, ed., *The Church in Town and Countryside* (Oxford, 1979), 137–48; J. Van Engen, "The 'Crisis of Monasticism' Reconsidered: Benedictine Monasticism in the Years 1050–1150," *Speculum* 61 (1986), 269–304, arguing that the idea of crisis has been overstated.

Lichfield, in 1131.[11] The terminology, "hermit," "anchorite," and "eremitical," however, does not do justice to the types of monastic life. Everyone knows what a hermit is, but to isolate a single example to define a category would be misleading. As Jean Leclercq argued, such terms as *eremus, solitudo,* and *vita solitaria* implied a number of different and sometimes conflicting priorities. Was the important feature of the monastic life emphasized by the term "solitude" or by "poverty," or, as Leclercq argues, by separation from the world and from other communities?[12] Each eremitical case must, in the end, be treated on its own merits. As we shall see, Gerard of Nazareth's *De conversatione* includes conventual monks, hermits, and individuals who tried both forms of Religious life.

Perhaps inevitably, our knowledge of eremitical life comes not only from hermits themselves but also from others' perceptions of their activities and ideals. Not all monks believed the fluidity between cloister and wilderness beneficial. Sometimes perceptions of hermits could be hostile, as, for example, in the attack on eremitism by Ivo of Chartres published by Dom G. Morin, or in Payin Bolotin's celebrated poem "De falsis heremitis qui vagando discurrunt," or in Peter the Venerable's letter of warning to the hermit Gislebertus.[13] This is not to imply that there was a consistently hostile dialogue (or indeed, a consistent dialogue at all) between conventual monks and hermits. Peter the Venerable envied Gislebertus the opportunity to live as a solitary but doubted whether he himself would be able to maintain such a strict regime for long. The objections Ivo of Chartres had to the eremitical life, expressed in a letter to the hermit Rainaud, were more fundamental but based on the same doubts. Ivo was convinced that there was a greater degree of the certainty of salvation for the cloistered monk than for the solitary hermit, who could easily be led astray spiritually and who lacked the corporate discipline necessary for monastic virtue.[14] This

11. Leyser, *Hermits and the New Monasticism*, 1; see also Leyser's appendix 2, 113–18, for a list of houses with eremitical origins.

12. Leclercq, "La crise du monachisme," 19, n. 1. On eremitism in the West generally, see the collection of papers *L'eremitismo in Occidente nei secoli XI e XII,* Miscellanea del Centro di Studi Medioevali 4 (Milan, 1965).

13. G. Morin, "Rainaud l'ermite et Yves de Chartres: Un épisode de la crise du cénobitisme aux XIe–XIIe siècles," *Revue Bénédictine* 40 (1928), 99–115; J. Leclercq, ed., "Le poème de Payen Bolotin contre les faux ermites," *Revue Bénédictine* 68 (1958), 77–84; Peter the Venerable, *Letters,* 1:28–39, Ep. 20.

14. Ivo of Chartres, *Epistolae, PL* 160:260–62. Rainaud's response, the treatise *De vita monachorum* (see Morin, "Rainaud l'ermite," 99–115), makes use of an alleged letter by Lanfranc of Bec in which Lanfranc argues that diversity of religious profession is necessary

was the opinion of an individual, however, and must not be taken as representative of all monks in the eleventh and twelfth centuries. Gerard of Nazareth shows that some monks, even a monk who became a bishop (as both Gerard and Ivo did), found distinctions between cloistered monks and hermits to be obstructive of the real qualities of their professions.

Descriptions of eremitical ventures, such as Gerard's *De conversatione*, or the Life of Stephen of Obazine (a Western hermit and monastic founder whose career I shall use as a basis for comparison with Gerard's examples), are particularly useful because they enable us to study the hermit or the foundation on their own terms, according to the ideals the monks themselves expressed. Gerard began his career, which was to take him to the heights of the episcopacy in Syria, as a hermit, and Stephen's biographer was a monk at Obazine; both, therefore, understood what was meant by use of the words *eremus* and *eremita* in a specific case.[15]

The Rule of Saint Benedict allowed no distinction between an anchorite—such as Wulfric of Haselbury, who became a focal point of everyday life in a twelfth-century Somerset village[16]—and one like Peter the Venerable's correspondent Gislebertus, who lived in complete solitude in the woods. The eremitical life, to Benedict, was simply the perfection of the monastic training received in the cloister. The monk who had advanced beyond the need for a structured community might become a hermit. Peter Damian saw his community of hermits at Fonte Avellana as following Benedict's advice in going one stage beyond the conventual monastery. The difference between true monks and false monks was not, Damian emphasized, whether one lived in a monastery or in the wilderness, but whether one remained obedient to a Rule. "Custom makes a cell sweet for a monk, but wandering makes it seem horrible."[17]

The profusion of new Orders and Rules for the monastic life from about

---

(*Epistolae* 9, *PL* 150:549). This letter, however, is not included in the more recent edition of Lanfranc's letters (*The Letters of Lanfranc, Archbishop of Canterbury*, ed. and trans. H. Clover and M. Gibson [Oxford, 1979]), and may be considered apocryphal. In general, see Leyser, *Hermits and the New Monasticism*, 78–86.

15. *Vita Stephani Obazinensis*, ed. with a French trans. by M. Aubrun (Clermont-Ferrand, 1970); Leyser, *Hermits and the New Monasticism*.

16. *Wulfric of Haselbury by John, Abbot of Ford*, ed. M. Bell (London, 1933); H. Mayr-Harting, "Functions of a Twelfth-Century Recluse, Wulfric of Haselbury," *History* 60 (1975), 337–52.

17. Peter Damian, *De contemptu saeculi* 12.35, *PL* 145:278. In *De monasticae institutionis observantiae* 11, *PL* 145:344–45, Damian adopts Benedict's rulings on the comportment of monks for his own community, esp. chaps. 5, 33, 42, and 52–55 of the Rule of Saint Benedict.

1050 to 1150 meant that a bewildering number of choices had become available for the aspiring monk and that, consequently, there was a fluidity between the states of cenobitic and eremitical monasticism that eludes precise terminology. A hermit such as Godric of Finchale, who lived in various parts of County Durham, sometimes in the open air but often in a hut, appears to have chosen physical wilderness and solitude in preference to cenobitism. Yet a monk of Durham wrote a contemporary biography of Godric, and Godric himself had obtained permission from the bishop in the first place to settle in his hermitage. Even after his withdrawal, Godric regularly attended feast-day services at Durham Cathedral Priory.[18] It was possible for monks to straddle the monastic world, tasting the extremes of eremitical solitude and institutional cenobitism.

Gerard's *De conversatione* shows the flexibility and vitality of religious life in Outremer during the twelfth century. From another point of view—that of Peter the Venerable, for example—it might also be argued that it exposes the failure of monasteries to attract and keep recruits within the cloister. Whether one chooses to interpret the flourishing of eremitical life as a sign of strength in the Christian life or as a sign of weakness, there is no doubt that, from the early days of the Frankish conquest, monks sought the ideals of the monastic life outside the established monasteries described in Chapter 2.

Gerard himself did not make formal distinctions between types of monastic living. His monks came from varied backgrounds (see Table 1). Some were native to the Latin East, but others had come overseas as pilgrims or crusaders and stayed behind. Some had specific pastoral vocations, such as the hermits Ralph and Alberic who worked in a leper hospital in Jerusalem.[19] Ralph is also an example of a baron who abandoned his fief to live in Jerusalem. All were Franks. Gerard did not write about Orthodox, Armenian, or Georgian hermits and monks, though there is abundant evidence for their presence throughout the Holy Land.

The nature of the survival of Gerard's work makes it extremely hazardous to interpret such data too freely. In the absence of a fuller version of the *De conversatione*, it is impossible to read the extracts preserved by the Centuriators except as comparative material. The extracts furnish further examples of

18. Reginald of Durham, *Libellus de vita et miraculis S. Godrici, heremitae de Finchale*, Surtees Society (London, 1847), 66, 225–26.

19. *Duodecima centuria*, col. 1603.

Table 1.   Gerard's Monks

Name & Origin	Type of Monastic Life	Past History
From *Duodecima Centuria*, 1603–1610		
Ralph (French)	Hermit working with lepers in Jerusalem	Lord with 70 vassals
Alberic (Unknown)	Hermit working with lepers in Jerusalem	Unknown
Cosmas (Hungarian)	Hermit enclosed in Jerusalem	Priest
John (Unknown)	Monk/solitary	Monk in Jerusalem
Walter (Unknown)	Monk at Machanath (Black Mountain)	Unknown
Rainald (Galilee)	Monk/solitary	Monk at Mount Tabor
Henry (Unknown)	Solitary on Black Mountain	Unknown
Dominic (Unknown)	Hermit enclosed in Nazareth	Unknown
Bernard (Unknown)	Solitary	Nazareth?
Bartholomew (W. Europe)	Worked with lepers in Jerusalem, then hermit on Black Mountain	Templar
Bernard (Blois)	Monk at Jubin, then Machanath, on Black Mountain	Unknown
Porphyry (Unknown)	Monk at Machanath	Jubin?
William (Unknown)	Monk at Machanath	Knight
Hugh (Unknown)	Monk at Machanath	Unknown
Hugh (2) ("Transalpinus")	Monk at Jubin, then Machanath	Crusader

Name & Origin	Type of Monastic Life	Past History
From *Duodecima Centuria*, 1603–1610 (cont'd)		
Ursus (Unknown)	Monk at Jubin	Unknown
Valerius (Burgundy)	Monk at Jubin, then solitary on Black Mountain	Knight
John (2) (Lucca)	Solitary on Mount Tabor	Monk at Carraria
Sigerius (Unknown)	Abbot of Carraria	Unknown
Elias (Narbonne)	Hermit in community, then abbot of Palmaria	Teacher
Robert (Jerusalem)	Monk at Jubin (then Machanath?)	Unknown
From Oxford, Bodleian Library Selden Supra MS 41, fol. 147v:		
Galfridus (Unknown)	Abbot	Unknown
Nicholas (Unknown)	Monk	Unknown

the type of monasticism found in eleventh- and twelfth-century western Europe, but they do not represent the extent of monasticism in the Latin East and cannot tell the historian much about the relative popularity of eremitical and cenobitic monasticism. As comparative examples, however, the surviving portions of the *De conversatione* allow us to assume that the type of eremitically inspired monastic reform common to France between about 1080 and 1150 was equally important in the establishment of Latin conventual life in the crusader states in the wake of the First Crusade.

Gerard wrote about cloistered monks (such as Walter and Sigerius), about anchorites (such as Dominic and Cosmas), and about hermits, who combined both aspects of the monastic life. It is hermits that most interested Gerard and that stand out as the most intriguing in his work. Of the twenty-four names known to us from Gerard's *De conversatione*, only seven were "genuine" hermits living a solitary life, as opposed to twelve who were cenobitic monks, albeit in new foundations that owed their origins to eremitical ideals. Six (Bernard of Blois, Elias of Narbonne, Bartholomew, John of Jerusalem, Valerius, and Ursus) moved easily from cenobitism to eremitism or vice versa. Yet Gerard's introduction to the lives of his monks, preserved in the Carmelite treatises of the fourteenth century, leaves no doubt that he considered his subjects "genuine" hermits and outstanding for their dedication to the solitary life as adopted by the Old Testament exemplars of Elijah and Moses:

> These are they who, after the example of Elijah, prefer the silence of solitude to the tumult of cities; they love the hidden contemplation of God. Thus David, fleeing from the troubles of the world, stretched himself out in solitude. "In a deserted, pathless and parched land," he said, "I appeared to you in holiness, that I might see your glory." This glory Moses sought to see in the desert, and finally Elijah in solitude. And hence the Savior shone in glory on the mountain, cut off from the crowds, between Moses and Elijah.[20]

In abandoning the formal distinctions between the hermit and the monk, Gerard was making explicit the tendency apparent in western European practice of a generation earlier. It is easy to see where Gerard's loyalties lay. According to separate extracts in the *Duodecima centuria*, he had himself been a hermit on Mount Tabor and the Black Mountain before becoming a Benedictine monk and, around 1140, bishop of Laodicea.[21] He was naturally sympathetic, therefore, to the idea of fluidity between the cloister and the wilderness.

Gerard's own career, and those of his primary examples, particularly Bernard of Blois and Elias of Narbonne, invite comparison with some of the leading lights of the "new monasticism" of western Europe, particularly Stephen of Obazine, Robert of Molesme, and Norbert of Xanten, just as the Carmelites of the early thirteenth century parallel the foundation of La Chartreuse one hundred years earlier. What these monks shared was an

---

20. Philip Ribot, *De institutione et peculiaribus gestis religiosorum Carmelitarum* 3.8. I have used Daniel a Virgine Maria's edition of *Speculum Carmelitanum*, 4 parts in 2 vols. (Antwerp, 1680). Citations will be made to Ribot's divisions of books and chapters only, because Daniel's pagination is not continuous.

21. *Duodecima centuria*, cols. 12, 987, 1379–80. The suggestion that he was a Carmelite is a later Carmelite interpolation and seems to appear first in Bale's *Cronica*, Oxford, Bodleian Library Selden Supra MS 41, fol. 148.

understanding that eremitism was not incompatible with features of the cenobitic life. As Henrietta Leyser has argued, personal solitude and anchoresis do not necessarily define the hermit of the eleventh and twelfth centuries. "What did matter was that the communities founded in 'forests and deserts' should be cut off and isolated from the world."[22] Thus such foundations as Stephen's Obazine, Bernard of Blois's Jubin, John Gualbert's Vallombrosa, and even Cîteaux could be perceived by their founders as eremitical even while the hermits appeared to live a cenobitic life. In the same way, Gerard's Bernard of Blois, though never apparently a hermit, was perceived to be following an eremitical way of life. The foundation of Jubin should be seen as an example of the same reforming impulse that led to the creation of, for instance, Prémontré at roughly the same period in northern France. This impulse can be described as "eremitical" because the monks themselves took as their models the heroes of the desert and wilderness. The reforming principle, the newness of the foundation, and thus its freedom from existing associations was more important than the conditions under which the monks lived together. Gerard's De conversatione reveals the same phenomenon in the Latin East, in the period roughly from the 1120s to the 1160s.

What features of a monastic career made it, in Gerard's eyes, eremitical? The monk John of Jerusalem performed wonders of abstinence, fasting completely three days of the week. He tried to live alone in a deserted monastery on the Black Mountain near Antioch, but hunger drove him back to the cloister in Jerusalem.[23] He had failed the test of eremitism, but for Gerard the attempt was what counted. Ursus, a monk of Jubin, was a "part-time" hermit, who would leave the cloister periodically to wander in remote parts of the Black Mountain, calling on the Lord and the Blessed Virgin. This is a model we encounter again in an Orthodox monk; it does not seem to owe anything to Western practice.[24] Valerius, a knight who had come to Jerusalem on pilgrimage from his native Burgundy, entered the cloister at Jubin but left again to live in a more deserted spot on the Black Mountain. Like Godric of Finchale in northern England, however, Valerius remained in contact with his monastery and was visited occasionally by a

---

22. Leyser, Hermits and the New Monasticism, 20.
23. Duodecima centuria, col. 1603.
24. Ibid., col. 1607.

priest from Jubin who celebrated Mass and gave him Holy Communion.[25] He returned to Jubin after being attacked and severely wounded by two Armenian shepherds, and died two months later.

The fullest accounts given by Gerard are those of Bernard of Blois and Elias of Narbonne, both of whom lived on the uncertain frontier between the cenobitic and eremitical life. Bernard is described as *vir eloquens et zelo iusticiae fervidus*, but his eloquence is not to be measured according to "scientia," a human attainment.[26] Nothing is known of Bernard's birth-place or parentage, but sometime before 1123 he went with a few companions (among them Robert of Jerusalem, another of Gerard's examples) to found a priory on the Black Mountain. Gerard speaks of a Rule devised by the new community, but of its contents mentions only the prohibition of all personal wealth. The priory might accept a donation of up to three bezants but no more. Whether this was one of a number of new strictures in a comprehensive Rule, or simply a reemphasis of one aspect of the Benedictine Rule, is not clear from Gerard's account. The fact that Bernard and his companions left to found a new house suggests that they had in mind a community that was not necessarily bound by the closest adherence to any existing Rule: there were Latin Benedictine or Cluniac monasteries available in the Holy Land.[27]

In any event, the new foundation was not a success and dissolved into a schism within the community. With the consent of Bernard, patriarch of Antioch, Bernard of Blois left the new foundation and entered the monastery of Machanath, near the Black Mountain. In 1123 he visited King Baldwin II of Jerusalem, who was languishing in a Turkish prison—although he had openly criticized the king in the past for his *vitia enormia*. He used the visit as an opportunity to preach to Balaq, the Turkish emir who had captured Baldwin, though apparently without success.[28]

---

25. Ibid.

26. Ibid., col. 1605. This theme deserves fuller treatment elsewhere. Late Antique sources often speak of solitary holy men as practicing "philosophy" by the manner of their lives, e.g., Gregory of Nyssa, *Vie de Sainte Macrine*, ed. and trans. P. Maraval (Paris, 1971), 18: passim; 20: 6; Theodoret of Cyrrhus, *Religiosa historia*, PG 82:1285, 1468.

27. *Duodecima centuria*, col. 1605. The refusal to accept donations was not unknown among hermits and "new" monastic communities in the eleventh and twelfth centuries. The English hermit Godric of Finchale rejected most of the offerings brought to him (Reginald of Durham, *Libellus* 72), while John Gualbert, founder of Vallombrosa and incensed at a rich man's donation to his new house, tore up the deed and called on the vengeance of God—to be rewarded by a fire that consumed the cloister (*AASS*, July III, 335).

28. *Duodecima centuria*, col. 1606. As Kedar, "Gerard of Nazareth," 67, points out, this

Gerard describes no stage of Bernard's life when he lived an eremitical life in the conventional sense. Rather, Bernard simply rejected the traditional forms of Benedictine monasticism for a new community based on a Rule. What made Bernard a "hermit"—his asceticism, or the foundation of a new house with a few companions? If the former, he was a failure as an eremitical leader, for it was the severity of his asceticism that contributed to the collapse of the venture and sent him into the cloister to follow a conventional monastic life. The formal elements of the monastic career seem to be less important to Gerard, in this case, than the spiritual impetus. A monk did not necessarily commit himself to a lifetime in the cloister, nor did a hermit commit himself to one in the wilderness. Indeed, a hermit might simply appear remarkable for the quality of his life, regardless of where it was lived.

Elias of Narbonne provides a fuller example of the same phenomenon.[29] A teacher of grammar from Narbonne, he went on pilgrimage to Jerusalem during the reign of King Fulk (1131–43). "Turning aside on his journey to a certain monastery of hermits, he accepted ordination to the priesthood there."[30] Later he hid himself away with some like-minded companions in a cave near Jerusalem. Despite his careful concealment, he seems to have attracted notice and admiration, for he was persuaded by the monks of Notre-Dame de Josaphat to enter their monastery. Their "continuous prayers," coupled with the exhortation of the patriarch of Jerusalem (so far had his reputation spread!), eventually won him over.

Elias's progression is difficult to define in precise terms. What does the phrase *eremitarum monasterium* signify? According to the strict conventional

---

episode predates Francis's more celebrated attempt to convert al-Malik al-Kamil on the Fifth Crusade by almost one hundred years. Balaq had a reputation for tolerance which Bernard may have been aware of. According to a Syriac chronicler, he "would not let any harm the Christians even by word" ("The First and Second Crusades from an Anonymous Syriac Chronicle," trans. A. S. Tritton with notes by H.A.R. Gibb, *Journal of the Royal Asiatic Society*, 1933, 92). On Baldwin's disastrous attempt to escape from captivity see Fulcher of Chartres, *Historia Hierosolymitana* 3.23–26, ed. H. Hagenmeyer (Heidelberg, 1913), 679–93.

29. Gerard wrote a separate biography of Elias, which has survived in fragments in the *Duodecima centuria* alongside the *De conversatione*. An entry in Josias Simmler's edition of Conrad Gesner's *Bibliotheca universalis* (Zurich, 1574), lists Gerard's works: "scripsit ad Guilhelmum presbyterum, De conversatione servorum Dei, lib. 1. Vitam Abbatis Heliae, Lib 1. De una Magdalena contra Graecos Lib 1. Ad ancillas Dei in Bethania, Lib 1. Contra Salam templarium, Lib 1. Atque alia. Claruit anno Domini 1140." See also Kedar, "Gerard of Nazareth," 60, n. 21.

30. *Duodecima centuria*, col. 1603.

definitions of historical scholarship it is paradoxical, for the *eremus* and monastery appear to represent distinct ideals of the Christian life. In fact they could be complementary. Contemporaries were clearly prepared to accept the flexibility of the monastic vocation. It may be assumed that Elias's first community, where he was ordained priest, was not unlike Bernard of Blois's attempted foundation on the Black Mountain, probably following some form of Rule but perceiving itself as distinct from the traditional idea of a monastery. Elias's withdrawal to the cave represents a further step away from mainstream Benedictine monasticism, but Elias was eventually to give up that form of life. Perhaps he never regarded it as permanent, but only as a stage in the monastic life.

Gerard's account implies that Elias was quite a catch for the monks of Notre-Dame de Josaphat, but this may be too flattering an interpretation. The initiative clearly did come from the monks, supported by the patriarch. It is possible, however, that Elias's removal to Notre-Dame may represent a general trend within the Latin Church in the Holy Land. To outside observers, his ascetic life in the caves may have appeared impressive, but the church authorities could never be sure that priests like Elias were fasting at the proper hours or following the correct liturgical observances, or even using the right calendar. For just such reasons, Ivo of Chartres had told Rainaud that his best chance of salvation lay in the cloister.[31]

Elsewhere Gerard refers to the activities of Aimery of Limoges, patriarch of Antioch, whom he describes as *sedulus vitae monasticae promotor*.[32] He goes on to describe how Aimery prohibited any monk from living alone on the Black Mountain without proper supervision (*sine maiore inspectore*). Gerard, who as bishop of Laodicea was Aimery's suffragan, would have been required to enforce this ruling in his own diocese. Aimery's conception of monasticism (as we see it through the Centuriators' paraphrasing of the *De conversatione*) was much narrower and more "traditional" than his subordinate's. It would be wrong, however, to suppose that he disapproved of eremitism per se. No other evidence from Aimery's long career survives to flesh out the single suggestive sentence in the *Duodecima centuria*, and there is no trace from an independent source of the *lex* referred to by the Centuriators. It is impossible to judge whether he shared Ivo of Chartres' skepticism about the intentions of hermits or, like Peter the Venerable,

31. Ivo of Chartres, *Epistolae*, PL 160:260–62.
32. *Duodecima centuria*, col. 1373.

doubted whether hermits could survive the harsh conditions of a self-sufficient life and at the same time retain a monastic discipline.

In any case, Aimery's "law" (which may have taken the form of either a judgment in a single case, or a synodal decree) is not particularly radical. It represents the same monastic ideal as that glorified by the doyen of eleventh-century monastic reform, Peter Damian. Aimery did not forbid eremitism in the form of such communities as Jubin, or even necessarily Elias of Narbonne's shadowy group in the cave outside Jerusalem, but he did forbid solitary hermits who lived under no established Rule or superior. The type of hermit he sought to bring into the fold of "traditional" monasticism was Gerard of Nazareth's Rainald of Galilee, who lived alone on the banks of the Jordan equipped with only a trowel to dig up the roots on which he subsisted; or John of Carraria, who was so removed from society that he did not even know Antioch was held by the Latins; or perhaps the Hungarian Cosmas, in his cell built into the walls of Jerusalem.

The pressure exerted on Elias by the monks of Josaphat and the patriarch of Jerusalem may have been inspired by the same concerns as Aimery's ruling: the desire to enforce the strict observance of the Benedictine Rule for monks who preferred to see themselves as living outside mainstream monasticism. Elias conformed to the wishes of the monks, but after an unspecified time he was elected abbot of Palmaria, not far from Tiberias in Galilee. Palmaria, as B. Z. Kedar showed, was probably an eremitical foundation quite similar to Jubin or to that in which Elias had started his monastic career.[33] The circumstances of Elias's election are unknown, but he may have become well-known (or notorious) as leader of the community in the Valley of Jehosaphat for an exploit in which he tried to offer himself and his brethren as hostages to the Muslim garrison of Ascalon in return for Christian prisoners.[34] On that occasion he was disappointed by the luke-warm response of his companions; at Palmaria he encountered problems with his new flock. He seems to have been both unhappy and ineffectual. He was not a good monastic administrator. Said Gerard, "He gave so liberally that his left hand did not know what his right was doing."[35] This may have been a virtue in purely human terms, but it was disastrous for the

---

33. For the location and history of Palmaria, see B. Z. Kedar, "Palmarée, abbaye clunisi-enne du XIIe siècle en Galilée," *Revue Bénédictine* 93 (1983), 260–69. Jacques de Vitry, *Historia Hierosolymitana* 53 (Bongars, 1075–76), mentions monks (or hermits) settling "in that wilderness lying by the Sea of Galilee."

34. *Duodecima centuria*, col. 1608.

35. Ibid. "Egenis liberaliter dedit, ita ut sinistra manus nesciret quid faceret dextra."

abbey. Elias managed to escape the burdens of office by obtaining a highly irregular exemption from Queen Melisende. He returned to Jerusalem[36] but was later forcibly reinstated at Palmaria by his superior, the archbishop of Nazareth. We do not know what Elias did in Jerusalem, but perhaps he took up the anchoritic life again.

Back at Palmaria, Elias provoked the hostility of the brethren by adhering to a stricter regime than that enjoined by the Benedictine Rule.[37] He admired the Cistercians and wanted to send a monk to France to learn the customs of Cîteaux, but his monks refused to wear the Cistercian habit, protesting, quite reasonably, that the rough wool was too uncomfortable for the Galilee climate.[38] Elias died in 1140, about the time that Gerard himself became bishop of Laodicea. His interest in the Cistercians shows that he was not in principle opposed to cenobitic monasticism, but there is no doubt that he was happier and more successful in a smaller, less structured group, unhindered by the demands of ecclesiastical superiors and the responsibilities of a monastic estate. Nevertheless, he was a sincerely holy man, an assiduous scholar of the Scriptures, and even a would-be missionary.[39] His talents, never quite fulfilled in the cloister, still made a valuable contribution to the Christian life of the Latin East.

Because of the circumstances of its survival, it is impossible to be sure of Gerard's purpose in recording the lives of Frankish hermits in Syria and Palestine. Clearly, he was trying to promote the ideals of eremitical monasticism. The interpolation of a hostile passage in the life of Bernard of Blois, added uncritically by the Centuriators, confirms the opposition of a more traditional element within the Latin Church to the "monastic fluidity" celebrated by Gerard.[40] As has been argued, Gerard's inclusion of such a "mixed bag" of hermits and monks appears to argue for a genuinely catholic view of the monastic life, such as that celebrated by the anonymous author of the *Libellus de diversis ordinibus et professionibus qui sunt in aeccle-*

36. Ibid.
37. Ibid., 1609. "De ambitione solitus est dicere, omnia vitia divino auxilio superari posse, unicum hoc illis sese insinuare, qui sanctius prae aliis vivere studerent."
38. Ibid. There is no evidence that Elias was successful in engaging the services of a French Cistercian.
39. Ibid. Elias had considered the idea of preaching the gospel to the Muslims in Spain before his pilgrimage to the Holy Land, but he never carried it through.
40. Ibid., col. 1230. This critical account of Bernard's career does not seem to be a commentary by the Centuriators themselves. If that were the case, it would surely form part of the rest of the section on Bernard, ibid., cols. 1605–6.

sia.[41] The passage from the preface to the *De conversatione* preserved by the Carmelite authors celebrates solitary living. But there may also be signs that Gerard was troubled by the same concerns as critics of unsupervised eremitical life, such as Peter the Venerable. The description of Rainald of Galilee's fasting practices concludes: "O ineptum simiarum genus, ieiuniam Christi sine mandato Dei et citra omnem necessitatem imitari praesumens," a fairly clear condemnation of excessive asceticism.[42] Further hints of a distaste for such excesses emerge from a close reading of the *De conversatione*. The penance Alberic imposed on himself for his disgust at the lepers' sores (to immerse his face in the blood and discharge collected from the washing and dressing of the sores) is described with the parenthetical comment "horribile dictu."[43] There is an implicit criticism in the wry account of John of Jerusalem's attempt to live in a deserted monastery on the Black Mountain and his return to Jerusalem when he had run short of food.[44] Gerard tried to teach the illiterate anchorite Dominic (who lived in the porch of a church in Nazareth) to read so that he could manage the psalms, but Dominic, to Gerard's regret, regarded it as a waste of time.[45]

Are these to be taken as the interpolated comments of the Centuriators themselves or as Gerard's own doubts? If the former, the Protestant compilers could have gone a good deal further in their condemnation of medieval Catholic practices—indeed of monastic vows themselves. But the highly favorable account of Elias of Narbonne is presented without any adverse comment at all. Assuming that they derive from Gerard himself, we should see these occasional gestures of disapproval not as opposition to solitary living but as warnings of the distractive extremes to which it could lead genuinely godly people. In the case of Elias of Narbonne, a propensity to an asceticism regarded as extreme by his monks at Palmaria is praised in glowing terms.

---

41. *Libellus de diversis ordinibus et professionibus qui sunt in aecclesia*, ed. and trans. G. Constable and B. Smith (Oxford, 1972), 13. Compare Lanfranc of Bec's letter (perhaps apocryphal) to Abbot Rudolph: "Non enim plures sunt Ecclesiae, sed una est toto urbe diffusa, et uni Deo ubique servitur, et uni Regi militatur" (*Epistolae* 9, PL 150:549). Rainaud the hermit quoted this to Ivo of Chartres (see n. 14 above).

42. *Duodecima centuria*, col. 1604. "O foolish race of monkeys, who presume to imitate the fasting of Christ without the command of God and against all necessity." The possibility remains that this sentence might be an interpolation of the Centuriators, but if so it would be an uncharacteristic intrusion by the otherwise scrupulous compilers of sources.

43. Ibid., col. 1603.

44. Ibid.

45. Ibid., col. 1604. Here the Centuriators (we assume, rather than Gerard himself) commented: "Tales sanctos hoc nimirum seculum produxit."

If the monastic life in the East was broad enough to include eremitical communities and individual anchorites as well as cloistered monks, what difference did other contemporaries see between these forms of life? Elias was implored to enter the cloister, but both he and Bernard of Blois provoked resentment by their austerity—in the case of Bernard, resentment even from his "eremitical" brethren. This sounds like the echo of an older refrain: Symeon the Stylite had begun his monastic career as a conventual monk in fifth-century Syria but was turned out of the monastery by his superior when he refused to accept his authority in the matter of personal, unregulated ascetic practices.[46] Many undoubtedly left monasteries in the Middle Ages because they found the life there too lax (many also because they found it too harsh), as the hermit Rainaud complained to Ivo of Chartres.[47]

The formal distinctions between the hermit and the monk become meaningless when we consider the life of, for example, Saint Bruno. After abandoning his career in the secular church, Bruno became a hermit at Sèche-Fontaine, in Champagne, in 1080. Four years later he and six companions sought a deserted place to settle in the Alps and founded La Chartreuse.[48] It is natural to think of La Chartreuse as a monastic institution because it had permanent buildings and a Rule of its own, and because it became a distinct Order in the church. It makes little sense, however, to label Bruno a hermit at Sèche-Fontaine but a monk while he was at La Chartreuse and a hermit again after he had left the papal court for the wilds of Calabria in 1090. His conception of his own career, after all, had not changed. Bernard of Blois's foundation at Jubin raises similar problems of definition. Each brother lived in his own cell, yet Gerard calls them *coenobii monachi*.[49] They were hermits in that they lived far from habitation, but cenobitic in that they lived as a community, eating and worshiping together. More important, they had opted to found a new community with their own rules rather than join an existing one.

The same fluidity of expression is found in the contemporary French foundation of Obazine. The biography of the founder, Stephen, by an anonymous monk who himself "crossed the lines" from a Benedictine house to a Cistercian and then to Obazine, provides us with the anatomy of

46. Theodoret, *Religiosa historia* 26, *PG* 82:1468.
47. Morin, "Rainaud l'ermite," 102–3.
48. Guiges I, *Vita Sancti Hugonis Gratianapolitani*, *PL* 153:769.
49. *Duodecima centuria*, col. 979.

a monastic foundation of the same era as Gerard of Nazareth. Stephen and his companion Peter were initiated into the solitary life by an anchorite in their native Limousin.[50] After six months they left to settle in a heavily wooded region of the Corrièze valley. They survived on uncertain alms and on what they could forage from the forest until Peter and a priest, Bernard, who had joined them, went to Limoges to obtain the blessing of the bishop. Bishop Eustorgius consecrated a cross for them and gave Bernard the authority to celebrate Mass and permission to build a monastery, provided they follow a "custom."[51] This marked the official beginning of the foundation and gave the hermits the credibility to attract recruits and patronage.

The monastic buildings at Obazine followed a typical Benedictine plan, with a dormitory for the monks, a refectory, a kitchen, and a cloister. The monks used the office of Regular canons and the schedule of a Benedictine monastery. But the quality of their lives, the author stresses, was eremitical, for while canons do not work, Stephen insisted that his monks spend much of each day in manual labor.[52]

The monastery at Obazine grew as greater numbers were attracted to the forest. Stephen dodged the issue of formal leadership of the community until it became impossible to ignore it, then the bishop of Chartres, asked to mediate, chose a reluctant and still unordained Stephen as prior.[53] Gradually Obazine took on the very formalism of a Regular monastery that Stephen had gone to the forest to avoid. Even while describing the permanent buildings, the singing of the office, and the Masses said for the souls of benefactors, Stephen's biographer insists that the brethren were still hermits. This may not be convincing until we are reminded that the foundation still had no Rule, but only the personal direction of Stephen. This was a vexing problem for Stephen. He visited other monasteries to observe their customs and make comparisons with his own,[54] but he found nothing satisfactory until he made the arduous journey to La Chartreuse. Stephen's formal request to associate Obazine with La Chartreuse was gently but firmly rejected by Chartreuse's prior, who instead recommended Cîteaux as

50. *Vita Stephani Obazinensis,* 1.1–3 (Aubrun, 42–50).

51. Ibid., 1.7 (Aubrun, 54). "Ita dumtaxat ut morem a patribus traditum per omnia sequerentur."

52. Ibid. (56).

53. Ibid., 1.14 (66).

54. Ibid., 1.23 (78). The undefined nature of Stephen's community is emphasized by the bad treatment he received at the hands of the canons of Lyons, who would have nothing to do with "irregular" monks.

a more appropriate model for the large foundation that Obazine had by now become.[55] Stephen's somewhat surprising response, once he had returned to Limousin, was to embark on more building in order to accommodate the ever-increasing numbers. A new church was added for pilgrims and their guests, as well as a convent for women recruits.[56]

Obazine still had no Rule. Stephen was forced to adopt one when his brethren pointed out that nobody was immortal and that his customs, developed over a number of years, would not outlive him—even though, as his biographer says, no written Rule could add anything Stephen had not already conceived. To the biographer, adoption of a Rule was a rite of passage by which an eremitical community slipped into the institution of monasticism, regardless of its size, longevity, or achievements before that point. The Obazine monks did not discuss the possibility of writing down Stephen's customs or forming a distinct Order. Rather, they simply debated whether to adopt the Rule of Saint Benedict or Augustine's Rule for canons.[57] With the advice of Aimery, bishop of Clermont (and himself a Benedictine), they chose to receive instruction in the Benedictine Rule from the nearby house at Dalon. On Palm Sunday 1142, twenty years after the foundation of Obazine, Stephen was made a monk in the presence of the bishop of Limoges and immediately promoted to abbot.[58] The formal adoption of the Rule of Saint Benedict marked the end of Obazine as an eremitical foundation, even if it changed little of the everyday life of the community.

By the yardstick of Obazine, Bernard of Blois's community at Jubin remained eremitical. Rather than adopting an existing Rule, they founded their priory on the single principle of absolute poverty.[59] It was on this principle that Jubin eventually foundered, as had Molesme a generation earlier. The prior of Jubin, who remains unknown, relaxed so far from the strict observance laid down in the original settlement as to permit gifts of money, wine, and foods to be accepted.[60] Bernard "and other hypocrites"

---

55. Ibid., 1.26 (82).

56. Ibid.

57. Ibid., 2.1 (96).

58. Ibid., 2.7 (106). "Interea fratres Obazine monachi ex eremitis effecti, novis legibus novisque institutionibus quotidia informabantur et quamquam esset in celesti militia veterani, monasticis tamen studiis adhuc videbantur indocti erantque rudes monachi qui jam fuerant in religione perfecti."

59. *Duodecima centuria*, col. 1605.

60. The chapters in the *De conversatione* dealing with Bernard are scattered across three chapters of the *Duodecima centuria*. The passage dealing with the schism is hostile to Bernard

chastised the prior for his laxity. When this proved ineffective, Bernard, impatient by disposition, became "stirred up like a gadfly and ran through the woods, prepared rather to die of hunger than to permit such an unspeakable thing."[61] Even Gerard of Nazareth apparently condemned Bernard's "insanity," until Bernard left Jubin to return to Jerusalem, where he began to harangue King Baldwin II. Eventually Bernard received permission from the patriarch of Antioch to become a monk at Machanath instead of returning to Jubin.[62] This solution worked for a while. The Jubin monks continued to accept gifts—a great scandal, comments the author sarcastically—while Machanath took the recruits who, like Bernard, "did not want to drink sweet wines." Later, and under circumstances not mentioned in the *De conversatione*, Bernard returned to Jubin, which was by now empty, "doubtless due to the persecution of those men."[63] The account favorable to him adds the detail that Bernard was made prior of Machanath by order of the papal legate.[64]

The schism at Jubin is presented in the *De conversatione* (our only source) as having erupted over the question of poverty and the observance of a specific ascetic regime. Molesme, a reformed Burgundian house founded in 1075 by a group of hermits, had suffered a similar split. By 1083 the monastery had been established on land granted by Hugh de Maligny and expanded by further donations on the specific appeal of the bishop of Langres.[65] The donations that made the foundation possible also sucked the community of hermits into the human society from which they had sought refuge. Grants of land brought with them, particularly in an inhabited area, feudal obligations and responsibilities. Abbot Robert and a few others, including Stephen Harding, left Molesme for the hermitage at

---

and fits so poorly with the tone of the eulogistic notices in the rest of Gerard's work that it must be the work of another author, perhaps a later interpolation.

61. *Duodecima centuria*, col. 1230. ". . . impatienti animo Bernhardus saepius velut oestro concitus, in sylvas excurrit, potius fame periturus, quam rem tam infandam, ut ipse quidem habebat, inspecturus."

62. Machanath, also on the Black Mountain, attracted (in addition to Bernard of Blois) the Frankish knights William and Hugo and three other hermits mentioned by Gerard of Nazareth (ibid., col. 1606).

63. Ibid., col. 1230.

64. Ibid., col. 1605.

65. *Cartulaires de Molesme*, ed. J. Laurent, 2 vols. (Paris, 1907–11), 2:7.

Aulps (later a daughter-house), in order to observe more closely the Benedictine Rule.[66]

Once again the comparison with Obazine is instructive. Well before the adoption of a Rule, Stephen struggled with doubts about the course his foundation seemed to be taking. His harsh asceticism had been conducive to the original recruits, who observed absolute silence day and night and subjected themselves to a rigorous personal discipline that excluded even raising one's eyes or smiling without permission.[67] Stephen's biographer suggests that his personal direction of the community became an increasing problem as the number of recruits grew. It was easier, he admits ruefully, to impose discipline on the monks when they were fewer and their lives more perfect.[68] Stephen himself expressed regret at taking in such large numbers. "His mind was stung and bitterly grieved, desiring solitude; he was impatient of the troubles he reaped from the perpetual government of so many people."[69] He had come to Obazine not to gather people together but to escape them. When Stephen spoke of solitude, he did not mean that he wanted to live alone (he had embarked on the eremitical life with his companion) but simply that he wanted to live in a secluded place, with few people. The model for his ideal foundation was La Chartreuse. There is a poignant irony in the Carthusian rejection of Obazine: Stephen agreed with them on the merits of a small community, but by then it was too late.

Size, of course, could not be attained without wealth. Even before the visit to La Chartreuse, Obazine had expanded beyond its original settlement into a new part of the forest,[70] and Stephen had begun to accept the sons—and the patronage—of nobles.[71] In a fascinating parenthesis, the biographer tells the story of how the devil, watching the new building, argued with a carpenter about the monks' virtue: they could not be genuine, the devil claimed, for they came to the forest simply to accumulate riches and property.[72] Stephen was aware of the need to steer a course

---

66. Ibid., 14. See also Lackner, *Eleventh-Century Background of Cîteaux*, 236, 250–55, for the controversy over the chronology of the split at Molesme and the foundation of Cîteaux.

67. *Vita Stephani Obazinensis*, 1.9 (Aubrun, 58). A visitor complained that he was unable to describe the manner of life of the Obazine monks because it was impossible to talk to them.

68. Ibid., 1.16 (68–70).

69. Ibid., 1.10 (58). "Mordebatur tamen et vehementius angebatur mens eius solitudinis cupiditate, curarum impatiens, quas se ex multorum gubernatione perpetui metuebat."

70. Ibid., 1.11 (60).

71. Ibid., 1.16 (68–70).

72. Ibid., 1.12 (62).

between a settlement that was too impermanent—lest he and his followers be dismissed as gyrovagues—and building too grandly.

The church hierarchy in Syria was instrumental in the Jubin controversy. Patriarch Bernard of Antioch seems to have supported Bernard of Blois in his desire to found a genuinely ascetic cenobitic community. Because it was the papal legate himself who appointed Bernard as prior (thus interfering with the canonical process of election), this support must have been confirmed by the highest authorities.[73] Moreover, if Jubin was indeed left empty, as the author claims, it cannot have received much support at the critical time. It is difficult to resist the conclusion that Jubin was left either to put up with Bernard and his demands or to founder without him—much as Palmaria foundered under Elias.

A different picture of the role of the church authorities emerges at Obazine, where nothing was done without the supervision and approval of the hierarchy. The intervention of the episcopacy can be seen as a series of signposts marking Stephen's career. Stephen's initial decision to become a hermit was made with the encouragement of the abbot of La Chaise-Dieu.[74] When the three founder-members were struggling to survive and to establish their credentials with locals faced by the appearance of a false hermit (*pseudochorita*), it was the authority of Bishop Eustorgius of Limoges that ensured their foundation.[75] When controversy arose in Obazine over the direction of the monastery, arbitration by the bishop of Chartres settled the matter.[76]

Finally, Obazine was received into the Benedictine Order with the advice of Bishop Aimery of Clermont and with the instruction of Regular monks.[77] The three decisive stages in the history of the foundation—the initial withdrawal from the world, the official recognition of the settlement,

---

73. *Duodecima centuria*, cols. 1605–6. The opposition to Bernard seems to have come from the Jubin community itself. Had a higher authority supported the prior, the account hostile to Bernard would surely have said so. As it is, the statement "ac reprehendit istam Bernhardi insaniam etiam Gerardus a Nazareth" is puzzling. If Gerard was involved in the controversy, it must have been when he was still only a monk at Nazareth, not yet bishop of Laodicea, because he is described as "flourishing" around 1140 (ibid., cols. 112, 1379; *Willelmi Tyrensis Archiepiscopi Chronicon* [hereafter referred to as William of Tyre], ed. R.B.C. Huygens, *CCCM* 63 [1986], 845).

74. *Vita Stephani Obazinensis*, 1.2 (Aubrun, 46).

75. Ibid., 1.3 (52); 1.7 (54).

76. Ibid., 1.14 (66). Close association with the episcopacy was also a feature of the early Cistercians (C. Bouchard, *Holy Entrepreneurs* [Ithaca, 1991]).

77. *Vita Stephani Obazinensis*, 2.1 (96).

and the adoption of the Benedictine Rule—all happened with the guidance or intervention of an ecclesiastical authority. If Jubin failed because of neglect or mismanagement, Obazine prospered because it enjoyed careful support.

This is not to suggest that the hierarchy in the crusader states was uninterested in new foundations. As has already been shown, Patriarch Aimery of Antioch insisted on proper supervision for all hermits on the Black Mountain. The most durable of all crusader monastic foundations began from the eremitical community on Mount Carmel. At the beginning of the thirteenth century, the Frankish hermits occupying the site of the "spring of Elijah" on Carmel applied to the patriarch of Jerusalem for supervision. The result was the Rule of Saint Albert and the rapid development of the Order of Mount Carmel.[78]

Episcopal control of a new foundation might be established, as at Mount Carmel or Obazine, by direct appeal on the part of hermits who had already settled on an uninhabited site. Hermits in Latin Syria were fortunate in their landscape: there was an abundance of mountains, semi-deserts, and wilderness from which to choose. They could settle either on land that was uninhabitable by secular Frankish populations because it was too exposed to Muslim raids, and thus unlikely to entail feudal obligations, or on cult sites such as Mount Carmel, the Black Mountain, or the Jordan Valley near Jericho, which had long histories of eremitical habitation. At Obazine, Stephen and his companions found a clearing in a dense forest, an area that was neither inhospitable (there was a river nearby)[79] nor yet claimed for habitation. At least initially, then, they were able to avoid the complexities of land tenure that plagued Molesme.

Other eremitical foundations dealt with the problem of settlement in similar ways. Bruno's venture at La Chartreuse—his third attempt at retirement from the world since fleeing episcopal preferment in 1080— succeeded largely because he and his companions were able to find the right location. Instead of striking out on their own, they applied specifically for an *eremum* from Bishop Hugh of Grenoble.[80] They were fortunate to find a bishop sympathetic to their needs, but they had also learned from experience that the site for an eremitical foundation could not be chosen too carefully—as Stephen of Obazine would find, to his cost. La Chartreuse

---

78. See Chapters 5 and 6, below.

79. *Vita Stephani Obazinensis*, 1.3 (50).

80. *Recueil des plus anciens actes de la Grande Chartreuse, 1086–1196*, ed. B. Bligny (Grenoble, 1958), 3.

was built in a narrow valley framed by the escarpments of high cliffs on either side.[81] The Carthusian success in preserving the eremitical quality of their foundation was ensured by the inaccessibility of the site. When Prior Guy I placed the *eremum* under the care of a bridge-keeper whose duty was to keep women and other undesirables from entering the valley,[82] he could be sure the measure would work because the site could be entered only by a single gap in the rock-face. The question of numbers is raised toward the end of the customary: there were to be thirteen monks and sixteen *conversi*.[83] In answer to the question "Why so few?" Guy replies that the hermits came to the *eremum* and instituted customs in the first place in order to shut themselves off from human contact.[84] Thus Stephen found that Obazine was considered too diluted by lay society to attract Carthusian interest.

One clause in Guy's customary forbids the community to accept any possessions outside the *eremum*. It could hold no fields, vineyards, gardens, churches, or cemeteries and collect no tithes.[85] By the time Guy's customs were written and adopted (between 1121 and 1128), the community had already become involved in problems arising from land tenure. The lands originally granted to La Chartreuse by Hugh of Grenoble were part of the demesne of the abbey of La Chaise-Dieu, given with the consent of Abbot Seguin.[86] When Bruno was summoned to Rome in 1090, his companions wanted to abandon La Chartreuse and gave up their rights to the valley. Urban II had to petition the abbot and Bishop Hugh to ensure that the Carthusians, having been persuaded to stay, could have the land returned to them.[87] Moreover, from 1099 onward the community received a series of land grants from individuals, sometimes solicited or encouraged by Bishop Hugh.[88] This led inevitably to territorial disputes with other landowners.[89]

81. See ibid., 5, for the extent of the original donation.

82. Guiges I, *Coutumes de Chartreuse*, 54 and 21, ed. and trans. "un chartreux" (Paris, 1984), 272, 210.

83. As observed and appreciated by Peter the Venerable, *De miraculis* 2.28, *PL* 189:944.

84. *Coutumes de Chartreuse*, 79 (1984 ed., 286). This principle was tested in 1132, when after seven monks died in an avalanche Guy could have taken in a mass of new recruits; he chose rather to stick to the ideal of minimum numbers.

85. Ibid., 41 (244).

86. See *Recueil des plus anciens actes*, 1 (Bligny, 1–8), for the original grant of land signed by Seguin on December 9, 1084. In 1082–83 Hugh had lived in retirement at the abbey of La Chaise-Dieu; P.-R. Gaussin, *L'abbaye de la Chaise-Dieu, 1043–1518* (Paris, 1962), 134–36.

87. *Recueil des plus anciens actes*, 2/3 (Bligny, 10–12).

88. E.g., ibid., 12 (31–32).

89. Ibid., 18/19 (46–50).

If Guy's customary was written expressly at the request of the five "imitator" Carthusian houses founded in 1115 and 1116 (Portes, Les Ecouges, Durbon, La Sylve-Bénite, and Meyriat), it may also have served to ensure that La Chartreuse itself had authority to refuse to administer further grants.

The hermits of La Chartreuse retained a genuinely eremitical way of life for longer than the monks at Jubin, or Obazine, or Silvanes, largely because they were so inflexible. Stephen's biographer, writing in the 1160s and 1170s, looked back to the adoption of a Rule as the turning-point, from which time Obazine ceased to be eremitical. This seems as artificial a definition of eremitism as any. The Carthusian Customary adopted in the 1120s was based, according to Guy, on Saint Benedict, the epistles of Jerome, and other patristic writings, yet there is no acknowledgment of the Benedictine Rule anywhere in the text,[90] and the Carthusian practice of monasticism continued to be genuinely eremitical rather than cenobitic. Similarly, the Rule of Saint Albert, in the early thirteenth century, would emphasize rather than diminish the eremitical quality of Carmelite monasticism. By contrast, Obazine slipped into cenobitic monasticism with its first permanent buildings.[91]

Stephen of Obazine had his overtures to the Carthusians turned down. The prior of La Chartreuse, however, acted as a "monastic broker," recommending Cîteaux as the most appropriate model for their needs. It was accepted practice in the twelfth century for monasteries to send "consultants" to new houses on request. Elias of Narbonne's request to send one of his monks to France to learn the customs of Cîteaux thus fits into a standard code of behavior.[92] At Obazine, Stephen initially ignored the Carthusian recommendation of Cîteaux as a model for a larger community. The Cistercians were not mentioned when the monks discussed the adoption of a Rule.[93] Later, once Obazine had become Benedictine, Stephen applied to Pope Eugenius III to have his house affiliated with Cîteaux. The special request to the pope was necessary because, as the biographer explains, it was against Cistercian custom to permit double houses for men and women.[94] Eugenius, himself a Cistercian, promised Stephen that the prohibition could be changed, but only little by little, "lest a foundation

---

90. *Coutumes de Chartreuse*, 69 (1984 ed.). See also "La chronique des premiers chartreux," ed. A. Wilmart, *Revue Mabillon* 16 (1926), 126.

91. *Vita Stephani Obazinensis*, 1.7 (Aubrun, 56).

92. *Duodecima centuria*, cols. 1608–9.

93. *Vita Stephani Obazinensis*, 2.1 (96).

94. Canivez, *Statuta*, 1:19.

which is still new be unable to bear a sudden change."[95] As a compromise, two Cistercian monks and two *conversi* were sent to teach the monks Cistercian customs. This was the new Cistercian office of 1134, revised by Bernard, and, as the biographer remarked, it was a hard new course of training.[96]

Elias of Narbonne's attempt to have Palmaria incorporated into the Cistercian Order,[97] by contrast, met with failure. As at Jubin, the austerity of the regime was unpopular, and the monks' refusal to countenance a change in the Rule forced Elias into exile in Jerusalem. It would be instructive to know what Rule, or customs, were followed by the monks of Palmaria before Elias's arrival. It was a relatively new foundation, and like Jubin and Obazine eremitical in origin.[98] Elias, however, seems to have imposed new observances that were regarded as unnecessarily harsh. Like Bernard at Jubin, he would not accept gifts of money. He so exhausted himself with nocturnal vigils that he used to fall asleep at the refectory table. It seems probable that he attempted to coerce his monks into following the same ascetic practices, but rather than writing his own Rule he wanted to adopt the Cistercian Rule. Gerard does not say what happened to the monk sent to France to learn Cistercian observances, but, if we can even assume that he returned with his mission accomplished, the customs he brought back with him were probably rejected along with the Cistercian habit.[99] Gerard's brief account of the episode implies that Elias's authority over his monks was frail. This seems consistent with the picture he paints of an unworldly ascetic incapable of exercising the responsibility of the abbacy. Yet Elias was not unused to heading a community of monks. He had been the leader of the band of hermits in the cave, or tomb-chamber, near Jerusalem, and had been a prominent enough figure to have been "head-hunted" both by Notre-Dame de Josaphat and by Palmaria.[100]

95. *Vita Stephani Obazinensis*, 2.12 (112). ". . . ne repentinam mutationem novella adhuc domus ferre non posset."

96. Canivez, *Statuta*, 1:13–33, for the revised Cistercian office; and 1:37–38 for the formal adoption of Obazine in 1150. See also J.-B. Auberger, *L'unanimité cistercienne primitive: Mythe ou réalité?* Cîteaux: Studia et documenta 3 (Achel, 1986), 25–41, 61–62.

97. Gerard's statement "Habitum et mores Cisterciensium unice adamavit, ita ut suorum unum mitteret Hierosolyma in Gallias, pro adducendo eius ordinis monacho, ex quo omnia quae ad eam sectam pertinerent, addiscere posset" (*Duodecima centuria*, col. 1603) can hardly be given any other interpretation than that Elias wanted Palmaria to join the Order.

98. Kedar, "Palmarée, abbaye clunisienne," 261.

99. *Duodecima centuria*, cols. 1608-9.

100. Ibid., col. 1603. Gerard describes Elias's companions in the cave as "suis."

Gerard's account reveals important clues about the administration of monasteries in the crusader kingdom. As abbot of Palmaria, Elias recognized the supervision of the archbishop of Nazareth and the patriarch of Jerusalem, both of whom he exhausted with his pleas to be released from his office. Yet it was from Queen Melisende that he obtained an exemption to leave Palmaria, and only the exhortation of the archbishop of Nazareth persuaded him to return to his abbey. Perhaps he had managed to secure a post in the queen's household that liberated him from the burden of office, but given his administrative shortcomings and his eremitical credentials, this seems unlikely. Palmaria, like Jubin, could not remain outside episcopal control, but it seems to have been easy for both Bernard and Elias to abandon their offices. Palmaria later became a Cluniac house, at the instigation of Thierry of Vermandois, a visiting Cluniac abbot,[101] and of King Amaury I. In his letter to Cluny lamenting the sad condition of the abbey, Amaury refers to the *advocatus, patronus et fundator* of Palmaria as Gormund, lord of Baisan.[102]

The abbey, then, was founded by a group of hermits with the help of a layman, who may have provided land or buildings and who continued to be interested in the abbey, but was not so closely involved that he could save it from virtual ruin. It would be intriguing to know what Gormund's relations with Elias were. In any case, although the archbishop of Nazareth tried to keep the abbot at his post, it was ultimately the king and a visiting Cluniac, Thierry, who saw to the future of the abbey. Episcopal control, in this case at least, seems to have been less useful than at Obazine in the same period.

Gerard's description of the Palmaria affair, which attributed the blame for Elias's failure to the laxity of his monks, bears similarities to the conflicting accounts of the Jubin schism. Both of Gerard's major examples of eremitical heroism, Elias and Bernard of Blois, fell victim to the rebellion of their brethren. Neither, however, exhibited extremes of ascetic behavior unusual for their age. It is only by stretching vocabulary that Bernard can even be called a hermit. If Elias was indeed forced out of Palmaria by his own monks, we are presented by Gerard with a picture of monasticism in the Latin East in the 1130s as turbulent and mutinous in the face of

---

101. Thierry undertook the journey to Jerusalem in 1170 both on behalf of his own Order and on behalf of Louis VII of France (*Recueil des Historiens des Gaules et de la France*, vol. 16 [Paris, 1878], 149–51, 408). Thierry was abbot of Cluny from 1179 to 1183.

102. A. Bernard and A. Bruel, *Recueil des chartes de l'abbaye de Cluny*, vol. 5 (Paris, 1894), no. 4234; Kedar, "Palmarée, abbaye clunisienne," 263. Gormund witnessed several charters between 1132 and 1174.

reforming zeal. It would be impetuous to conclude from this that Latin monasticism in Outremer was less rigorous, or disciplined, than in western Europe. It might be fairer to characterize the crusader church, on the whole, as lagging behind developments in the West—as less educated and less equipped to create lasting foundations based on reforming ideals.[103]

Gerard's collection of monks shows the eclecticism of the religious life in Outremer. More than this, the *De conversatione* reflects a transitional stage in the life of the church in the Latin East, representing as it does conventional cenobitic forms, new foundations both cenobitic (such as Jubin) and eremitical (such as Elias's community in the cave), hermits working within society (such as the leper-nurses), and extremes of solitary eremitism. Although these types were not unknown in the West, the particular forms of observance chosen by Gerard's hermits were determined by the special conditions, topographical and political, of crusader society. Gerard appreciated the value of all these forms of monastic life, but his ideal, typical of a reform-minded bishop, was the monk who was able, like Elias, to provide spiritual leadership and enterprise within a regulated community. We might, reading the surviving fragments of Gerard's *Life of Elias*, consider his career a failure. It is clear that to Gerard he was a hero of the church in the Latin East.

103. Kedar, "The Patriarch Heraclius," in B. Z. Kedar et al., eds., *Outremer: Studies Presented to Joshua Prawer* (Jerusalem, 1982), 184; and B. Hamilton, *The Latin Church in the Crusader States: The Secular Church* (London, 1980), 134–35, paint a general picture of the Latin Church as wanting in purely spiritual qualities. Although both deal exclusively with the secular church, their arguments suggest by extension a relatively undeveloped monastic culture in the Latin East compared with the West, since unless it can be proved that monasteries were able to recruit largely from Europe, they had the same pool of human resources available to them.

2

The Character of Latin Monasticism in the Crusader States

Gerard of Nazareth's heroes of the eremitical life can be seen to have drawn inspiration from the example set by the monastic reformers of the previous generation in the West. Reform presupposes a state of perceptible decay or weakness in the institution itself. In the case of the Latin East, however, men like Bernard of Blois and Elias of Narbonne were not so much changing an existing monastic culture as helping to create one almost from the beginning. Their achievement must be seen in the context of the monasteries established in the crusader states in the first years after the Frankish settlement.

The universal virtue of life in the cloister emphasized by such monastic leaders as Bernard of Clairvaux and Peter the Venerable at the expense of the holiness of a particular place was characteristic of monastic reform in the eleventh and twelfth centuries. Reformed houses, from Cluny in the tenth century to Fontevrault, Vallombrosa, La Chartreuse, and Cîteaux in the eleventh century, and Prémontré, Obazine, and the Cistercian abbeys in the twelfth, were situated far from the hubs of society. Cîteaux and its daughter-house Rievaulx were in marginal lands recently reclaimed from woodland. Cistercian houses were deliberately not affiliated with a saint or a place. They were all dedicated to the Virgin Mary, and their names—in Latin, "Clare Vallis," "Vallis Paradisi," "Hortus Dei," "Castrum Dei"— underline the detached quality of each house. Without obligations or attachments to cities, regions, or noble families, Cistercian monasteries could concentrate on building the New Jerusalem on earth. By contrast, the established Benedictine houses—for example, Saint Denis, Saint Martial at Limoges, Saint Martin at Tours, Saint Remi at Rheims, Saint Bénigne at Dijon, or, in England, Bury Saint Edmund's or Saint Alban's, were centered on a specific shrine or relic. The function of the monastery was at least in part to safeguard the saint's relics for the town or region.

If we distinguish monasteries of this period according to dependence on or independence from a specific location, the major foundations in the Holy Land appear to have conformed to the more traditional pattern. The great landowning houses of the Latin East owed their foundation to the presence of a shrine, such as the Holy Sepulcher or the Tomb of the Virgin, or to a place with clear scriptural associations, such as Mount Tabor or the Mount of Olives. These celebrated the uniqueness of a particular place rather than the universal ideal of the cloister. This is not to say that the monks of, for example, Mount Tabor, denied the validity of such an ideal. Rather, for them the fact of living in a place celebrated in the liturgy itself enhanced the quality of their spiritual lives. To be a monk, a nun, or a hermit was already to renounce the world; to be "drawn by the sweet odor of the holy places," in Jacques de Vitry's phrase, was to reassure oneself of the reality of the new world thus attained by perpetual contact with the physical framework and liturgical content of Christianity.

Jacques de Vitry noticed an unequal pattern of settlement in the Latin monastic foundations in the Holy Land. If in western Europe new foundations tended to be situated as far as possible from existing habitation, in the Latin East the monastic vocation was no guarantee of solitude:

> And although crowds and hordes of people are a hindrance to religion, they have chosen to live bodily among crowds of people, rather than deprive themselves of living in the holy cities of Jerusa-

lem, Bethlehem, and Nazareth, which, like pots of frankincense, give off the odor of the Savior's presence.[1]

Settlers in the newly conquered East were naturally drawn, as Jacques de Vitry observed, to special places with a proven spiritual charge—in other words, to the shrines that had been the goal of pilgrims for centuries. The pattern of monastic foundation was thus determined by the spiritual contours of the land, which corresponded to scriptural locations. Jerusalem, the place of the Savior's death and the site of the Temple to which the church was the successor, was naturally the most important center, but Nazareth, Sebastia (Samaria, the site of John the Baptist's martyrdom), and Hebron were also important. Insignificant villages, such as Bethany and Capernaum, were fitting places for new foundations because they were important in the Gospel narratives.

Jacques de Vitry's picture should not mislead us. The wildernesses of Judaea, the banks of the Jordan, and the hills of Galilee were no less important in the Gospels and thus in the Christian liturgy and the Christian consciousness. Monasteries were also founded on Mount Tabor, the site of the Transfiguration, on Mount Quarantana, the mountain identified with the place of Jesus' temptation, and on Mount Carmel, the site of Elijah's triumph over the priests of Baal. In general, however, the pattern of Latin religious settlement reflected the concentration of Franks in towns, particularly those on the coastal strip between Jaffa and Beirut, rather than in the hinterland of the new kingdom. In Europe, monastic reform impinged on areas that were, if marginal, at least solidly Catholic. In Outremer, by contrast, the monastic foundations had to establish themselves in territories that had already been settled for centuries by the Greek Orthodox, Jacobite, Maronite, and other Eastern churches. The question of mutual influences between Latin and Eastern monastic houses will thus be particularly important in the context of unregulated and eremitical settlement.

Twelfth- and thirteenth-century sources do not always distinguish between types of monastic vocations that are strictly delineated by modern historians. Thus Jacques de Vitry speaks broadly of monks, canons, and hermits without distinguishing between their foundations. This broad brush

---

1. Jacques de Vitry, *Historia Hierosolymitana* 52 (Bongars, 1076). ". . . licet turba & tumultus hominum plerumque religioni sint impedimentum, maluerunt tamen inter turbas populorum corporaliter habitare, quam a sanctorum civitatum Hierusalem, Bethlehem & Nazareth, quae tanquam cellae aromaticae Salvatoris redolent conversationem, habitatione privari."

may account for his picture of a largely urban settlement. Most of the important shrines were in cathedrals served by chapters of canons rather than in monasteries. The chief exception to this rule, Notre-Dame de Josaphat, may have predated the First Crusade in its original foundation. For the purposes of this book, Latin monastic settlement in Outremer may be divided into three main groups: the reinforcement of foundations pre-dating the First Crusade, the assumption of shrine churches by the Franks, and the foundation of new monasteries. The following pages are not in-tended to provide a catalog of monastic or eremitical foundations, but to furnish examples of the types of foundations found in the Latin East in the twelfth and thirteenth centuries.[2]

Latin Foundations Before the First Crusade

The first Latin monks to settle in the Holy Land were individual hermits, not members of a monastic community. It is impossible to determine how many such hermits lived in a particular site at any one time, but the evidence of the *Commemoratorium de casis Dei vel monasteriis* (ca. 808) suggests that their presence before the eleventh century may have been consistent if not continuous. The *Commemoratorium*, which lists the num-ber and type of clergy serving at each church or monastery, mentions five Latin hermits among the large numbers whose permanent residence was the site of the ruined abbey of Saint Mary on the Mount of Olives.[3]

This settlement, or group of settlements, should be distinguished from the permanent foundation of Saint Mary's, an Orthodox church served by two priests, and from Saints Peter and Paul, an Orthodox monastery with

2. In general, see D. Pringle, *The Churches of the Crusader Kingdom of Jerusalem: A Corpus*, vol. 1 (Cambridge, 1992). When completed, Pringle's architectural survey, undertaken for the British School of Archaeology in Jerusalem, will be the basis for future discussions of Latin ecclesiastical foundations in the Holy Land. Pringle's preliminary work, "Les édifices ecclési-astiques du royaume latin de Jérusalem: Une liste provisoire," *Revue Biblique* 89 (1982), 92–98, has been an essential guide for this chapter.

3. *Itinera Hierosolymitana et descriptiones Terrae Sanctae*, ed. T. Tobler and A. Molinier, 2 vols. (Geneva, 1879–95), 1:302. The other hermits included eleven Greeks, four Syrians, four Georgians, two Armenians, and an Arab "qui Sarracenica lingua psallit" and who may have been a Muslim convert. Two more, a Greek and a Syrian, lived by the steps of the foot of the Mount of Olives, and a Greek, a Syrian, and a Georgian lived at the top of the Garden of Gethsemane.

thirty-five monks, also located on the Mount of Olives. Franciscan archaeologists suggest that the strikingly "international" composition of the Mount of Olives settlements in the ninth century might represent the survival of disparate communities from the huge monastic foundations on the Mount before the Arab invasion.[4]

A Latin monastic community did, however, exist on the Mount of Olives between the date of the *Commemoratorium* and the Frankish occupation of the Church of the Ascension in 1099. Evidence for this is contained in the letter of its monks to Pope Leo III, in which they complain that John, an Orthodox monk of the monastery of Saint Sabas, has accused them of heresy.[5] Around 870 the pilgrim Bernard, a Frankish monk, reported the existence of a hospital catering to Latin pilgrims in Jerusalem.[6] The ninth-century settlement must have owed its existence to the patronage of Charlemagne, to whom, as Einhard reports, the Khalif Harun al-Rashid had given a measure of control over certain holy sites.[7]

The Latin presence on the Mount of Olives is difficult to determine topographically and chronologically, and there is similar uncertainty about the establishment before the First Crusade of a Latin monastery in the Valley of Jehosaphat, just outside the eastern walls of Jerusalem. Notre-Dame de Josaphat had its origins in the hermits and monks who had probably always been a consistent presence around the tomb of the Virgin. The *Commemoratorium* establishes the existence of an Orthodox monastery with thirteen priests and six monks, a *monasterium puellarum* with twenty-six nuns and fifteen hermits, presumably in huts, cells, or caves.[8] According to a later tradition, at some point in the middle of the eleventh century a group of Amalfitan pilgrims founded the Benedictine monastery that was still in existence when the Franks captured Jerusalem in 1099. This tradition was accepted by one of the nineteenth-century editors of the monastery's cartulary, C. Kohler, but rejected by Berlière and the other editor, H.-F. Delaborde.[9] Delaborde, however, suggested that the charter of Baldwin I of

---

4. H. Vincent and F. M. Abel, *Jérusalem, recherches de topographie, d'archéologie et d'histoire*, 3 vols. (Paris, 1912–26), 2:398.

5. Ibid., 398–99, n. 7; U. Berlière, "Les anciens monastères bénédictins de Terre-Sainte," *Revue Bénédictine* 5 (1888), 443.

6. *Itinera Hiersolymitana*, 1:314. "De Emmaus pervenimus ad sanctam civitatem Ierusalem, et recepti sumus in hospitale gloriosissimi imperatoris Karoli, in quo suscipiuntur omnes qui causa devotionis illum adeunt locum, lingua loquentes Romana."

7. Einhard, *Vita Karoli magni*, chap. 16, ed. G. H. Pertz (Hannover, 1863), 14.

8. *Itinera Hierosolymitana*, 1:302.

9. C. Kohler, "Chartes de l'abbaye de Notre-Dame de la vallée de Josaphat en Terre-

1113, in which an abbot is mentioned for the first time, might simply mean that a prior had previously headed the community.[10]

There is no doubt, however, that by 1099 the monastery was in ruins. William of Tyre attests to its foundation by Godfrey de Bouillon, and the monastery was functioning at the time of Saewulf's pilgrimage in 1102–3.[11] If a Latin community had existed before the First Crusade, the monks would almost certainly have been expelled by the Fatimids, who recaptured the city in 1098, if not long before. The likeliest explanation may be that the community did not outlast the destruction of Christian shrines by al-Hakim at the beginning of the eleventh century and was not rebuilt until 1099. There is no evidence that an Orthodox convent had survived to the eve of the Frankish conquest. Orthodox monks clearly did remain, however, living outside a monastic community, and throughout the twelfth century the valley was an important site for hermits.[12]

Whatever the date of the original foundation, the monastery of Notre-Dame flourished from the first years of the Frankish occupation, thanks to the prominence of the shrine. The Romanesque church built over the shrine, which still survives, probably dates from the earliest years of the settlement. Essentially it was a crypt in a cross plan, with an apse at the eastern and western ends, and the tomb itself in the middle of the nave.[13] Queen Melisende had herself buried in the church, halfway down the steps to the shrine of the Virgin.[14]

A papal charter of 1255 confirming the privileges of the abbey lists properties and other interests in Jerusalem, Nablus, Acre, Jaffa, Hebron, Caesarea, Haifa, Tiberias, Tyre, and Sidon.[15] Saladin destroyed the con-

---

Sainte," *Revue de l'Orient Latin* 7 (1899), 108–10; Berlière, "Les anciens monastères," 548; H.-F. Delaborde, ed., *Chartes de la Terre-Sainte provenant de l'abbaye de Notre-Dame de Josaphat*, Bibliothèque des écoles françaises d'Athènes et de Rome, fasc. 19 (Paris 1880), 1.

10. Delaborde, *Chartes de la Terre-Sainte*, no. 3, p. 24.

11. William of Tyre, 9.9 (Huygens, 431); Saewulf, *De situ Ierusalem* 5, in S. De Sandoli, ed., *Itinera Hierosolymitana Crucesignatorum*, 4 vols. (Jerusalem, 1980), 2:18.

12. John Phocas, *Descriptio Terrae Sanctae*, PG 133: 945. This phenomenon is discussed in more detail in Chapter 3, below.

13. C. Enlart, *Les monuments des croisés dans le Royaume de Jérusalem: Architecture réligieuse et civile*, 2 vols. (Paris, 1925–28), 1: pl. 107, 2:230–33, suggests an artistic milieu originating in the Rhône Valley.

14. William of Tyre, 18.32 (Huygens, 858). The tomb of Melisende can still be seen today.

15. Delaborde, *Chartes de la Terre-Sainte*, no. 49, pp. 100–105. Du Cange listed the military service of the abbey in the twelfth century as 150 sergeants (*Les familles d'Outremer de Du Cange*, ed. E. Rey [Paris, 1869], 819–20). There is an extensive discussion of the abbey's

ventual buildings in 1187, using its stones to rebuild the city walls, but left the church intact.[16] Even so, the chapter had moved to Acre after the fall of Jerusalem, and by 1197 had also formed an association with the Benedictine Abbey of Saint Paul in Antioch.[17] In the charter of 1255 Alexander IV reassured the monks that the "difficulty of the times" would not cause them to suffer any loss in their privileges, but the community never returned to its original site. Like other great monastic foundations in the Latin kingdom, however, Notre-Dame had extensive properties and dependencies in Europe. The most important of these were in Sicily, where Roger I founded the priory of Saint Magdalene de Josaphat in Messina as a daughter-house.[18]

Foundations at Shrine Churches

Notre-Dame de Josaphat is an example of a traditional Benedictine house founded on an important shrine and thus serving a specific cult. The only other Latin monastery to predate the Frankish conquest, Saint Mary Latin, had no such resources. Like Notre-Dame, Saint Mary Latin was founded by Amalfitans, probably between 1014 and 1023.[19] Because of its central position in Jerusalem, Saint Mary's and its sister foundation, Saint Mary the Less, achieved prominence by catering to Latin pilgrims. Saint Mary Latin continued to be an important house during the First Kingdom, but

properties in H. E. Mayer, *Bistümer, Klöster, und Stifte in Königsreich Jerusalem* (Stuttgart, 1977), 258–372.

16. *L'état de la cité de Iherusalem*, in De Sandoli, *Itinera*, 2:416.

17. Delaborde, *Chartes de la Terre-Sainte*, no. 44, pp. 92–94.

18. Ibid., no. 3, pp. 24–26. For the Sicilian possessions, see L. T. White, *Latin Monasticism in Norman Sicily* (Cambridge, Mass., 1938), 207–13. After 1291 the community settled in Sicily. In 1269 the abbot of Notre-Dame was given permission by the patriarch of Jerusalem, in his capacity as papal legate, to visit the abbey's western possessions to collect unpaid dues (Delaborde, *Chartes de la Terre-Sainte*, no. 69, pp. 120–21).

19. William of Tyre, 18.5 (Huygens, 815); Jacques de Vitry, *Historia Hierosolymitana*, 58 (Bongars, 1078); Albert of Aix, *Historia Hierosolymitana* 6.25, *RHC Occ.* 4:481. Berlière, "Les anciens monastères bénédictins," 443, incorrectly attributes the origin of the Hospital of Saint John to this double foundation. Although the Hospital's extent eventually bordered Saint Mary Latin to the south, it is now agreed that its origin was on the site of the church of Saint John the Baptist, an Orthodox church to the southwest of the Church of the Holy Sepulcher (J. S. Riley-Smith, *The Knights of St. John in Jerusalem and Cyprus* [London, 1967], 32–37).

after 1187 the community was transferred to Acre and never returned.[20] Its wealth and importance never approached that of Notre-Dame because it could claim guardianship over no shrine, even though it was a stone's throw from the Holy Sepulcher.

The major shrines, the targets of pilgrimage, remained throughout the Muslim occupation of the Holy Land before the First Crusade in the hands of the Orthodox. This did not prevent Latin access to them. Richard of Saint Vannes, visiting Jerusalem in 1026–27, was allowed to celebrate Mass in the Church of the Holy Sepulcher at Easter.[21] After 1099, however, the crusaders took all the shrine churches into their possession, replacing the serving Orthodox, Armenian, Jacobite, and Georgian clergy with Franks.[22]

The Church of Mount Zion, which in 808 had seventeen priests and was described by Saewulf in 1102–3 as "still in existence," was refounded by Godfrey de Bouillon in 1099–100 as a house of canons dependent on the Latin patriarch of Jerusalem.[23] The canons' possessions are known from a confirmation of Alexander III in 1178 and include property in Jerusalem, Bethlehem, Mahumeria (a settlement north of Jerusalem), Jaffa, Nablus, Sebastia, Caesarea, Acre, Sidon, Tyre, Gibelet, and Antioch, as well as churches in Sicily given by Count Roger.[24] After the fall of the First Kingdom in 1187, the canons settled in their own Church of Saint Leonard in Acre, and after 1291 in Santo Spirito in Catalanizetta, in Sicily.[25] The migration had in a sense begun in the twelfth century, however, for Louis VII brought back with him from the Second Crusade some Mount Zion canons and settled them in the Church of Saint Samson in Orléans.[26]

The Franks also took possession of the Church of the Ascension on the Mount of Olives, entrusting its care and offices to a local stylite and a Latin priest called Hermann in 1101; the church subsequently became a house of

20. *Les familles d'Outremer*, 824–25; Mayer, *Bistümer*, 215–21; White, *Latin Monasticism*, 214–27; Enlart, *Les monuments*, 2:182.

21. Hugh de Flavigny, *Chronicon Hugonis monachi* 2.21, *MGH SS* 8:396.

22. This caused great scandal even among those who, like the Armenians, had welcomed the Frankish conquest, as Matthew of Edessa attests (*Chronique et continuation de Grégoire le prêtre* 2.170, ed. and trans. E. Dulaurier [Paris, 1858], 234).

23. *Itinera Hierosolymitana*, 1:301; Saewulf, *De situ Ierusalem* 6 (De Sandoli, 2:20); *Les familles d'Outremer*, 827. Du Cange's first mention of the church is from 1152, and his last is from 1289.

24. E. Rey, "Chartes de l'abbaye du Mont-Sion," *Mémoires de la Société Nationale des Antiquares de France*, 5th ser., 8 (1887), 40–53.

25. The Sicilian possessions are discussed fully by White, *Latin Monasticism*, 231–34.

26. Rey, "Chartes de l'abbaye du Mont-Sion," 31–32.

Augustinian canons.[27] The local stylite was presumably a Melkite—that is, an Arabic-speaking Greek Orthodox monk. The fact that he was given joint care of such an important church, even in a makeshift arrangement, suggests a willingness on the part of the Latin ecclesiastical authorities to cooperate with the existing indigenous church and its priests on a parochial level. This did not happen everywhere. The Orthodox church of Saint Lazarus in Bethany, for example, became a convent of Benedictine nuns during the reign of Queen Melisende.[28]

The Byzantine Church of Saint Mary "in Probatica," in Jerusalem, was superseded by the new house of Saint Anne, founded by a few Frankish women soon after 1099 on the supposed site of the birth of the Virgin. Baldwin I forced his Armenian wife, Arda, into the community in 1104–5, in order to be able to remarry, and in so doing "enlarged their possessions and extended their patrimony."[29] The building of the monastery and church began before 1104 and included a chapel on the site of the Byzantine church, which had been located slightly to the north, directly over the pool of Probatica. Saladin converted the monastery to an Islamic school, but it was given back to the Catholic Church and restored in the nineteenth century. It still provides one of the finest examples of crusader Romanesque architecture.[30]

In Sebastia, the Orthodox monastery mentioned in the *Commemoratorium* had become Latin by 1106–7, when Daniel visited the town.[31] John Phocas also visited the Latin monastery, built on the site of Herod's palace, in 1185,[32] but one hundred years later the situation had changed. Burchard of Mount Zion, writing in about 1280, reported that the two churches of Sebastia—one the cathedral of the city, the other the shrine church built

27. Ekkehard of Aura, *Hierosolymita* 22, *RHC Occ.* 5:36.

28. *Itinera Hierosolymitana*, 1:302; *Les familles d'Outremer*, 822–23. In 1256 Alexander IV gave the house, long since abandoned by the nuns, to the Hospital of Saint John.

29. William of Tyre, 11.1 (Huygens, 496); John of Würzburg, *Descriptio Terrae Sanctae* 12 *PL* 155:1087. The patrimony included the great suq of Jerusalem.

30. Saint Anne's consists of a triple-aisle nave divided into three bays with three apses and a stunted choir. The transept crossing is covered by a cupola, but the arms extend no farther than the walls of the aisles. Enlart describes the structure of the nave as Burgundian in origin but compares the whole effect to Romanesque churches in Aquitaine, which seem to derive from a Byzantine model (*Les monuments*, 1:106, pl. 7; 2:193, 195).

31. Daniel the Abbot, *The Life and Journey of Daniel, Abbot of the Russian Land*, in J. Wilkinson, ed., *Jerusalem Pilgrimage, 1099–1185* (London, 1988), 156. However, an Orthodox church still seems to have been in place.

32. John Phocas, *Descriptio Terrae Sanctae*, *PG* 133:940.

over the tomb of John the Baptist—had been turned into mosques. However, a Greek monastery that seems to have occupied the same site as the Latin monastery visited by Phocas welcomed and sheltered Burchard.[33]

Perhaps the most important shrine church outside Jerusalem was the Church of the Nativity in Bethlehem. The church itself was virtually intact when the crusaders occupied Bethlehem in July 1099.[34] Indeed, it was the only major shrine church to have escaped vandalism or neglect since its foundation. In 808 there were fifteen monks and priests to serve the church, and two stylites living nearby. Between 1100 and 1110 a community of Augustinian canons was founded to serve the shrine, and in 1110 Baldwin I elevated it to a bishopric (to replace Ascalon, still in Muslim hands) and endowed the community with the town of Bethlehem and other *casalia* in the kingdom.[35] Saewulf's description of Bethlehem in 1102 mentions the monastery of the Blessed Virgin Mary, "which is greatly celebrated."[36] This must refer to the Orthodox monastery, because even if the Augustinian canons had been installed so early, the monastery would scarcely have become, in only three years, "magnum preclarum." In any case, as Mayer argues, the establishment of a chapter of Regular canons took place gradually, with the support of King Baldwin but against the opposition of the patriarch.[37]

The case of Bethlehem is complicated by the possible survival, or reestablishment, of a community of Orthodox monks. In the Church of the Holy Sepulcher too the indigenous clergy turned out from their shrines in 1099 were soon permitted to return. By the middle of the eleventh century the Holy Sepulcher was already architecturally the most complex of all the shrine churches. The fourth-century church of Constantine consisted of two distinct churches built over the sites of Calvary and the tomb of Christ and joined by an open courtyard. After the destruction of the early Christian

---

33. *Peregrinatores medii aevi quatuor,* ed. J.C.M. Laurent (Leipzig, 1864), 53. Both Phocas and Burchard describe the monastery as occupying the site of Herod's palace.

34. Saewulf, *De situ Ierusalem* 7 (De Sandoli, 2:22).

35. William of Tyre, 11.12 (Huygens, 512). A full list of the properties of the bishop and canons is in P. Riant, *Etudes sur l'histoire de l'église de Bethléem,* 2 vols. (Genoa, 1889; Paris, 1896), 1:131–35 and app. 4, 140–54. For the complex arguments over the exact date and circumstances of the creation of the bishopric, see Mayer, *Bistümer,* 44–80.

36. Saewulf, *De situ Ierusalem* 7 (De Sandoli, 2:22). "Ibi nichil a sarracenis est remissum habitabile, sed omnia devastata sicut in aliis omnibus sanctis locis extra murum civitatis ierlm, preter monasterium Beate virginis Marie matris domini nostri, quod est magnum atque preclarum."

37. Mayer, *Bistümer,* 50–56.

church in 1009, Constantine Monomachus rebuilt the Anastasis church on a smaller scale, centered on the rotunda of the sepulcher itself. The crusader enlargement completed in 1149 took account of the use of the church by the Orthodox and Eastern churches, but from 1099 onward the church functioned as the cathedral of the patriarch of Jerusalem, staffed by a chapter of canons that was at first secular but from 1114 Augustinian. The dominant role of the canons in the ecclesiastical politics of the kingdom of Jerusalem, and the extent of their possessions in the Latin East and in Europe, makes the chapter worthy of study by itself,[38] a task that is beyond the scope of this book.

Most of the major shrine churches were served by communities of canons, often as cathedral chapters, rather than by monks. Aside from Notre-Dame de Josaphat and Mount Tabor (founded early in the twelfth century as a Benedictine abbey to replace an Orthodox house), the only shrine served by monks rather than canons was the tomb of John the Baptist at Sebastia. Some but not all Western pilgrims visited this shrine, and it may not have been considered an important stop on the itinerary of holy places. The Church of the Holy Sepulcher (containing the most important shrines), the Church of the Nativity in Bethlehem, the Church of the Annunciation in Nazareth, and the Church of Saint Abraham in Hebron, which attained new significance after the discovery of the tombs of the Patriarchs in 1119, were all served by Augustinian canons rather than monks, as was another important shrine church, the Templum Domini (sometimes identified as Solomon's Temple but actually the Dome of the Rock on the Haram as-Sharif).[39]

New Monastic Foundations

The number of entirely new monastic foundations on sites previously uninhabited by religious was relatively small. The Premonstratensians had two houses in the kingdom of Jerusalem, Saints Joseph and Habbakuk at

---

38. This is particularly so since the appearance of the critical edition of the cartulary of the chapter, *Le cartulaire du Saint-Sépulcre de Jérusalem*, ed. G. Bresc-Bautier (Paris, 1984).

39. For the community of the Templum Domini, see William of Tyre, 9.9 (Huygens, 431). The earliest evidence for a prior in 1112 is in J. Delaville Le Roulx, ed., *Cartulaire général de l'Ordre des Hospitaliers de St. Jean de Jérusalem, 1100–1310*, 4 vols. (Paris, 1894–1906), 1: no. 25.

Ramla[40] and Saint Samuel at Montjoie. Saint Samuel was, Rey believed, founded by Baldwin III in 1156.[41] It is perhaps surprising to find the Premonstratensians taking so long to establish themselves in Outremer. As Bernard Hamilton has pointed out, one would expect to find this evangelical order making an attempt to settle in rural areas, where the opportunities for conversion of Muslims and Eastern Christians would have been greatest.[42] The Cluniacs too showed a reluctance to establish daughter-houses in the East and eventually arrived in the Holy Land on the backs of established houses so to speak. Palmaria, in Galilee, originally a reformed house with no affiliation, became Cluniac because of the intervention of the future abbot of Cluny, Thierry de Vermandois, and was ceded to Mount Tabor before 1180.[43]

Doubtless discouraged by Bernard of Clairvaux, the Cistercians did not arrive in Outremer until 1157. The first two houses—Belmont (founded in 1157), in the mountains of Lebanon southeast of Tripoli, and Salvatio (1161)—were dependencies of Morimond. The buildings at Belmont may have replaced an Orthodox abbey, but the only evidence for the previous site is a reversed Byzantine capital reused in the Frankish church as a baptismal font. The abbey was built according to a typical Cistercian plan, the oldest phase of building dating to 1157–69 and the most recent phase dating to 1289.[44] Salvatio is not mentioned after 1174 and was probably abandoned,[45] leaving Belmont the only Cistercian house in Latin Syria until 1209, when the Cistercian monk Peter of Ivrea became patriarch of Antioch. Peter, a monk of La Ferté, had tried to abandon Ivrea to become a hermit but was persuaded by Innocent III to resume his responsibilities.[46]

40. Les familles d'Outremer, 817; William of Tyre, 17.26 (Huygens, 797).

41. Les familles d'Outremer, 832; Enlart, Les monuments, 1: pl. 123; 2:277–82. Saint Samuel united with Saint Lazarus at Bethany in 1259.

42. Hamilton, The Latin Church in the Crusader States, 101–2.

43. Kedar, "Palmarée," 265–67. Thierry, at the time abbot of Saint Basil's, a Cluniac house, was in the Holy Land on royal business and on the business of his Order; see Recueil des historiens des Gaules et de la France 16 (Paris, 1878), 149–51, 408. Mount Tabor became Cluniac after 1130, as G. Constable determined from a letter of Peter the Venerable, Letters, 1:214–15, Ep. 80.

44. Enlart, Les monuments, 1: pl. 60–68; 2:45–63. Enlart argues (2:48) that the abbey church, with its single nave and apse and no aisles, is more typical of a Grandmontine plan than a Cistercian plan.

45. B. Hamilton, "The Cistercians in the Crusader States," in One yet Two: Monastic Tradition East and West, ed. M. B. Pennington, Cistercian Studies 26 (Kalamazoo, Mich., 1976), 406.

46. Innocent III, Regesta 9.172, PL 215:1004–8.

After his transfer to Antioch, he worked hard to establish the Order in his patriarchate, offering to incorporate any unaffiliated house on the Black Mountain into the Cistercian Order.[47] Saint Mary's in Jubin was thus added to the Order. As the register of Gregory IX's pontificate shows, however, a specter of the dissent that had dogged the foundation of the house in the 1120s seemed still to hang over it. In 1232 there was apparently a dispute between the abbey and the patriarch of Antioch, Albert de Rezato (1228–45). According to papal letters of 1233–34, the abbot of Jubin had refused to pay tithes from certain properties settled on the patriarchate when Peter of Ivrea conceded the abbey to the Cistercian Order and had forged a document freeing the abbey from payment.[48] The internal troubles that exploded into violence in 1237 may have arisen from the handling of the dispute with the patriarch. In that year a quarrel between the prior and the subprior became so severe that the prior used knights (presumably the abbey's own) to expel the subprior and thirty of the monks who supported him.[49] At the request of the abbots of Jubin and La Ferté (the mother-house), the pope agreed to let the matter be settled internally by the Cistercian Order rather than by the ecclesiastical authorities in Syria, as he had originally proposed. Jubin's tradition of independence thus seems to have been upheld.

Despite the gap of one hundred years between them, this incident suggests parallels with the schism of Bernard of Blois described in the previous chapter. If, as I have surmised, the troubles of 1237 arose from the withholding of the tithes in 1232–33, there seem to have been two factions in the abbey: one in favor of complete independence from the patriarch of Antioch—even to the point of breaking a financial contract—and the other in favor of appeasement. Because the abbot who had withheld the tithes seems not to have been replaced in the settlement of the original dispute, it can further be assumed that he presided over the quarrel of 1237, though whether he took sides is unclear.[50] In any case, he was instrumental in

47. *Les Registres de Grégoire IX*, ed. L. Auvray, Bibl. des écoles françaises d'Athènes et de Rome (Paris, 1896–1910), vol. 1, no. 3468. This was a continuation of the policy of Peter's twelfth-century predecessor Patriarch Aimery, as reported by Gerard of Nazareth, *Duodecima centuria*, col. 1373.

48. *Registres de Grégoire IX*, vol. 1, nos. 1101, 1887. In 1237 the pope confirmed the patriarch's sentence of excommunication on Jubin (no. 3466). For a fuller discussion of the documents, see Hamilton, "The Cistercians," 415–16.

49. *Registres de Grégoire IX*, vol. 1, no. 4020. The letter is dated January 6, 1238.

50. There are several possible reconstructions, but the most likely is that the sentence of excommunication confirmed by the pope in March 1237 (ibid., no. 3466) prompted a faction (the subprior's?) to stage a coup within the monastery.

keeping the settlement of the affair out of the hands of the patriarch. Having already suffered excommunication, he probably feared deposition. In the event, the Cistercian Order settled the affair in 1238 and demoted Jubin to the status of daughter-house of Locedio, itself a daughter of La Ferté.[51] The schism of the 1120s had also erupted over monastic finances in a general sense, but in that case over the observance of the strict rule of poverty adopted by the founding monks. The parallel occurs in the reluctance, or inability, of the ecclesiastical authorities to intervene in either case. Jubin was left denuded of monks in the 1120s and had to be restored by Bernard and his fellow rebels of Machanath by the papal legate.[52] By the 1230s, Jubin was able to resist the patriarch because of the immunity granted by membership of the Cistercian Order.

The foundations of the thirteenth century in Outremer were not, strictly speaking, new, but refoundations of abandoned or destitute houses.[53] Thus Bishop Vassal of Gibelet offered the site of the abbey of Saint Sergius to two Cistercian monks of La Ferté, Andrew and Giles, in 1231. Judging from the dedication, this must have been an Orthodox house that either fell into disuse or was taken over by a Latin community and then dwindled. Andrew and Giles were given land that included two casalia, a garden, a vineyard, and an olive grove.[54] Vassal explained to the abbot of La Ferté that the paucity of new vocations made it impossible to staff the monastery from Latin Syrian monks. Hoping for fresh vocations from the mother-house, he transferred the original grant directly to La Ferté, and ultimately to the abbot of Cîteaux.[55] In 1238, however, the Chapter-General of the Cistercian Order advised the removal of the monks who had gone out to Gibelet to a safer place.[56] This episode fits into the thirteenth-century pattern of surviving Latin communities founding daughter-houses in the Lusignan kingdom of Cyprus. In 1268, for example, following the fall of Antioch, the

51. Canivez, *Statuta*, 2:172, no. 18; Hamilton, "The Cistercians," 417.

52. *Duodecima centuria*, cols. 1230, 1605.

53. The exception is the foundation of Cistercian nuns at Saint Mary Magdalen's in Acre. Cîteaux and Belmont both claimed authority over the convent; the Chapter-General of 1239 upheld Cîteaux's claim, but as a compensation Belmont was given the convent of Episcopia (Hamilton, "The Cistercians," 410–12).

54. E. Petit, "Chartes de l'abbaye cistercienne de Saint-Serge de Giblet en Syrie," *Mémoires de la Société Nationale des Antiquaires de France*, 5th ser., 8 (1887), 23–24.

55. Ibid., 25–26.

56. Canivez, *Statuta*, 2:192. An attempt to rebuild the community in 1241 by Guy I, lord of Gibelet, seems to have failed (Petit, "Chartes de l'abbaye cistercienne," 26–30).

Cistercians of Saint Mary's in Jubin went to Beaulieu in Cyprus,[57] while the Benedictine monks of Saint Paul's in Antioch took over the Orthodox monastery of Stavrovouni.[58]

The most celebrated new foundations of the twelfth century in Europe were characterized by the desire to strike out into the wilderness, away from settled places. Houses like Cîteaux, Prémontré, and La Chartreuse owe their origins to dissatisfaction with established houses and to obligations imposed by local attachments. The Syrian wilderness, however, was more extreme than France, northern Italy, or England. It was also more danger-ous, as the evacuation of Gibelet and Mount Carmel testifies. Pilgrims in the first decade after the Frankish conquest traveled at considerable peril. The Russian abbot Daniel, for example, needed a military escort to travel through Samaria,[59] and Saewulf found entire areas still outside Frankish control. Muslim raids, even at a time when the Latin kingdom appeared reasonably secure, could threaten monasteries, as the Greek monks of Mount Tabor found in 1183.[60] Monastic foundations in rural areas, which had to be able to defend themselves, therefore tended increasingly to seek protection from the military Orders. Grants of land and gifts of churches that we might expect in the West to be made to monasteries were in Latin Syria made to the Hospitallers or the Templars. The pilgrim Theoderic observed, in the 1170s:

> It is not easy for anyone to understand the power and wealth of the Templars. They and the Hospitallers have taken possession of al-most all the cities and villages with which Judaea was once enriched and which were destroyed by the Romans, and they have built castles everywhere and filled them with soldiers; and this is in addition to the many and infinite estates which they are well known to possess in their lands.[61]

57. Hamilton, "The Cistercians," 416.

58. L. de Mas Latrie, "Documents nouveaux servant de preuves à l'histoire de l'Ile de Chypre sous le règne des Princes de la Maison de Lusignan," *Colléction de documents inédits sur l'histoire de France, Mélanges historiques: Choix de documents*, vol. 4 (Paris, 1882), 588, n. 1.

59. Daniel the Abbot, *Life and Journey*, in Wilkinson, *Jerusalem Pilgrimage*, 154.

60. William of Tyre, 22.26 (Huygens, 1052).

61. *Theoderici libellus de locis sanctis editus circa A.D. 1172*, ed. T. Tobler (Saint Gall, 1865), 27. According to the chronicler Ernoul, the Armenian king attributed the weakness of the crown of Jerusalem to the power of the Hospital (*Chronique d'Ernoul et de Bernard de Trésorier*, ed. L. de Mas Latrie [Paris, 1871], 27–28).

In the 1160s the conventual brethren of the Hospital themselves demanded a moratorium on new acquisitions on Saracen frontiers, not wanting to burden the Order with responsibilities it could not manage.[62] The Order nevertheless continued to acquire new possessions, and especially, in the thirteenth century, to take over ailing monastic institutions, such as Mount Tabor in 1255 and Saint Lazarus in Bethany a year later.[63] Riley-Smith argues that by 1154, thanks to the papal bull *Christiane fidei religio*, the Hospital had been granted exemptions from tithes and episcopal control that were equaled in twelfth-century Europe only by those granted to the Temple and the Cistercians, and in the thirteenth century to the friars.[64]

It is surely no coincidence that the foundations that survived into the thirteenth century, and particularly beyond the 1240s, were connected to or owned by a flourishing international Order—the Temple, the Hospital, the Cistercians, or the Carmelites—all of which were run by a carefully structured central organization and divided into provincial governments. By the middle of the century it was apparent to astute observers like Louis IX that the kingdom of Jerusalem could no longer provide a viable system of defense or self-government. From here it was a short step to entrusting the defense and administration of the Latin East entirely to the military Orders.

The contribution of the monasteries to the ecclesiastical administration of the kingdom of Jerusalem was surprisingly modest. As Hamilton has pointed out, few bishops of the Latin kingdom were monks. Of the patriarchs of Jerusalem before 1220, three out of twelve—Stephen of Chartres (1128–30), Fulcher (1145–57), and Aimery II (1197–1202)—had been monks, and Stephen and Fulcher had professed in France before emigrating to the Holy Land. Albert, bishop of Tripoli, had been abbot of Saint Evrard's in Marseilles, and Bernard, bishop of Lydda, had been abbot of Mount Tabor. The only canon Regular to become a bishop was Guernicus, archbishop of Tyre. Hamilton has argued that the necessary requirements of a bishop in the Latin kingdom were the virtues of pragmatism and a firm grasp of the affairs of state.[65] These were more likely to be found in a bishop like Ralph of Bethlehem (1155–74), an Anglo-Norman courtier who had

62. Riley-Smith, *The Knights of St. John in Jerusalem and Cyprus*, 61–63.

63. Ibid., 401–3.

64. Ibid., 376–77.

65. Hamilton, *The Latin Church in the Crusader States*, 136. This point should not be overstressed. C. Bouchard's study of the church in Burgundy in this period reminds us that the normal path to the bishop's throne in the West was not through the cloister (*Sword, Miter, and Cloister: Nobility and the Church in Burgundy, 980–1198* [Ithaca, 1987], 67–76).

served as chancellor of the kingdom, than in a cloistered monk. But after all, abbots were called to be administrators of estates, and the influence of a monk such as Bernard of Clairvaux in affairs of state was unparalleled even in the secular world.

Monasteries in Outremer may, rather, appear to have been uninfluential and insignificant when compared with the shrine churches, which could tap the wealth of the pilgrim traffic and attract patrons among the powerful of the realm. The appeal of Vassal of Gibelet for Cistercian monks seems symptomatic of the plight of the monasteries. In 1233, when Saint Sergius was given to La Ferté, the kingdom of Jerusalem appeared to have regained much of the territory lost in 1187. Above all, Jerusalem itself had been returned to the Latins. What better time could there have been, in the lifetime of most monks, to have settled in the Holy Land? Ten years later the trend was instead to resettle Palestinian foundations in Cyprus, or to withdraw altogether to European possessions. We have already seen that monastic settlement in the Holy Land was regarded with ambivalence or suspicion by twelfth-century reformers. These doubts could have stemmed the tide of foundations we might have expected from a comparison with western Europe. However, Andrew and Giles, the enterprising Cistercians, are not isolated examples but representatives of the phenomenon described by Gerard of Nazareth and Jacques de Vitry: the desire of religious to settle in the Holy Land. Unlike most of Gerard's examples, they chose an established and powerful Order. The kind of irregular monastic enterprise the course of which Gerard traces was no longer a popular choice in the thirteenth century. A group of hermits still living on the Black Mountain in 1235 applied directly to the pope for guidance and were steered firmly toward the Benedictines.[66] The age of the "new monks" was over.

---

66. *Registres de Grégoire IX*, no. 2660.

3

Orthodox Monks and Monasticism in the Holy Land

The examples of Frankish eremitical life encountered in Gerard of Naza-reth's *De conversatione servorum Dei* fit into a broad pattern of monastic life in western Europe. Bernard of Blois and his associates, Elias, and the solitaries of Galilee had their counterparts throughout France, England, Germany, and Italy. In Palestine and Syria, however, they took their place among many native hermits and monks in the laurae and caves of Judaea and the Jordan. Even by settling in places native monks had for centuries regarded as holy sites, Frankish hermits acknowledged the influence of Orthodox monasticism.

But how extensive was the contact between Orthodox and Frankish monks and hermits? In this chapter we examine the most notable examples of Orthodox monasticism from which Western monks might have drawn

inspiration, and point out essential differences between Western and Orthodox monastic practices in the crusader states. In the process, we see that
Greek monasteries underwent a revival under crusader occupation and that
the traditions of the solitary life practiced in the early church were still
known in the twelfth century. Although Orthodox and Frankish monks and
hermits may have interacted little with one another, they were both clearly
aware of these traditions.

Monks, solitary or in communities, had been a feature of the Near
Eastern landscape since the fourth century. Gerard's hermits were pioneers
only if viewed from a purely European perspective. Such a perspective is
based on the assumption that the relations between the Franks and the
"subject peoples" of the Latin East were necessarily always hostile, or at
least distant, and that Frankish monks, even those who abandoned the
cloister, could have had nothing to do with Orthodox. Such, indeed, is the
impression given by the largely inimical relations between the papacy and
the Greek Orthodox Patriarchate of Constantinople in the twelfth century,
and the general distaste or even contempt in which Franks and Byzantines
held one another.[1]

To assume, however, that such cultural conditions were universal and
applicable to all Latins and Orthodox in regular contact with one another
seems rash. The polemics produced by apologists of papal authority and
their Orthodox counterparts in the twelfth century[2] are of limited use as a
guide to Latin-Orthodox relations in the crusader kingdom. They seem,
simply, to have had little or no impact. Very little polemical literature from
the church in the Latin kingdom has come to light. As Bernard Hamilton
remarked, neither academic intellect nor spiritual fervor was a quality
greatly prized in potential bishops in the kingdom.[3]

---

1. The growth of anti-Latin sentiment in Constantinople has been well documented by,
among others, C. M. Brand, *Byzantium Confronts the West* (Cambridge, Mass., 1968); A.A.M.
Bryer, "Cultural Relations Between East and West in the Twelfth Century," in D. Baker, ed.,
Relations Between East and West in the Middle Ages, Studies in Church History 10 (Edinburgh,
1973); and D. M. Nicol, "The Byzantine View of Western Europe," *Greek, Roman, and
Byzantine Studies* 8 (1967), 315–39.

2. The course of papal-patriarchal relations has been sketched by J. Darrouzès, "Les
documents byzantins du XIIe siècle sur le primauté romaine," *Revue des Etudes Byzantines* 23
(1965), 42–88. See also D. M. Nicol, "The Papal Scandal," in D. Baker, ed., *The Orthodox
Churches and the West* (Oxford, 1976), 141–68.

3. Hamilton, *The Latin Church in the Crusader States*, 134–35. An exception to the rule is
Gerard of Nazareth, whose doctrinal works *De una Magdalena contra Graecos* and *Contra Salam
presbyterum* (known only from the titles and a few extracts preserved by the Centuriators of
Magdeburg) were written to challenge Orthodox views.

Even if such evidence were available, it probably could not shed light on the relations between Frankish eremitical communities of the type described by Gerard of Nazareth and Orthodox foundations, and still less between individual hermits. A chief attribute of the hermit was an unwillingness to accept authority, and the example of Bernard of Blois shows that it was as common a problem in the Latin East as in the West. It would have been impossible for bishops or abbots, even where they knew of their existence, to have prevented dialogue between Frankish and indigenous hermits. Aimery of Antioch's prohibition of unsupervised eremitism may indeed have been provoked by the fear that Frankish hermits on the Black Mountain might be unduly influenced by the customs or beliefs of Orthodox hermits with whom they came into contact. Given the popularity of the Black Mountain as an eremitical site among Latins and Orthodox, such contact was a real possibility.

Writing about European hermits in the eleventh and twelfth centuries, Henrietta Leyser was able to dismiss any putative influence of Orthodox monasticism on Latin.[4] The Latin East was a different matter. Here it is not necessary to establish a tentative chain of influence between individuals, or to trace the slow infiltration of Greek patristic texts into Western libraries. The countryside and cities were studded with functioning Orthodox monasteries and laurae throughout the Latin occupation. They provided venerable traditions and living examples from which the Latin eremitical settlements might draw their influences and inspiration.

As we have shown, Gerard of Nazareth's conception of the monastic life included both eremitical and cenobitic monks. This may reflect the prevailing understanding of monasticism in Europe (as espoused, for example, by the author of the *Libellus de diversis ordinibus et professionibus qui sunt in aecclesia*), but it may also have been inspired by the Orthodox examples of laurae or dependent groups of cells as outposts of monasteries. Were monks like Gerard's John of Jerusalem, who tried to resettle an abandoned monastery on the Black Mountain, conforming consciously to an Orthodox custom?

Godric of Finchale, the English merchant who became a hermit near

---

4. Leyser, *Hermits and the New Monasticism*, 24–25. Individual cases of Greek influences on Western monks in the tenth and eleventh centuries are discussed by B. Hamilton with D. A. McNulty, "Orientale lumen et magistra latinitatis: Greek Influences on Western Monasticism, 900–1100," *Le millénaire de Mont Athos, 963–1963: Etudes et mélanges* 1 (1963), 181–216. For Benedictine monks on Mount Athos, see A. Pertusi, "Nuovi documenti sui Benedettini Amalfitani dell'Athos," *Aevium* 27 (1953), 400–429.

Durham, visited the dwellings of hermits in the twelfth century while on pilgrimage to Jerusalem.[5] In particular, "he investigated very keenly the more secret tombs of the eremitical life." These tombs, described as being in the vicinity of the Mount of Olives, were known to Godric's biographer as traditional habitats for recluses:

> For there are in that area many underground caves, the work of nature, as if cut painstakingly but elegantly in the rocks and the cliffside without any tool. In these live several hermits, who are called by the neighboring people "The Hermit Workers" or "Worshipers in the Wilderness." He [Godric] often visited these dwellings and commended himself to their prayers.[6]

These cave tombs can still be visited in the Valley of Jehosaphat. Evidence for the use of such tombs by Orthodox hermits as early as the ninth and tenth centuries is provided by the monk Epiphanius.[7] The Cretan pilgrim John Phocas, who visited Jerusalem in 1185, saw in the valley "various artificial grottoes, which are named after the Virgin, and are inhabited by a few Orthodox and by a larger number of Armenian and Jacobite monks." A Georgian hermit lived in the conical tomb known as Absalom's Pillar.[8] About ten years earlier John of Würzburg had also noted the popularity of the valley with hermits.[9]

The first-century Hellenistic tombs in the Valley of Jehosaphat provided ready-made cells for hermits. Monumental tombs were located in the Kidron Valley, of which the Valley of Jehosaphat forms the westernmost and deepest part, from the Iron Age onward. The "artificial grottoes" mentioned by Phocas can be identified with the burial chambers known as

---

5. The date of his pilgrimage is uncertain. A. Grabois, "Anglo-Norman England and the Holy Land," *Anglo-Norman Studies* 7 (1984), 138, identifies Godric of Finchale with the English merchant (or pirate) Godric who rescued King Baldwin I after the battle of Ramla in 1102. If this connection is valid, the episode must have occurred on his first pilgrimage. His second must have been after 1106, but it is impossible to be more explicit. Godric died in 1170. See Reginald of Durham, *Libellus de vita et miraculis S. Godrici*, 169 (Surtees Society [London, 1847], 326).

6. Reginald of Durham, *Libellus S. Godrici* 15 (1847 ed.), 57–58. The Latin phrase *eremi cultores*, as Bernard Hamilton has pointed out to me, is probably meant to be a pun: I have given both senses in the translation to bring out the full sense.

7. Epiphanius, *Enarratio Syriae*, PG 120:268.

8. John Phocas, *Descriptio Terrae Sanctae*, PG 133:945.

9. John of Würzburg, *Descriptio Terrae Sanctae*, PL 155:1073.

the Tomb of Absalom, the Tomb of Jehosaphat, and the Tombs of the Bene Hezir and Zechariah. These complexes stretch about 75 meters along the valley, about 350 meters to the south of the Latin monastery of Notre-Dame de Josaphat, in the gorge immediately beyond the present eastern wall of the Old City. The Tomb of Absalom ("Absalom's Pillar") consists of a square courtyard cut out of the rock-face of the valley, in which the monument itself, part masonry and part cut from the rock, sits on a podium. The whole is about 16.5 meters high, and the court is about 12.5 meters long. The Tomb of Jehosaphat is a series of chambers cut into the rock-face beginning immediately behind the Tomb of Absalom; the Tomb of the Bene Hezir is a similar complex; and the Tomb of Zechariah is a pyramidal monument similar to Absalom's Pillar, about 10 meters to the south of the Bene Hezir complex.[10]

The tombs were fitting dwellings for people dead to the lure of the world. The image of the hermit as the "living dead" was common in the medieval West, where hermits could choose to be walled up in their cells in a ceremony of dying to the world.[11] Such vocabulary ultimately derived from the practice of early Christian hermits in Egypt of choosing empty tombs as their cells.[12] Doubtless there was more to this than the simple convenience of an empty tomb if no cave was available. The Egyptian bishop Pisentius, for example, found tomb complexes in the desert filled with mummies useful for teaching moral lessons to his disciples on the inescapability of death.[13]

The additional presence of the Latin monastery of Notre-Dame de Josaphat made the Valley of Jehosaphat a center for monks that was no less eclectic than the Black Mountain. Godric's curiosity about the eremitical life—natural in one who had himself become a hermit—must have been exercised by the different religious traditions represented in the valley.

10. For a full architectural description of the tombs, see Kay Prag, *Jerusalem*, Blue Guides (London, 1989), 247–51.

11. Anne K. Warren, *Anchorites and Their Patrons in Medieval England* (Berkeley, 1985), 92–100: "The psychological impact of the walling up of the recluse forces the modern mind to thoughts of incarceration as punishment, the cell as a prison, and the anchorite existence as a living death. All of these themes were in fact accepted and even utilized in the medieval period." See also L. Gougaud, *Ermits et reclus: Etudes sur d'anciennes formes de vie réligieuse* (Vienne, 1928), 71; and J. Leclercq, "Le cloître est-il un prison?" *Revue d'ascétique et de mystique* 47 (1971), 407–20.

12. J. Dorèsse, "Saints coptes de Haute-Egypte," *Journal Asiatique* 236 (1948), 257.

13. *The Arabic Life of St. Pisentius*, trans. De Lacy O'Leary, *PO* 22:420–29. Pisentius told his disciple John: "Thou hast seen, my son, all these dead cast aside to warn us that we shall be like them."

Figs. 1 and 2. First-century B.C. tombs in the Valley of Jehosaphat, later used as hermits' cells. *Above*: "Tomb of Absalom," also known as "Absalom's Pillar." *Facing page*: "Tomb of Zechariah" (right) and "Tomb of Bene Hezir" (left). The presence of both Orthodox and Latin monks made the Valley of Jehosaphat an eclectic monastic center in the twelfth century.

There is no mention of an interpreter being needed to converse with the hermits in the rock tombs, which may suggest that by the time of Godric's pilgrimage, probably in the second quarter of the twelfth century, the site had been occupied by Frankish hermits as well as Orthodox, and that it was these hermits with whom Godric was acquainted.

Elias of Narbonne and his companions settled in "a certain large cave near Jerusalem"[14] that was almost certainly in the Valley of Jehosaphat. From there he entered the cloister at Notre-Dame de Josaphat. What seems most likely is that Frankish and Eastern hermits—a Georgian as well as Armenians, Jacobites, and Greek Orthodox—frequented the tomb complexes throughout the twelfth century and lived in close proximity. Elias was known to have formed a community, while the Georgian mentioned by Phocas clearly lived in solitude.

Both anchoritic and communal or semi-communal forms of eremitical life were thus possible in the Valley of Jehosaphat during the course of the twelfth century. The tomb complexes, however, do not cover a wide area, and even the solitary Georgian in Absalom's Pillar would have been close to the hermits occupying the chambers behind his monument. Fellow hermits so close by must have been impossible to ignore, even if they spoke a different language and observed different customs.

14. *Duodecima centuria*, col. 1603.

For a reasonably enterprising and well-informed pilgrim with genuine interest, such as Godric, it would have been easy to observe Orthodox, Armenian, or even Georgian hermits. His contact with the varied eremitical life outside Jerusalem shows how easy it was for a Frankish hermit to absorb different traditions. Simply by observing a hermit at work one could collect a store of information on types of habitat, diet, liturgical practices, the way in which the day was divided between prayer and meditation, and the type of manual work done, if any.

Such observation almost certainly helped Godric to determine his own pattern of eremitical living. When he returned to England after giving up his mercantile career, Godric sought the wilderness, living first in caves and later in woods, where, "after the example of John the Baptist, he used to eat grass and wild honey."[15] One can find inspiration from the Baptist's example without going to the Holy Land, but his biographer's account suggests a strong Eastern influence on Godric's diet. The verse from Matthew's Gospel on which this passage is based says that the Baptist's food consisted of locusts and wild honey.[16] The Vulgate reading of *locustae* is a direct translation of the Greek ἀκρδες, a perfectly good Homeric word for "locust." By the Middle Ages, however, a different tradition about the Baptist's diet was common in Palestine. In the early thirteenth century, Jacques de Vitry asked a Syrian monk from a monastery near the Jordan about the locusts John was supposed to have eaten and was told that in the refectory of his monastery they were often served a type of plant or vegetation called *langustae*, or *locustae*, which grew copiously in that region. It was doubtless this plant that John the Baptist had eaten.[17] A confusion thus seems to have arisen between the insect and a shrub similar to the North American *robinia pseudoacacia*, which is known as the "locust tree." This plant, despite a rather prickly aspect, produces an edible seedpod called the "locust bean." Locust trees are, however, not indigenous to Britain and could not have been eaten by Godric in the woodlands of County Durham. The likeliest explanation for the substitution of *virecta* for *locustae* in Reg-

15. Reginald of Durham, *Libellus S. Godrici* 10 (1847 ed.), 42–43. "In silvis denique sic diutius demoratus, juxta typum Beati Johannis Baptistae, virecta herbarum aliquandiu comedebat, et mel silvestre."

16. Matthew 3:4 "esca autem eius erat locustae, et mel silvestre." Mark 1:6 uses identical words.

17. Jacques de Vitry, *Historia Hierosolymitana* 53 (Bongars, 1075). "Qui mihi statim respondit, quod frequenter in refectorio suo quaedam herba monachis ad edundum apponebatur, quam ipsa 'langustae,' id est, 'locustam' nominabant, cuius circa monasterium suum magna habebantur copia; adiungens quod illa esset, quam edebat beatus Iohannes."

inald's *Life* of Godric is that Godric himself was following, insofar as he was able with his native vegetation, the exact dietary customs of Orthodox monks or hermits whom he had observed in the Holy Land, not just the example of John the Baptist.[18] It would not have been necessary for him to have traveled to the Jordan if the custom of eating the locust bean were widespread among Orthodox monks. If Godric could find this out, so could other Franks who had already adopted the eremitical profession. Jacques de Vitry, after all, not known for his sympathy for Orthodox practices, showed sufficient interest to ask a Greek monk about the local tradition; other Franks probably made the same discovery.

The Valley of Jehosaphat was just one place where a pilgrim might expect to encounter Orthodox monks. According to the *Commemoratorium*, there were thirty-eight Orthodox monasteries, or *casi Dei*, at the beginning of the ninth century. Many of these were shrines taken over by the Franks after 1099, and others were simply small churches served by a single priest. Of the monasteries listed in Prawer and Benvenisti's "Map of Crusader Palestine,"[19] at least seventeen can be corroborated by literary evidence to have been functioning in the twelfth century as Orthodox institutions. The most celebrated Greek monastery, Saint Catherine's on Mount Sinai, maintained an unbroken existence from its foundation in the sixth century, largely because of its inaccessibility. A center for the production of icons, it is now the major source of our knowledge of pre-Iconoclast Byzantine painting. Saint Catherine's was a popular pilgrimage site for those with time and energy to spare for the difficult journey. The guide now known as the *Work on Geography* enthused over the piety of the monks:

> The monks and hermits are so devoted to religion that they are free from passions of the body or spirit, and only fight for God. They are so famous that from the borders of Ethiopia up to the furthest bounds of Persia they are spoken of with respect. . . . They freely

18. The appearance of this passage in the *Libellus S. Godrici* before the story of his pilgrimage to Jerusalem can be explained by the biographer's imposing on events a slightly mistaken order and assuming that Godric's eremitical practices had already been established before his second journey to Jerusalem.

19. J. Prawer and M. Benvenisti, "Crusader Palestine," in *Atlas of Israel* (Jerusalem, 1960), sheet 12/9. The anonymous *Anon. de locis Hierosolymitani, PG* 133:985, 988, probably from the twelfth century, claims that under the Byzantine emperors the Holy Land contained 365 churches and monasteries, all of which have ceased to function "under the impious rulers." The later reference to Agarenes suggests that the Muslims, rather than the Franks, were intended, and thus that a much earlier date is meant.

and quietly possess monasteries in Egypt and Persia, around the Red Sea and Arabia, from which their livelihood is abundant. . . . They live alone in individual cells, not together, yet sharing a communal life.[20]

In 1106–7, a Russian abbot, Daniel, made a pilgrimage to the Holy Land, and his own account has survived. While in Jerusalem he was a guest in the hospice of the monastery of Saint Sabas, just inside the walls of the city near the Tower of David. He also visited the monastery itself, about 12.5 kilometers east of Bethlehem in the Kidron Valley:

> The Laura of St. Sabas was established by God in a marvellous and indescribable way: there was a river bed, fearful and very deep and dry and with high walls and to these walls cells are attached and held there by God in a marvellous and fearful manner. On the cliffs on both sides of this terrible ravine stand cells fixed to the rocks like stars in the sky.[21]

Sabas, a disciple of the great monastic founder Euthymius (376–473), founded the Great Laura, as his monastery became known, in the last quarter of the fifth century. Sabas's original cave in the high cliff walls of the wadi became the pattern for the cells cut by his followers into the rock. The present monastery, built around the cave church dedicated in 491, is situated on a wide ledge overlooking the wadi.[22] This site was already in use in Daniel's time, but he was evidently more interested in the original cells. This may suggest that they were still in use by monks of the community who wanted to intersperse communal life with periods of eremitism.

20. *Work on Geography*, 35, in Wilkinson, *Jerusalem Pilgrimage*, 186. Also in De Sandoli, *Itinera*, 2:84–86.

21. Daniel the Abbot, *Life and Journey*, 140. The Anglo-Saxon pilgrim Saewulf, ca. 1102–3, described Saint Sabas as "a very beautiful and large monastery," housing more than 300 monks (*De situ Ierusalem* 21 [De Sandoli, 2:22]). But he had not been there himself, and erroneously located it west of the Georgian Holy Cross monastery, now on the western outskirts of Jerusalem. The laura of Saint Sabas is also described by John Phocas, *PG* 133:948. For some possessions of the monastery, see *Regesta regni Hierosolymitana, 1097–1291*, ed. R. Röhricht (Berlin, 1892), no. 409.

22. The early history and topography of Saint Sabas and other Judaean monasteries is extensively described by Y. Hirschfeld, *The Judaean Desert Monasteries in the Byzantine Period* (New Haven, 1992). For an entertaining nineteenth-century description of a visit to Saint Sabas monastery, complete with an ambush by local Beduin, see Lord Curzon's *Visits to Monasteries in the Levant* (London, 1865), 180–87.

Fig. 3. Monastery of Saint Sabas in the Kidron Valley of the Judaean desert. The surrounding cliffs contain the original caves of Sabas and his followers. The monastery is built around the cave church dedicated in 491. The present buildings are on the same site Daniel visited in the twelfth century.

Eighty years after Daniel, the Cretan pilgrim John Phocas described a similar type of laura at Saint Mary Choziba, 4 kilometers southwest of Jericho in the wadi Qilt, as:

> something unbelievable when described, and inspiring wonder when seen; for the cells of the monks are the mouths of caves, and the church itself and the cemetery has been excavated out of the solid rock, and is heated to such a degree by the rays of the sun that one sees pyramid-shaped tongues of flame bursting out of the rock. . . . I climbed into and out of this monastery not without some danger, both because of the precipitous nature of the place and because of the overpowering heat of the sun.[23]

23. John Phocas, *PG* 133:949. The approach is no longer dangerous, but something of the awe it inspired in Phocas can still be experienced by walking along the wadi Qilt from Jerusalem to Jericho.

Fig. 4.   Monastery of Saint George Choziba (Saint Mary Choziba in the twelfth century) in wadi Qilt of the Judaean desert. Orthodox monasteries carved out of desert cliffs formed part of the itinerary of medieval pilgrims and inspired awe and devotion.

Orthodox laurae were founded in such places precisely to produce the effects remarked on by Daniel and Phocas—wonder, disbelief, and awe at the devotion necessary to live on inaccessible cliff-tops. That two pilgrims from different ends of the Orthodox world—Russia and Crete—exposed themselves to considerable danger to visit these sites is testimony to the importance of the monasteries among members of the Orthodox community. The links between Orthodox monastic communities were firm enough for a Russian monk to be received as a guest at the hospice of Saint Sabas in Jerusalem, to be guided around the holy sites by a monk of Saint Sabas, and even to participate with the community in the Holy Fire ceremony at Easter 1107 in the Church of the Holy Sepulcher.[24]

24. Daniel the Abbot, *Life and Journey*, 121, 166, 168. Daniel does not say what relations he enjoyed with the Latin Church hierarchy, but he knew King Baldwin I personally and applied to him for permission to hang a lamp dedicated to Russian saints from the Holy Sepulcher at Easter 1107.

A comparison of the accounts of Daniel and Phocas reveals a healthy revival in Orthodox monasticism in Palestine during the twelfth century. In 1106–7 Daniel found many convents and churches abandoned, ruined, or in disrepair. The "great square church" over the Virgin's tomb in Gethsemane (the Valley of Jehosaphat) had been "destroyed by the pagans." There is no mention of the Latin monastery or the new church over the tomb.[25] The convents of Saint Euthymius at Khan al-Ahmar (now Mishor Adummim), 10 kilometers east of Jerusalem on the road to Jericho, and of Saint Theoctistus, 15 kilometers southeast of Jerusalem, lay in ruins in 1106–7.

By 1185 John Phocas was able to describe Saint Euthymius's as being fortified with towers and ramparts.[26] These houses, only six kilometers apart, had been founded from a laura established by the saints in 411 and by the time of Council of Chalcedon (451) had grown into the center of Palestinian Orthodoxy. They were originally sister-houses, or at least associated closely with each other, but the communities seem to have fallen out in the 480s. By the early eleventh century Saint Euthymius was being used as a repository for unsatisfactory monks: Saint Lazarus of the Gelasian Mountain was relegated there by the abbot of Saint Sabas for disobedience.[27] Neophytus, a Cypriot monk who traveled extensively in Palestine in 1158 and wrote a life of the Georgian monk Gabriel the Stylite, indicates that around 1185 the monastery was still being used for the same purpose.[28] This piece of evidence is testimony to the capacity of the Orthodox community to retain the memory of certain monastic traditions over several

25. Ibid., 134.

26. Ibid., 141; John Phocas, *PG* 133:949. Daniel's account is enigmatic, and might be taken to mean that only Saint Theoctistus monastery was in ruins in 1107. The bodies of the saints had, Daniel thought, been preserved. Y. E. Meimaris, *The Monastery of St.-Euthymius the Great at Khan al-Ahmar, in the Wilderness of Judaea: Rescue Excavations and Basic Protection Measures, 1967–1979* (Athens, 1989), 17–18, understood Daniel to mean that the monastery in 1106–7 occupied the site of a small chapel of the Byzantine period. Another monastery, Saint Theodosius (now in the village of 'Ubeidiyya, southeast of Bethlehem), was alluded to by Daniel the Abbot (*Life and Journey*, 139), but whether it was standing in his day, we do not know. It had been fortified with a wall and towers by 1185.

27. *Vita Sancti Lazari, AASS*, Nov. III, 514.

28. H. Delehaye, "Saints de Chypre," *Analecta Bollandiana* 26 (1907), 171–72. Delehaye's edition of Neophytus's "Life of Gabriel the Stylite," 162–75, is from Bib. Nat., Paris, MS Grec. 1189. For the Byzantine history of the monastery and an archaeological survey, see D. J. Chitty, "Two Monasteries in the Wilderness of Judaea," *Palestine Exploration Fund Quarterly Statement 1928*, 134–52; D. J. Chitty and A.H.M. Jones, "The Church of St. Euthymius at Khan el-Ahmar, near Jerusalem," ibid., 175–79; and subsequent reports in ibid., *1930*, 43–47, 150–53; and *1933*, 188–203.

centuries, even where the conditions under which those practices had developed had changed beyond recognition, and to reemploy them once again once the situation allowed. It is a theme that lies immediately beneath the surface of twelfth-century descriptions of Orthodox communities.

Another early Christian foundation provides evidence for the most tangible form of influence of the Orthodox monastic tradition on Frankish monks. A monastery had been founded on Mount Quarantana (Jebel Quruntul), about 2.5 kilometers northwest of Jericho, by Saint Chariton in the fourth century. By the crusader period this had been abandoned by the Greek Orthodox community, and in 1116 a Frankish eremitical community had evidently been in occupation of the site, if not the original buildings, for some time.[29] In 1133 William the patriarch of Jerusalem gave the priory of Quarantana (as it was now known) the full tithes of Jericho and consecrated a new altar, evidence that a church had been built there. But this was the prelude to a takeover—a year later the patriarch gave the whole community and its possessions to the Latin canons of the Holy Sepulcher, who elected Rainald, one of their number, as prior.[30] A German pilgrim, Theoderic, visited Mount Quarantana in the 1170s. His description shows us a Latin monastery following the same model as Choziba and Saint Sabas. The path leading up the mountain to the monastery is so twisting and steep that one has to use hands as well as feet. A gate across the path leads to a chapel dedicated to the Blessed Virgin; the path then continues, snaking back on itself up the mountain, passing an altar and a tomb, until it reaches the spot where Jesus was tempted by the devil and fasted for forty days. The tremendous view from the summit—one can see beyond the Jordan and into "Arabia"—had by 1172 been turned into strategic advantage by the Templars, who used the mountain as a watchtower and its subterranean caves as a munitions store.[31]

Theoderic was primarily interested in the scriptural site, and his descrip-

---

29. G. Bresc-Bautier, ed., *Le cartulaire du Saint-Sépulcre* (Paris, 1984), no. 94. In 1116 Constantius, *sancte Quarantane servus*, and another monk, William, requested from the lord of Jericho, Eustace Grenier, the land that the *habitatores* of Quarantana had once possessed. This, and a water-mill, was returned. In 1124, the monks successfully petitioned Eustace's widow, Emma, to extend the period during which use could be made of the water. For this episode, see H. E. Mayer, "Studies in the History of Queen Melisende of Jerusalem," *Dumbarton Oaks Papers* 26 (1972), 103.

30. Bresc-Bautier, *Cartulaire du Saint-Sépulcre*, nos. 21–22.

31. *Theoderici libellus de locis sanctis*, 70–73. Henry the Lion, duke of Saxony and Bavaria, visited the monastery in 1172 (Arnold of Lubeck, *Chronica Slavorum* 1.7, *MGH SS* 21:121).

Fig. 5.   Cave cells on Mount Quarantana, where an Orthodox monastery had been founded in the fourth century. During the crusader period a Frankish eremitical community occupied the cells, following an Orthodox model.

tion is disappointingly uninformative regarding the monastery. This in itself points to a difference in the Western and Orthodox perceptions of monasteries in the Holy Land. Daniel and Phocas made sure that their pilgrimages included early Christian monasteries, even when they were abandoned, because to them the sites settled by Chariton, Sabas, and Euthymius were hallowed. Sacred history, in the Orthodox tradition, continued into the early Christian period in a way that it did not for a Western pilgrim like Theoderic, who limited his interest to biblical sites. Our knowledge of Orthodox monasteries in the medieval period is thus enhanced by narrative descriptions, whereas for the Latin monasteries we are more reliant on the documentation of land tenure provided by the cartularies.

Abbot Daniel also visited the site of the Transfiguration on Mount Tabor, where he found churches dedicated to Moses, Elijah, and the Transfiguration but no sign of the Orthodox monastery mentioned in the *Commemoratorium*. Instead, the site was surrounded by the "solid stone walls and iron gates" of a Latin monastery.[32] By 1185 the situation on the mountain had changed:

> On the top there are two monasteries, in which Christians who are vowed to the same life invoke the mercy of God in hymns of various tongues. The monastery where the Transfiguration of Christ took place for our salvation is inhabited by a number of Latin monks; but to the left the holy place is sanctified by the holy presence of Nazarenes of our Church.[33]

The Franks had taken over the actual site of the miracle, presumably guided by the Orthodox tradition. Later they allowed the Orthodox to build their own monastery next door. Like the Saint Euthymius and Saint Theodosius monasteries, it was strongly fortified, but not sufficiently to withstand determined assault. Two years before John Phocas visited, Muslim soldiers had stormed the mountain during Saladin's raid of Galilee. According to William of Tyre, they treated the Greek monastery of Saint Elias "according to their own good pleasure," and even tried to break by force into the great cloister itself. The Latin monks and the local inhabitants retired behind their walls and were able to drive the Muslims off the mountain.[34] Ninety-five years later, Burchard of Mount Zion would find only the ruins of "palaces, towers, and Regular buildings, now the lairs of lions and other wild beasts."[35] The Franks had left in 1187, after the fall of the First Kingdom, and the Greeks left in the following century, perhaps as a result of the Kharasmian invasion of 1244.

The largest concentration of Orthodox monasteries was on the banks of the Jordan, to the east and south of Jericho. An anonymous pilgrimage guide dating to before 1114, the *De situ urbis Ierusalem*, mentioned about twenty Orthodox monks at the convent of Saint John the Baptist on the

---

32. Daniel the Abbot, *Life and Journey*, 161. Daniel was impressed by the treatment he received from the Frankish monks, who allowed him to worship in their church.

33. John Phocas, *PG* 133:951. Theoderic mentioned only one monastery, thinking presumably of the Latin (*Theoderici libellus de locis sanctis*, 103).

34. William of Tyre, 22.26 (Huygens, 1052). ". . . monasterium Grecorum, quod dicitur Sancti Helie, pro libero tractantes arbitrio, ipsum etiam maius cenobium effringere temptaverunt, sed receperant se infra septa monasterii, que muro et turribus erant valleta, tam monachis quam eorum universa familie et de viculis nonulli finitimus, qui eos, qui in montem ascenderant, hostes ab universo monasterii ambitu viriliter abegerunt."

35. *Peregrinatores medii aevi quatuor*, 47.

Jordan.[36] In 1106–7, Daniel had found a new monastery built on a hill. The old monastery, on the site of John's baptism of Jesus, was identifiable from a surviving altar and a small arch.[37] By 1185, when Phocas visited it, the monastery had been rebuilt again with the patronage of Manuel Comnenus. Also in the same region was a convent dedicated to Saint John Chrysostom, and another, whose name is missing in Phocas's text but may have been the Saint Michael in Prawer and Benvenisti's map.[38] Farther south, on Mount Horeb by the Dead Sea, Fulcher of Chartres, accompanying the royal army in 1100, passed the Orthodox monastery of Saint Aaron, which was still functioning, perhaps without a break, in 1217, when the pilgrim Thietmar saw two monks there.[39]

Approaching Jericho from the austere wilderness of the Judaean desert to the west, the traveler is struck by the sudden descent into the fertile plain of the Jordan. The Orthodox monasteries were largely concentrated around the oasis of Jericho. "The land, divided and shared out among these holy monasteries, is full of woodland and vineyards, as the monks have planted trees in the fields and reap rich harvests from them."[40] Whether this is to be understood as meaning that a system of communal landownership and cultivation was in operation among the surviving Orthodox monasteries is uncertain. The restoration of Saint John the Baptist by Manuel Comnenus, as will be seen from other examples, is indicative of a wider policy of the Byzantine emperor to recreate the monastic culture of an earlier era. If this included the distribution of lands, we must assume that these lands had been respected as the property of the Orthodox monasteries by the Latin kings of Jerusalem.

Phocas met both cenobitic and eremitical monks in the Jordan Valley. To the west of Saint John the Baptist and Our Lady of Kalamon (whose church

---

36. *On the Site of Jerusalem, and of the Holy Places Inside the City or Round It*, in Wilkinson, *Jerusalem Pilgrimage*, 180.

37. Daniel the Abbot, *Life and Journey*, 136.

38. John Phocas, *PG* 133:952; Prawer and Benvenisti, "Crusader Palestine," sheet 12/9. According to Daniel the Abbot, *Life and Journey*, 138, the monastery of Saint John Chrysostom was very rich.

39. Fulcher of Chartres, *Historia Hierosolymitana* 2.5.9 (Hagenmeyer, 381); *Peregrinatores medii aevi quatuor*, 38. As Hamilton, *The Latin Church in the Crusader States*, 168, points out, the Orthodox monasteries on the Black Mountain near Antioch (some of which were Armenian or Jacobite) were also left alone by the Franks. According to Ordericus Vitalis, *Ecclesiastical History* 10.12, ed. and trans. M. Chibnall (Oxford, 1969–76), 5:278, Bohemond I confirmed the possessions of the Orthodox monks of the Black Mountain, installing Frankish monks only in the houses that fell into ruin before the First Crusade.

40. John Phocas, *PG* 133:949.

boasted an image of the Virgin allegedly painted by the hand of Saint Luke),[41] south of Jericho, were the ruins of Saint Gerasimus, which in Phocas's day had been washed away by the river to its very foundations so that only a few remains of the church were visible, with two grottoes and "a pillar for recluses, in which is bricked up a tall old Georgian, from whose conversation we benefited greatly."[42] Phocas found a hermitage with another Georgian monk, not far from the monastery of Saint John Chrysostom.[43] As we have seen, yet another compatriot lived in "Absalom's Pillar" in the Valley of Jehosaphat. The monastery of Kalamon itself ('Ain Hujla), founded 450–75, was still functioning in the beginning of the twelfth century, when Daniel found twenty monks there.[44] A surviving inscription from the 1150s–60s indicates some restoration in the middle of the century, perhaps, like Saint John the Baptist's, financed by Manuel Comnenus.[45]

Sometimes an Orthodox monastery known from precrusader literary sources is known to have continued into the twelfth century, even when the site can no longer be identified with certainty. Such is the case with Saint Michael the Archangel at Gilgal (Galgala), described by Daniel as the place where Saint Michael appeared to Joshua, and marked by twelve stones taken from the Jordan. The huge stones were lying behind the altar of a church by 570, where they were also described by Arculf in the 680s. At some point during the next forty years the church was ruined and replaced by the wooden structure seen by Saint Willibald in 724, but by 1106–7 it seems once again to have been rebuilt.[46] The monastery is not mentioned again by a twelfth- or thirteenth-century source, though the site of the Twelve Stones appears in topographical accounts. Thietmar, in 1217, saw the Twelve Stones but does not mention a church.[47]

---

41. Ibid., 953.

42. Ibid., 952. The Georgian apparently fed lions from his own hand. A. Stewart mistranslates the Greek *Iberus* as "Spanish" (*John Phocas*, PPTS 5 [1896], 27). Phocas appears to be confused about the location of Saint Gerasimus monastery, which he puts "between" Saint John the Baptist and Kalamon. He may have forgotten the precise topography by the time he wrote up his account, or he may have been mistaken about the site because it was in ruins in 1185.

43. John Phocas, PG 133:953.

44. Daniel the Abbot, *Life and Journey*, 138.

45. Pringle, *Churches of the Crusader Kingdom*, 1:197, 201. By the 1280s Kalamon was being wrongly identified as Saint Gerasimus, which apparently never recovered under Frankish rule.

46. Daniel the Abbot, *Life and Journey*, 139; Pringle, *Churches of the Crusader Kingdom*, 1:221.

47. *Peregrinatores medii aevi quatuor*, 31. Pringle, *Churches of the Crusader Kingdom*, 1:222,

The status of some remaining structures is still uncertain. A monastic church of Saint George at al-Ba'ina (Dair al-asad) in the lordship of Acre is described in an anonymous pilgrimage account of around 1230, *Les sains pèlerinages*, as being occupied by Greek monks. Two near-contemporary French accounts, however, the *Pèlerinaiges* and the *Chemins et pèlerinages*, mention only "black monks," which may refer to Benedictines or to Orthodox, who commonly wore black. Pringle identified the monastic buildings at Dair al-asad as being twelfth-century in date, and described a courtyard with individual cells built around an upper storey. Such a layout might be reminiscent of a Carthusian house, "or possibly an ascetic strain of Augustinian canons," but because there were no Carthusian houses in Palestine in the twelfth or thirteenth centuries, Pringle concluded that it must have been an Orthodox monastery.[48]

The individual cells, however, do not necessarily rule out a Frankish presence. The structural layout of Bernard of Blois's foundation at Jubin in the Black Mountain is unknown, but our knowledge of such irregular foundations, based on particularly ascetic Rules, must suggest the possibility that Saint George's was a semi-cenobitic Latin foundation run along Carthusian-inspired lines. Given the fragility of such foundations, it might of course have been abandoned and taken over by Orthodox monks by the thirteenth century.

The revival of Orthodox monasticism in Outremer is a testimony to the modus vivendi established by the rulers of the kingdom of Jerusalem and the Byzantine emperors. Manuel Comnenus was instrumental in the physical reconstruction of such monasteries as Baptisma Christi, and his patronage seems to have met no opposition. On the road from Jerusalem to Bethlehem, for example, was the monastery of Elijah, "which was built by religious men in very ancient times, but subsequently completely destroyed in an earthquake. The universal benefactor, my master and emperor [Manuel Comnenus], has raised it from its foundations, answering the prayers of the Syrian who is the chief of the community."[49]

Manuel's patronage in the kingdom of Jerusalem stands in contrast to his

---

discusses various possibilities for the site of the monastery—notably Tall Matlab, northeast of Jericho, where there is evidence of Byzantine buildings.

48. Pringle, *Churches of the Crusader Kingdom*, 1:91.

49. John Phocas, *PG* 133:956. Manuel Comnenus also donated books to monasteries. A manuscript of John Chrysostom now in the Greek Orthodox Patriarchate in Jerusalem has a note recording the occasion of its being given to the monastery of Saint Euthymius by the emperor (Chitty, "Two Monasteries," 138).

general monastic policy nearer home, where he was hostile to the extension of monastic property, particularly to the foundation of new monasteries.[50] In the Latin kingdom he seems to have been willing to respond to the request even of a single monk, if Phocas is to be believed. A brief comparison of the general position of Orthodox monasteries in another frontier society, the Norman kingdom of Sicily, serves to underline the nature and importance of Manuel's policy. The revival of Orthodox monasticism in Sicily was, as Lynn White showed, largely a matter of Norman royal policy. It was designed to keep at bay the centralized Western Orders, such as the Cistercians, lest papal influence intrude with them through the back door.[51] This policy did not entail a privileged status for the Orthodox population as a whole. Orthodox monasteries, in Sicily and elsewhere, were autocephalous institutions with no formal connections to Constantinople. This makes Manuel's interest in the monasteries of Palestine, and his success in sponsoring their redevelopment, the more remarkable.

In a general sense, Manuel's policy supports the assumption already made that the Orthodox Church understood its role in Palestine in the context of its own history there, specifically as interpreted by the great monasteries of the early Christian period. By restoring the monasteries of Saint John the Baptist, Saint Elijah, or Saint Euthymius, Manuel was restoring a Byzantine religious past within the frontiers of the new Latin kingdom. There is thus a sharp political edge to his patronage. Recent study by art historians has shown how Manuel deliberately fostered the work of Byzantine artists in crusader churches as an expression of religious imperialism.[52] Besides the monasteries already mentioned, the rebuilding of Saint Mary of Choziba (described by John Phocas) occurred during the reign of Manuel Comnenus (1143–80)[53] and may have been made possible by his patronage. Manuel gave money for the gilding of the cupola of the Lord's Sepulcher and for the extensive redecoration of the mosaics in the Church of the Nativity in Bethlehem.

There is, of course, a distinction between local monastic culture and the

---

50. F. Chalandon, *Les Comnènes: Jean II Comnène et Manuel I Comnène* (Paris, 1912), 633. P. Magdalino, *The Empire of Manuel I Komnenos, 1143–1180* (Cambridge, 1993), 113–15, points out that the Comneni patronized private foundations rather than public churches or monasteries.

51. White, *Latin Monasticism*, 53–57.

52. A.-M. Weyl Carr, "The Mural Paintings of Abu Ghosh and the Patronage of Manuel Comnenus in the Holy Land," in J. Folda, ed., *Crusader Art in the Twelfth Century* (Jerusalem, 1982), 215–44.

53. Pringle, *Churches of the Crusader Kingdom*, 1:184.

patronage of shrine churches. A monastery such as Saint Sabas, with 300 monks at the beginning of the twelfth century,[54] could do its own business with the Latin Church. In 1163–64 the abbot of Saint Sabas, Meletios, sold to the Church of the Holy Sepulcher three villages with their villeins, so that they could buy the casale of Thora from King Amaury.[55] Ten years later Meletios appears as a *confrater*, or "associate member," of the Hospital of Saint John, in a charter recording the cession of the monastery of Saint George at Beit Jibrin to the monastery of Saint Sabas. Meletios is called "archbishop of the Syrians and Greeks at Gaza and Eleutheropolis."[56] Saint George's had apparently been recently rebuilt and would revert to the Hospital when Meletios died, as part of the terms of the deed, but whoever was resident in the monastery was required to pray for the souls of Meletios himself and Manuel Comnenus. The Byzantine emperor cannot easily be excluded from the dealings of indigenous monasteries with Latin houses.

As a suffragan of the Latin bishop, Meletios may have able to promote the cause of the Orthodox Church from within the episcopal structure of the ruling clique. The monastery of Saint Sabas had played a prominent role in the liturgy of the Easter celebration at the Holy Sepulcher as early as 1107,[57] and the evidence suggests that the abbots, who were significant landowners, were able to maintain a position of great influence in the Latin kingdom. This may be a further indication of the long arm of Manuel Comnenus. He had secured the replacement of Aimery of Antioch by a Greek patriarch in Antioch in 1165 in return for paying the ransom of Bohemond III to the Turks. It is not impossible that Manuel was able to foster the revival of Orthodox monasticism in the Latin kingdom by the same judicious use of money.[58]

54. Saewulf, *De situ Iherusalem*, 21 (De Sandoli, 2:22).

55. Bresc-Bautier, *Cartulaire du Saint-Sépulcre*, 259–60.

56. J. Delaville le Roulx, ed., *Cartulaire général de l'Ordre des Hospitaliers*, 1:305–6, no. 443. Another Orthodox monk used as a suffragan bishop by the Franks in the twelfth century was Paul of Antioch (P. Khoury, ed., *Paul d'Antioche, évêque melkite de Sidon* [Beirut, 1964]). Paul was an Arabic-speaking Christian, whereas the Orthodox Church before the Frankish occupation had appointed Greeks from the Byzantine territories.

57. Daniel the Abbot, *Life and Journey*, 166–69. Orthodox monks were allowed to maintain an altar in the church, and after the rebuilding of 1149 this was placed in front of the new choir (*Theoderici libellus de locis sanctis*, 20).

58. Hamilton, *The Latin Church in the Crusader States*, 183–84, suggests that Orthodox suffragans were in use from the early days of the Latin kingdom. The seventeenth-century Orthodox patriarch of Jerusalem, Dositheos, included in his Ἱστορια πατριαρχων (Athens, 1715), 752, three other Orthodox bishops in the twelfth century: Germanus, metropolitan of Baisan; Matus, bishop of Gaza; and Elias, bishop of Bethlehem. These names are taken

It should be noted that monasteries played a more dominant role in the Orthodox Church than in the Western Church. Orthodox bishops were elected from among the body of monks alone, so it was natural for the Latin hierarchy to select abbots such as Meletios, or the abbot of Saint Catherine's on Mount Sinai, as suffragan bishops.[59] Moreover, because monasteries were the epicenters of the spiritual life of the laity as well as of the monks themselves, they are a good indication of the spiritual health of the Orthodox population as a whole.

The best-documented case of Manuel's patronage of the Orthodox Church in the Holy Land is the redecoration of the Church of the Nativity in Bethlehem. During the 1160s an extensive program of wall mosaics was installed in the nave, transepts, and apse. An inscription in the apse, in Latin and Greek, dates the completion of the work to 1169 and attributes the workmanship to a Syrian, Ephraim, and the patronage jointly to Manuel Comnenus, King Amaury I of Jerusalem, and Ralph, bishop of Bethlehem.[60] Only the Latin inscription gives any clue to Frankish participation

---

apparently from an uncited charter from the monastery of Saint Euthymius and dated 1146. "Matus," an otherwise inexplicable name, looks like a contraction of Meletios, which suggests either that Dositheos's date is incorrect or that Meletios's period of office stretched for thirty-odd years. These bishops cannot refer to appointments made in exile by the patriarch of Constantinople, because the sees of Baisan and Bethlehem do not appear in contemporary Orthodox episcopal lists. Baisan was known in the Orthodox Church as Scythopolis, and Bethlehem was a see created by Baldwin I (1100–10) as a surrogate for the Orthodox see of Ascalon, then still in Fatimid hands. Such episcopal lists were being produced in Orthodox monasteries in the Latin kingdom—e.g., Jerusalem, Greek Orthodox Patriarchate MS 39, fols. 171–96.

59. The pilgrim Thietmar (in 1217) reports that the abbot of Saint Catherine's had the dignity of a bishop (*Peregrinatores medii aevi quatuor*, 41). In theory at least, the abbot was the suffragan of the archbishop of Petra. Y. Katzrir, "The Patriarch of Jerusalem, Primate of the Latin Kingdom," in P. W. Edbury, ed., *Crusade and Settlement* (Cardiff, 1985), 173, discusses briefly the issue of abbots as suffragans. It is difficult to know exactly what to make of the assertion here, taken from the *Livre* of John of Ibelin, that the abbots of the Templum Domini, of Mount Zion, and of the Mount of Olives were also suffragans of the patriarch of Jerusalem, except perhaps to suggest that the word "suffragan" is used by John, a layman, in a technically uncanonical sense.

60. H. Vincent and F. M. Abel, *Bethléem, le sanctuaire de la Nativité* (Paris, 1914), 157–58, published a reconstruction of the inscription. The nave mosaics survive only in fragmentary condition but have recently been cleaned by Gustav Kühnel. They were clearly described in 1626 by the Franciscan custodian of the Holy Places, Quaresmius, *Enchiridion locorum sanctorum*, ed. D. Baldi (Jerusalem, 1935), 203–7. In addition, the Italian traveler Ciampini published a description accompanied by an engraving of the mosaics of the north wall of the nave (J. Ciampini, *De sacris aedificiis a Constantino Magno constructis* [Rome, 1693], 153–56). There is an impressive bibliography on the mosaics, much of it recent. The thesis of H. Stern

in the program, so fully Byzantine is the style of the mosaicist. The south side of the nave also bears an inscription in Latin and Greek attributing the work in the nave to the artist Basil, who must have been either a Syrian trained in the Byzantine style or a Greek imported from Constantinople.[61]

While the apse mosaics followed a typically Byzantine scheme, the nave walls depicted a subject unique in ecclesiastical architecture: the seven ecumenical councils on one wall and, facing them, six provincial councils. These are extraordinary not simply in terms of subject matter but for their overtly Byzantine ideological stamp, depicting Byzantine Orthodoxy in a Latin cathedral church.[62] The Council of Constantinople of 381 is a good example of this boldness. The representation includes a text from the Nicene Creed, determining the procession of the Holy Spirit but omitting reference to the *filioque*. Such an omission naturally reflects the precise wording of the decree in the fourth century, but by the 1160s this formula was no longer acceptable in the West and proved to be the most trouble-some issue dividing Orthodox and Roman churches. It is difficult to escape the conclusion that the Latin bishop and cathedral chapter consciously allowed a doctrine they regarded as theologically incorrect to be published on the wall of their church. That this was done at the behest of Manuel Comnenus seems certain. The emperor's proclivities for theological dispu-tation were a source of scorn in Constantinople,[63] but in the Latin kingdom

---

that the nave scheme was based on an original to be dated ca. 700, of which only the north wall survives, is now largely discredited, but Stern's analysis of the mosaics is still worth reading: "Les représentations des conciles dans l'église de la Nativité à Bethléem," *Byzantion* 11 (1936), 101–52; 13 (1938), 415–59; "Nouvelles recherches sur les images des conciles dans l'église de la Nativité à Bethléem," *Cahiers Archéologiques* 3 (1948), 82–105; "Encore les mosaiques de l'église de la Nativité à Bethléem," *Cahiers Archéologiques* 9 (1957), 141–45. For refutations, see G. Kühnel, "Der Ausschmückungsprogramm der Geburtsbasilika in Bethle-hem: Byzanz und Abendland im Königreich Jerusalem," *Boreas* 10 (1987), 133–49; and L.-A. Hunt, "Art and Colonialism: The Mosaics of the Church of Nativity in Bethlehem (1169) and the Problem of Crusader Art," *Dumbarton Oaks Papers* 45 (1991), 69–85.

61. This may have been the same Basil who painted some of the miniatures in the "Melisende Psalter" (London, BL MS Egerton, 1139), made ca. 1140. On the influence of Byzantine styles in crusader art, see H. Buchthal, *Miniature Painting in the Latin Kingdom of Jerusalem* (Oxford, 1957); and G. Kühnel, *Wall Painting in the Latin Kingdom of Jerusalem* (Berlin, 1988).

62. For a full discussion of the significance of the conciliar mosaics in the context of Manuel I's religious policy, see A. T. Jotischky, "Manuel I Comnenus and the Reunion of the Churches: The Evidence of the Conciliar Mosaics in Bethlehem," *Levant* 26 (1994), 207–23.

63. *Nicetae Choniatae Historia*, ed. J. L. van Dieten, Corpus Fontium Historiae Byzantinae, 3 vols. (Berlin, 1975), 1:210–12.

they had the more serious purpose of ensuring the continuity of Orthodoxy at the Holy Places. It is significant that John Phocas attributed the mosaics in the Church of the Nativity to Manuel's patronage alone. The emperor wanted to leave no doubt that Manuel was responsible for establishing the Orthodox community in the Holy Land.

> In many places, and especially in the sanctuary itself, above the holy grotto, the priest in charge of those of that place who follow the Latin rite has placed the beautiful portrait of the Emperor, probably meaning thus to thank him for his magnanimity.[64]

The Bethlehem mosaics strongly suggest that an Orthodox monastic community was active in the Church of the Nativity in the 1160s. Manuel Comnenus did not bestow his patronage on Latin churches, but his interest in Bethlehem corresponds to his patronage of the Church of the Holy Sepulcher and other Orthodox monasteries, and makes sense if there were an Orthodox community in residence, or at least an Orthodox altar. The mosaics themselves must have been overseen by Orthodox clergy, since the inscriptions were, save for Nicaea II, all rendered in Greek.[65] The mosaics formed only a part of the extensive decorative program in the Church of the Nativity in the mid-twelfth century. The double row of columns on each side of the nave was decorated with paintings of saints ranging from the conventional, such as the Blessed Virgin, Saint James, and Saint Stephen, to the obscure or regional, such as the South Italian Saint Catald, the Scandinavian saints Olaf and Cnut, and the early Christian Eastern hermits Onuphrius, Macarius, and Theodosius. The latter group includes the great monastic founders of Byzantine Palestine, Sabas and Euthymius, and the exemplar of all hermits, the prophet Elijah. The column paintings, many of which bear inscriptions in Latin and Greek, are balanced more tentatively between Orthodox and Latin than the conciliar

---

64. John Phocas, *PG* 133:957.

65. Stern, "Les représentations des conciles," *Byzantion* 13 (1938), 447, argues that the texts for the Provincial Councils must have derived from oriental rather than Byzantine sources, since the lists of bishops recorded as present are taken from John of Damascus rather than from Constantinopolitan accounts. The ecumenical texts may have been supplied from an Orthodox library in the kingdom of Jerusalem or, conceivably, directly from Constantinople. On the complex subject of the origins of the Latin chapter at Bethlehem, see Mayer, *Bistümer*, 50-65.

mosaics. As G. Kühnel has shown, they were probably the result of a joint Byzantine-Frankish workshop.[66]

Whether the paintings should be seen as a random collection of votive paintings, or as a coherent series to be integrated with the nave mosaics,[67] it is unlikely that the Latin chapter of the Church of the Nativity would have chosen to represent Onuphrius, Euthymius, or Sabas without the initiative of Orthodox monks. If Kühnel is correct in insisting on a sophisticated and consistent program, the subject and style of the column paintings add further weight to the argument for an Orthodox monastic community in Bethlehem.

The inclusion of a text promoting Orthodox doctrine at the expense of Latin in a shrine church run by Latin canons raises the broader issue of the status of the Orthodox in the kingdom of Jerusalem.[68] The presence of Orthodox monasteries meant that Orthodox liturgies, rites, and doctrines were tolerated under Frankish rule. This does not mean that the Latin Church was being undermined by a "fifth column" within the fabric of the religious life of Palestine. Orthodox monasteries were autocephalous and did not entail the influence of the partriarchate in Constantinople or a central Chapter-General in the same way that a Cistercian monastery, for example, did.

Orthodox parochial life, moreover, was left almost untouched by the Frankish settlement of the Holy Land. Jacques de Vitry was scandalized to find, when he arrived to assume his new bishopric of Acre in 1216, that Orthodox and Jacobite (Syrian Orthodox) communities were continuing to practice the very cultural and religious customs that the Latin Church found offensive: they circumcised their young boys, used leavened bread in the Eucharist, did not have auricular confession, and so on.[69] This was to

66. Kühnel, *Wall Painting*, 138–39.

67. J. Folda, "Painting and Sculpture in the Latin Kingdom of Jerusalem, 1099–1291," in H. Hazard, ed., *The Art and Architecture of the Crusader States*, vol. 4 of K. Setton, gen. ed., *History of the Crusades* (Madison, Wis., 1977), 255, suggests that the paintings reflect the offerings and tastes of pilgrims to the church, but Kühnel, *Wall Painting*, 138–39, 145, suggests a deliberate iconographic program and sees a possible Italian provenance for the Western artists.

68. In general, see Hamilton, *The Latin Church in the Crusader States*, 159–88.

69. Jacques de Vitry, *Lettres*, ed. R.B.C. Huygens (Leiden, 1960), 83–84. Despite the apparent similarities of their religious customs, the Jacobite and Greek Orthodox churches were doctrinally distinct. The Jacobites were Monophysites who had rejected the Council of Chalcedon in 451 and remained a separate church. They were identical in doctrine to the Copts of Egypt and were largely based in Antioch (the seat of the patriarch) and in northern Syria.

be expected of the Jacobites, who had their own bishops and no claim to share the communion of the ecumenical church, but for the native Arabic-speaking Orthodox priests to wear their hair long and marry, *more Graecorum*, was intolerable. The appointment of suffragan or assistant bishops from among the Orthodox, such as Abbot Meletios, can only have strengthened the resilience of the Orthodox Church by ensuring that a vital artery was maintained between the lay communities in villages and towns and the monasteries where canonical texts were being copied, commentaries and treatises were being written, and doctrine was being fiercely protected. Jacques, indeed, provides a rare example of a Latin bishop in the kingdom of Jerusalem who found the situation disagreeable or offensive. During the twelfth century, nothing had apparently been done to disrupt the continuity of the religious life of the Orthodox.[70]

This chapter began with the premise that the conditions existed for extensive contact between Orthodox and Frankish monks and hermits. Specific examples of such conditions, such as the communities of hermits in the Valley of Jehosaphat, must be seen in the more general context of the revival of Orthodox monasticism in the crusader kingdom. But favorable conditions for contact do not necessarily make inevitable the influence of Orthodox monastic practice on Frankish hermits. Orthodox and Latin

---

70. The disapproval of Jacques de Vitry was doubtless matched by the disdain of the Orthodox clergy for the Latin. In 1948 R. J. Loenertz published a letter from the Greek philosopher in Manuel Comnenus's entourage, Theorianus, "L'épître de Théorien le Philosophe aux prêtres d'Oreine," *Archives de l'Orient Chrétien* 1 (1948), 317–35. Theorianus had been informed that disputes had arisen between the Orthodox priests and the Latins on various matters of religious observance: on keeping the Sabbath fast, on Holy Communion, on whether priests should marry or wear beards. He advised the priests to "love the Latins as brothers, for they are orthodox and the sons of the Catholic Church, just as you are." These questions were minor matters of custom, not articles of faith, and should not rupture fraternal relations. This remarkable statement of tolerance by the Greek theologian used by Manuel as an envoy to the Armenian catholicos, 1169–71 (*PG* 133:120–22), has been avoided by historians, perhaps because of the problem of the identity of the recipients of the letter. 'ορεινη (literally, "mountainous") was a common colloquial place name in the Greek-speaking world. In the 1160s the only region where such Orthodox/Latin friction might have occurred was the crusader states. Loenertz ("L'épître," 321), argued that 'ορεινη referred to "Beth Zechariah," the mountainous place in Judaea where Mary visited her cousin Elizabeth (Luke 1:39). The Greek text of Luke does indeed describe Mary's journey εἰς την 'ορεινη, "into the mountains." In the twelfth century the House of Zechariah was shown to pilgrims at 'Ain Karim, five miles southwest of the center of Jerusalem (Pringle, *Churches of the Crusader Kingdom*, 1:30–31). Phocas, moreover, refers to the area of 'Ain Karim as 'ορεινη, "and it is well-named, because it is more mountainous than any hill-country for a distance of many stades around it" (Wilkinson, *Jerusalem Pilgrimage*, 332).

communities must typically have lived independent of such contacts, by mutual choice. Those episodes of friction described in the sources, such as Jacques de Vitry's homilies to the Jacobites and Orthodox in Acre in 1216, stand out in sharp relief precisely because they were unusual. Jacques ingenuously informed his correspondent that the native Christians had promised to reform their ways. Undoubtedly they ignored him, but for all their lack of effect the efforts of Jacques are of great importance for historians as a point of reference. The single futile attempt to bring the Orthodox and Jacobite forms of worship in Acre into line with Latin practices stands for generations of omission or indifference on the part of the Latin authorities.

Another tangible point of reference reinforces the importance of monastic culture for the meeting of Frankish and native Christian practice. In Antioch in 1152 a Frankish boy had a bad fall from a tree and lay in a coma for days. Neither doctor nor priest seemed able to cure him. Eventually, in desperation, his mother prayed to Bar Sauma, a saint of whom she had heard from a Jacobite monk. The saint appeared simultaneously to the mother and to the monk, telling them to build a church dedicated to him in the garden of the Frankish house. A little later the boy suddenly gave a great cry and came out of his coma; he told of a remarkable vision that had appeared to him of Bar Sauma with a gold cross accompanied by a troop of monks. The saint had touched his head and healed him. The Frankish family subsequently built the required church, which was consecrated in December 1156, in the presence of the Armenian governor of Cilicia, Princess Constance of Antioch, and Frankish, Jacobite, and Armenian clergy. The church became a noted center for miracles of healing, venerated by the faithful of all three churches.[71]

The story is told less to glorify the harmony between Franks and Jacobites than to exclude the Greek Orthodox (who took no part in the cult and thus derived no benefit from the saint's works), but it has the effect of showing how easily patterns of "popular" religious practice could be transmitted from one church to another. Such contacts were lasting, and did not depend for their effect on the relations between prelates and pontiffs.

The cult of a saint was an obvious and easy form of religious devotion to spread in an urban environment. Statues of saints were visible, and processions on feast days were audible. The mother of a dying boy presumably did

---

71. Michael the Syrian, *Chronique*, ed. and trans. J.-B. Chabot, 4 vols., new ed. (Brussels, 1963), 3:300–304.

not care from which church the veneration of a foreign saint derived; she simply wanted the saint to be effective. From such accidental and unofficial contacts did influences spread. But such influence need not have been in one direction only. Saint Nerses of Lampron, the Armenian catholicos in the 1190s, learned Greek, Latin, and Syriac while a monk at the Armenian monastery on the Black Mountain. He admired the Franks for their piety, in contrast to his own people's negligence of the church: "Becoming masters of the land which had long been ruled by Armenian princes, who had founded no churches or bishoprics there, the Franks' first care was to found an institutional church, as we have seen for ourselves."[72] Nerses later wrote in defense of his decision to implement the reforms of his church demanded by the papacy as a condition for reunion. He was willing, he told King Leo II, to adopt the Benedictine custom of prayer at the third, sixth, and ninth hours, in addition to the Opus Dei seven times a day, simply because he believed they were worthwhile practices.[73] Although his pro-Western attitudes were unpopular with the Armenians, he cannot have been the only Eastern Christian to have approved of Latin piety.

A more problematical question, and central to the issue of Orthodox influence on Latin monasticism in the Holy Land, is what Frankish hermits could really have learned from contacts with indigenous monks that they did not already know. The importance of the "desert fathers" as exemplars was well known to educated Western hermits.[74] But this academic interest in the founders of monasticism cannot be compared to the Orthodox continuity of life in early Christian convents in Palestine or their restoration by the Byzantine emperor. The Orthodox monks whom Phocas, Daniel, and Godric met were conscious of their place in a religious tradition. But do the careers of monks like Bernard of Blois and his followers, or, more pertinent, Elias of Narbonne and John of Jerusalem, who moved from eremitical to cenobitic monasticism, show the absorption of a distinct Orthodox influence, or were they simply conforming to the examples of, for instance, Stephen of Obazine, but in a radically different environment?

The pattern of reformed foundations in western Europe, about which Henrietta Leyser has written so convincingly, was that of a progression from rude beginnings to a more rigid permanence, but as the example of Stephen of Obazine shows, this was often achieved at the expense of the hard-won

72. Nerses of Lampron, *Réflexions sur les institutions de l'église, RHC Arm.* 1:576.
73. Ibid., 598–99.
74. Peter the Venerable, *Letters*, 1:29, Ep. 20.

ideals of the founders themselves. The experience of such a community was the opposite of the individual monk's as conceived in the Rule of Saint Benedict. Instead of receiving a general training in cenobitic life leading to a sharpened spiritual awareness, building up a reserve of experience and inner strength that would enable the monk to embark on the perilous journey of anchoresis, Stephen of Obazine and Elias of Narbonne found themselves submerged in the very forms of cenobitism they had sought to evade. The patterns of Orthodox monasticism in Palestine, by contrast, show a balance between these types of monastic life, and an appreciation of the value of fluid cycles of eremitic and cenobitic living.

The account of Saint Catherine's on Mount Sinai in the *Work on Geography* shows us Orthodox monasticism at its grandest. But even this most prestigious of monasteries allowed for a degree of solitary living by supporting anchorites in clusters of cells outside the walls. "Everyone lives in separate cells round the Mount, and they live not in common, but of a common stock."[75] As a monk at Mount Zion in the first quarter of the eleventh century, the maverick Symeon of Trier had been permitted to live for long periods as an anchorite in the desert of Judaea and by the Red Sea, though he remained a full member of the community.[76]

The best example of this type of monastic life from the crusader period comes from the life and works of the Cypriot monk Neophytus. More than anything, his career and those he illustrated in his written works show how naturally Orthodox monks of the twelfth century followed the traditions of the early Christian monastic founders in Palestine. Neophytus's own career is known from a brief autobiography contained in the Rule he wrote for his foundation toward the end of his life.[77] Born in Cyprus in 1134, he left his family at the age of eighteen to escape a marriage that had been arranged for him, and entered the monastery of Saint John Chrysostom on Mount Koutsovendes. Although recovered by his parents after two months, he was able to persuade them to let him enter the monastery. Five years later, however, in 1158, he left suddenly and without permission for Jerusalem and spent six months touring the holy places. Neophytus was more than a pilgrim; he was an aspiring hermit, searching for an experienced eremitical master whose pupil he might become. He traveled north to the Galilee hills,

75. *Work on Geography*, 36, in Wilkinson, *Jerusalem Pilgrimage*, 186.

76. *Vita S. Symeoni*, *AASS*, June I, 87.

77. F. E. Warren, ed., "The 'Ritual Ordinance' of Neophytus," *Archaeologia* 47 (1882), 1–40. On Neophytus in general, see C. Galatariotou, *The Making of a Saint: The Life, Times, and Sanctification of Neophytus the Recluse* (Cambridge, 1991).

visited Mount Tabor (where there were cenobitic Orthodox monks), then went south again to Saint Sabas, to Saint Mary Choziba's, and to the monasteries in the Jordan Valley.[78]

Neophytus did not find what he sought, but the psychological effect of his wandering was to make him, on his return, abandon the monastery of Saint John Chrysostom. He hoped to travel to Mount Latros, near Miletus in Asia Minor, and join a famous community of monks and hermits there. He arrived at the port of Paphos but was mistaken for a fugitive, thrown into prison, and robbed of all the money he had for the journey. He contented himself on his release with settling in a cave in the nearby mountains, where he lived from June 1159. By September 1160 he had built a cell that included an altar and a tomb. In 1170 the bishop of Paphos persuaded him to become a priest and take on a disciple, and this relaxation of his strict solitude was further compromised by the growth of a monastic community around his cell.[79]

The *Ritual Ordinance* was written as a Rule (in Byzantine terminology, a *typikon*) for his monks.[80] It included a catalog of books in the library for the monks' edification. One of these was a collection of saints' lives that includes Neophytus's own account of the career of a near-contemporary stylite in Palestine, the Georgian Gabriel. The work is in the form of an instruction for monks on how to deal with evil spirits, but for the historian it is chiefly useful for providing a biography to hang on the bare pegs in John Phocas's account of Georgian hermits.[81]

After living as a hermit for eleven years in various sites in the Holy Land, Gabriel entered the monastery of Saint Sabas. But it was not long before he yearned for solitude again and obtained permission from the abbot to occupy a column in the desert not far from the monastery. There, however, he became subject to visitations from three demons, who lodged themselves in his ears and stomach. One appeared to him in the guise of Saint Sabas himself, the two others appeared as Symeon the Stylite and Stephen Trichinas. Gabriel's cries of despair, held as he was in the grip of this psychological torture, were heard from the monks in their monastery. Under the influence of the demons, Gabriel left his column and tried to murder a

---

78. Warren, "Ritual Ordinance," 12.

79. Ibid., 12–13; H. Delehaye, "Saints de Chypre," *Analecta Bollandiana* 26 (1907), 275.

80. The *typikon* was first written in 1177, but it is the revised version of 1214 that survives (Galatoriotou, *Making of a Saint*, 16).

81. *Narratio de monacho Palaestinensi*, from Bib. Nat., Paris, MS Grec. 1189, ed. H. Delehaye, "Saints de Chypre," 162–75.

neighboring hermit, David. This monk was able to persuade him to seek help at Saint Sabas. The abbot sent Gabriel to the monastery of Saint Euthymius, where he was to practice a strict regime of manual labor. The demons continued to torment him here, however, and in 1187, when that monastery was overrun by Saladin's conquering army, Gabriel was captured and taken to Damascus. A marginal note in the manuscript edited by Delehaye and dated to 1205 shows that Gabriel eventually continued his eremitical vocation in the region of Antioch, presumably on the Black Mountain.[82]

Gabriel's career is strikingly similar to that of one of Gerard of Nazareth's hermits. Ursus entered the cloister at Jubin under the influence of a demonic visitation, *illusione quadam diabolica persuasus*.[83] Like Gabriel, he was put to manual work, then rose to be sacristan and miller. But he kept the habit of leaving the monastery to wander alone on the Black Mountain whenever he was troubled in thought; he would call on the Lord and the Blessed Virgin to help him, then return to the monastery. This appears to be an example of a Latin monastery encouraging, if on a smaller scale, the type of fluidity regularly observed in Orthodox monasticism. Gabriel and Ursus were, perhaps, naturally more inclined to eremitism, but both needed the institutional support a cenobitic community provided. The abbot of Saint Sabas was prepared to let his new recruit live on his column as an "associate" member of the monastery. When Gabriel could no longer combat the demons on his own, Orthodox institutional support provided an appropriate place for him to deal with his problem.

It is significant that the same remedy for ridding monks of demons— manual labor—was known in both Latin and Orthodox monastic culture. Because no connection can be shown between Gerard and Neophytus, it cannot be proven that either author was dependent on the other—but the practice might have derived from Orthodox tradition and been learned in the course of personal contact by the monks of Jubin from Orthodox colleagues on the Black Mountain.[84]

Gabriel provides fascinating evidence for the vibrancy of Palestinian Orthodox monasticism. The same relationships between the monasteries of Saint Sabas and Saint Euthymius that had existed in the early eleventh century were still in place or had been restored effortlessly. The spiritual

---

82. Delehaye, "Saints de Chypre," 281–82.
83. *Duodecima centuria*, col. 1607.
84. Ibid.

practices of monks in the eastern deserts had not been eroded by the centuries of Muslim occupation. Gabriel was able to copy the example of the great Symeon the Stylite, and did so with such self-consciousness that he was tormented by a demon in Symeon's likeness.[85]

Neophytus was interested in Gabriel because he had, to a degree, foreshadowed the Georgian's career, fluctuating between extremes of cenobitism and solitude. He served his apprenticeship in the cloister, as Benedict had advised, before attempting to strike out on his own. His decision to go to Palestine to look for an eremitical teacher may have been inspired by the need to escape the ecclesiastical authority of his monastery, but it is testimony to the fame of Orthodox hermits there. Neophytus resisted attempts by the bishop of Paphos to ordain him and make him accept disciples for four years before giving in.

The involvement of the bishop shows us a pattern of institutional control that recalls Aimery of Antioch's legislative measures for the Black Mountain hermits. Once the foundation had started, however, Neophytus realized the importance of authoritarian control. Unlike the Frank Elias of Narbonne, who was drafted into an existing monastery, Neophytus could make his own rules. An Orthodox founder had more freedom here than his Frankish counterpart. Where Neophytus simply followed the centuries-old tradition of Orthodox monks in Palestine, of looking for an eremitical mentor,[86] and Gabriel arranged to live as a "part-time" monk of Saint Sabas, Elias was forced into a structure that could not properly accommodate him and that he himself served poorly.

Neophytus wrote his own Rule, specific to his own community. A Frankish community in Antioch that tried to do the same, Bernard of Blois's Jubin, did not long survive without a wider legislative framework.[87] Orthodox monasteries, in contrast, were by nature autonomous and ruled at the whim of the abbot or founder. To return for a moment to a Western

---

85. Galatoriotou, *Making of a Saint*, 104–5, discusses other incidences of stylites in later Byzantine monasticism and the degree to which they imitated Symeon.

86. For this theme in Orthodox hagiography, see ibid., 75–79.

87. A comparison with the Western example of Stephen of Obazine is also instructive. When urged by his monks to write a Rule, Stephen agonized over which alternative existing Rule to adopt. The monks' final choice of the Rule of Saint Benedict permitted them to retain an independence they would not have had if they had been successful in their application to La Chartreuse or Cîteaux. It is significant, however, that this independence was forced on them by the refusal of Stephen's original choices.

comparison, Stephen of Obazine's weakness in encouraging too many disciples narrowed his options when it came to choosing a Rule. The Carthusians rejected his community as too large. This was never a problem for Neophytus, partly because he was able to limit the numbers to between fifteen and eighteen,[88] but also because in the Orthodox Church a community could remain independent without thereby becoming the foundation-stone of a new Order. The community on Paphos bore the unmistakable stamp of the founder himself. He appointed his successor (his nephew Isaiah), gave directions for his funeral, and chose a burial place.[89]

The personalities of the monks and hermits whose careers I have discussed are now largely hidden from us. Yet it does not seem too bold to argue that Orthodox monasteries differed from Frankish monasteries in that in the Greek East the figure of the founder cast a longer shadow over the community, even after death, than in the West. Stephen of Obazine had to be begged to adopt a written Rule because his monks were sure that his precepts would not be remembered after his death. In the Western Church, only a foundation that spawned daughter-houses and established an Order retained the character of its founder.[90] In the East, by contrast, the founders continued to exert an almost physical influence on their followers, even centuries after their deaths.

Much of the *Ritual Ordinance* of Neophytus is a description of the buildings and structure of the new community. In the absence of any firm documentation of Orthodox monastic buildings in Palestine beyond the brief allusions in pilgrims' accounts, his description can be used to suggest a possible reconstruction of such a monastery.[91] Naturally Neophytus cannot be taken as an infallible guide, since each Orthodox monastery was unique, but it would be reasonable to assume that the general guidelines he established for his monks had been learned during his tour of the Holy Land.

88. "Ritual Ordinance," 13, 30. Too many monks, he explained, led to mad uproar and fostered scandals.

89. Ibid., 20, 34–35.

90. The Carmelite Order provides a lucid example of this contrast. Papal recognition for the "Order," then comprising only the single community of hermits on Mount Carmel, was obtained in 1226, at most twenty years after Albert's Rule. This degree of centralized control was absent from the Orthodox Church; for Neophytus's foundation of Paphos the approval of the local bishop was enough.

91. The monastic buildings of the twelfth century survived at least until the beginning of the twentieth, and were described at the end of the nineteenth by an English traveler, Mrs. Lewis (*A Lady's Impression of Cyprus in 1893* [London, 1894], 166).

Neophytus did not want a school in the monastery; instead, he emphasized a Rule of poverty rather than cultivation of learning.[92] He regulated against the admission of women into the convent—even she-asses were not allowed into the stables[93]—and drew up rules for confession, for fasting, for recreation and exercise, for bathing and sleeping, for food (about which no complaints were to be made!), for the monks' dress, for alms to be given to beggars, and for punishments assigned to disobedient monks.[94] None of these regulations would have been out of place, in style or content, in a Latin foundation, either in western Europe or in Outremer, of the twelfth century. In its comprehensive scope and concern for the minutest details of monastic life, Neophytus's Rule most closely resembles the Customs of Chartreuse drawn up by Prior Guy in the 1120s.[95]

Like Guy, and like Albert of Vercelli, the regulator of the Carmelite hermits in the early thirteenth century, Neophytus sought a balance between cenobitism and eremitism. Although they worshiped and ate in common, his monks were not to remain longer than necessary out of their individual cells, for a monk out of his cell—says Neophytus, repeating the old saw of the desert fathers—is like a fish out of the sea.[96] Indeed, the cells were the main feature of the monastery. The first disciples had simply occupied caves near Neophytus's own on the mountainside, and it was from there that the conventual buildings and church spread. The monastery was not complete until 1183, six years after Neophytus's first typikon.[97] Even after this, in 1197, Neophytus chose another cave retreat as his habitual residence (which he called "New Zion"), to be farther from people.[98]

Neophytus's foundation was an expression of his own experience as a monk and his convictions of how the monastic life should be lived. At its heart lay the balance between solitude and community, anchoresis and the support of the *coenobium*, the communal life. It is the same preoccupation that runs through his Life of Gabriel the Stylite and his collection of Lives of the Cypriot saints, which he made available for his monks in the library at

---

92. "Ritual Ordinance," 14. There was, however, a library, which Neophytus himself stocked with sixteen chosen texts, mostly standard commentaries and canonical collections.
93. Ibid., 21.
94. Ibid., 23–31.
95. Guiges I, *Coutumes de Chartreuse.*
96. "Ritual Ordinance," 27.
97. Delehaye, "Saints de Chypre," 275.
98. Ibid.

Paphos.[99] In contrast to this carefully considered relationship between solitude and community, monks like Elias of Narbonne or Bernard of Blois appear attenuated, tense, like men caught in the magnetic pull of opposing forces.

Gerard of Nazareth's *De conversatione* shows us Frankish hermits trying, with varying degrees of success, to break the bonds of monastic convention, to maintain the fluidity between cenobitic and eremitical monasticism that is so characteristic of Eastern monastic ideology. For the most part they failed, largely because they could not escape the structures of the Latin Church hierarchy imported to the Levant during the course of the twelfth century. More profoundly, perhaps, the careers of Gerard's hermits, when compared with the examples of a revived Orthodox monasticism, show the importance of historical focus in the monastic life. The Franks who settled in the Holy Land might choose any of an astonishing number of locations with biblical or early Christian associations in which to settle. But they had no historical presence, no traditions of the monastic life associated with the sites on which to draw. The Frankish comprehension of a holy site was based on its biblical associations, but not c.ı a continuous history of monasticism to which they were heirs.

The career and writings of Neophytus, so carefully reconstructed by Catia Galatoriotou, show us by contrast how rich was the archive of monastic history from which an Orthodox monk could draw to model his own life. Neophytus tried initially to follow the practice of the early Christian founders literally, by looking for a suitable *eremum* in the Holy Land. On his return to Cyprus he devoted himself to his own sanctification by following the examples he found in synaxaria and hagiographical accounts of monastic founders.[100] His own panegyrics of earlier monks and hermits were themselves expressions of his consciousness of what it meant to be a monk in the Orthodox tradition. Thus, "apparently trivial details from Neophytus's life have their parallels—reported by Neophytus—in other saints' lives."[101]

Such traditions would only crystallize in the West, ironically, after the Holy Land had been lost to the Franks. During the last quarter of the thirteenth century and especially in the fourteenth century, the only Frank-

99. Ibid., 175–232, for an edition of Neophytus's menologion from Bib. Nat., Paris, MS. Grec. 1189.
100. Galatoriotou, *Making of a Saint*, 85–146.
101. Ibid., 108.

ish contemplative Order native to the crusader states, the Carmelites, developed a historical tradition of their antiquity that provided precisely the historical focus that Orthodox monks had taken for granted. The fact that such a tradition relied heavily on spurious documentation is the matter for another book. What is important is that the displaced Carmelites recognized the need to be rooted in the fertile soil of Byzantine monasticism.

There were undoubtedly more Eastern-rite than Frankish monks in the crusader states. These were Arabic-speaking Greek Orthodox, Arabic-speaking Jacobites, Georgians, Armenians, and stray "visitors," such as Neophytus. In addition, Jerusalem had permanent communities of Copts and Ethiopians. The survey of Orthodox monasticism in this chapter shows that the revival of monastic communities and the restoration of actual buildings gave hermits a wider variety of choices than would have been available in the West. This variety, indeed, seems to have been bewildering to the Latin ecclesiastical authorities in the twelfth century. Although there are cases where Orthodox practice had a distinct influence on Franks—for example, in habitat, food, or spiritual life—no single community before the Carmelites could boast a mixture of Franks and Orthodox, and the Frankish eremitical communities known to us appear to have been unable to preserve their eremitical inspiration for long. The overriding impression is of Orthodox monasteries, self-contained and conservative, remaining tantalizingly exotic and out of the reach even of the Western hermits and monks who might have been interested in learning from them at close hand.

4

The Origins of Monasticism on Mount Carmel

The study presented in the following chapters is best approached as the concrete manifestation of the themes discussed so far in this book. The Carmelite Order arose from an unregulated hermitage on Mount Carmel, but the precise date and terms of the foundation are impossible to determine. The initial impetus for the foundation and development of the Order in the course of the thirteenth century are part of Western ecclesiastical history as much as crusader history. The Carmelites were the only Religious Order founded in the two centuries of the Latin East, at a time when the European church produced a succession of reform movements and monastic leaders, from Cîteaux to the Franciscans. The development of monasticism on Mount Carmel provides a contrast to the foundation of houses in the West in the late eleventh and twelfth centuries, such as La Chartreuse, Cîteaux, and Obazine.

The Carmelites "arrived" relatively late, a century or so after the initial Frankish settlement in the Levant. Any discussion of Carmelite origins must therefore take into account the previous history of monasticism, both Latin and Orthodox, in the crusader states. The hermits who adopted the Carmelite Rule in the first decade of the thirteenth century were following not only the tradition of Bernard of Blois, Elias of Narbonne, and Gerard of Nazareth's other hermits, but also that of Neophytus and the Orthodox hermits encountered by pilgrims in the Jordan Valley and in the Valley of Jehosaphat. The themes that have so far emerged in comparing the careers of Frankish hermits in the Latin East with hermits in the West and with native Orthodox hermits crystallize in the period from about 1160 to 1248 in the early history of the Carmelites: the importance of a specific place with an existing monastic tradition, the forms taken by Frankish eremitical monasticism in the Latin East, and the relationship between Frankish hermits and Orthodox who began to revive the early Christian monastic tradition on Mount Carmel in the last quarter of the twelfth century.

The Carmelites settled on a cult site that had attracted the devotion of indigenous Orthodox monks as early as the fourth century. Moreover, Mount Carmel had been a part of the revival of Orthodox monasticism in Palestine before the Latin hermits established a hermitage, probably at the end of the twelfth century. The early history of the Order is therefore the ideal example of the wider issues raised in this book—the forms of eremitical monasticism in the Latin East, and contacts between indigenous Orthodox and Frankish monks.

The evidence for the early history of the Carmelite Order is for the most part either unpublished or entangled in later medieval Carmelite collections. The historiography of the Order has been almost entirely the province of its own members, who have relied heavily on the traditional internal account of the foundation. Uncovering early Carmelite history therefore is an exercise in literary archaeology. It is impossible to discuss the origins of the Order, and the forms eremitism on Mount Carmel took in our period, without an appreciation of the later Carmelite reconstruction of the past. This Carmelite literature itself provides the footholds for the fragmentary external literary and archaeological evidence. It will first be necessary, therefore, to introduce the main body of apologetic material from which we must infer a more analytical reading of the real situation on Mount Carmel.

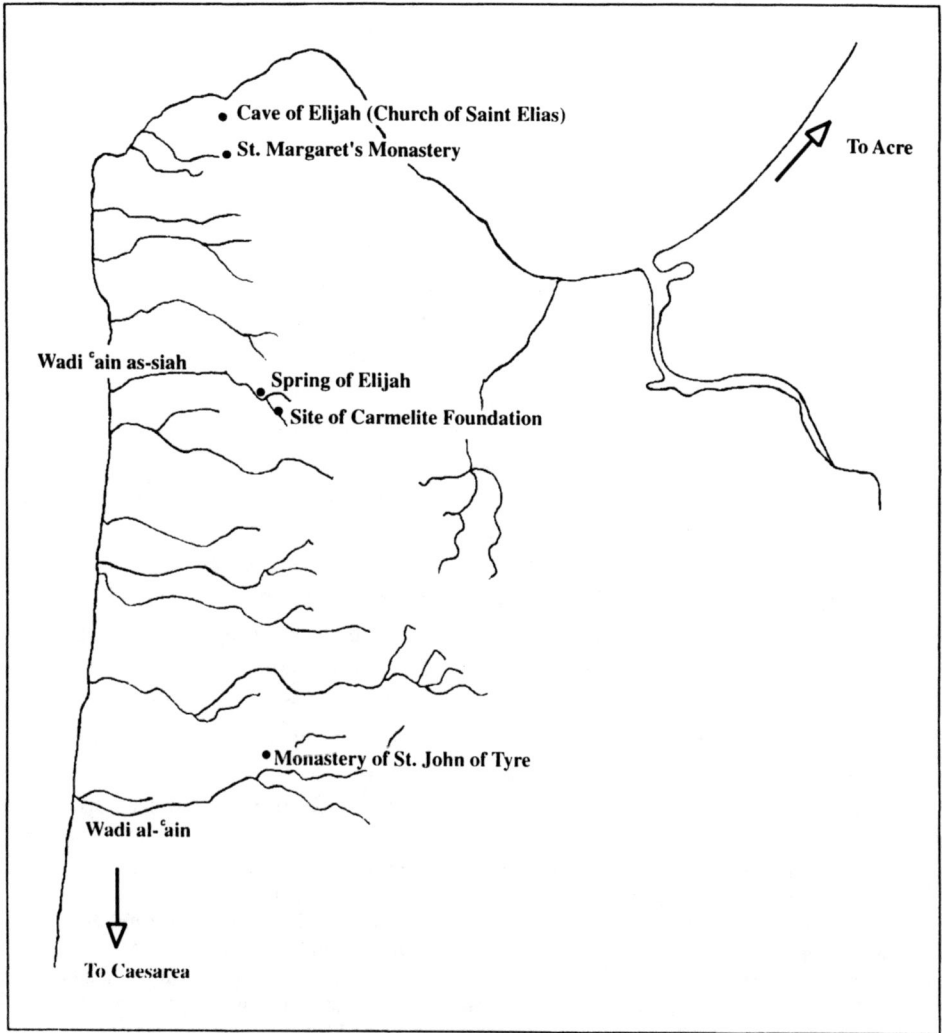

Map 2. Mount Carmel

The first surviving accounts of the history of the Carmelite Order date from the fourteenth century.[1] In this chapter I use one of these, which is summary in nature and presents the most coherent discussion of the Order's origins: the apologetic treatise *De institutione et peculiaribus gestis religiosorum Carmelitanum* of the 1370s by the Carmelite prior-provincial of Catalonia, Philip Ribot.[2] My choice is not arbitrary. Ribot offers a consistent narrative by presenting three works that he claimed were copies of earlier originals, along with his own interpretative glosses and general comments. The first of these was the *De institutione primorum monachorum* of John of Jerusalem, ostensibly the written form of the original Carmelite Rule, produced by a fifth-century bishop of Jerusalem. The *Letter to Eusebius* of Cyril of Constantinople, supposedly the third prior-general of the Order, provides Ribot with a narrative account of the Byzantine and Muslim periods of Mount Carmel. And the *Chronicle* of William of Sandwich takes Carmelite history from the beginning of the European expansion to the fall of Acre in 1291, of which William was himself apparently an eyewitness.

Ribot's treatise provided the standard chronology for the development of the Order even as late as the twentieth century, notably in Benedict Zimmerman's collection of Carmelite sources.[3] The authenticity of Ribot's "primary sources" is extremely dubious. William of Sandwich was indeed prior-provincial of the Holy Land in the 1280s and may have written an account of the recent history of the Order, but no independent testimony to this survives.[4] John, bishop of Jerusalem, was also a real figure, but there is no evidence of any written work by him, and the Cyril of Constantinople

1. For selections from some of these, see A. Staring, *Medieval Carmelite Heritage: Early Reflections on the Nature of the Order*, Textus et studia historica Carmelitana 16 (Rome, 1989).

2. Ribot's work is preserved in five manuscripts: Archivio Generale dei Carmelitani, Collegio Sant'Alberto, Rome, MS II C.O.II 35; Trier Stadtbibliothek, MS 155(80)/1237; Munich Staatsbibliothek, MS Clm 471; Bibliothèque de l'Arsenal, Paris, MS 779; and Lambeth Palace, London, MS 192. The London manuscript also contains a fifteenth-century English translation by Thomas Bradley. Ribot's treatise was edited in the seventeenth century by the Carmelite Daniel a Virgine Maria and is printed in full in vol. 1 of his compendium *Speculum Carmelitanum* (Antwerp, 1680) with separate pagination. Father Paul Chandler is currently preparing an edition of the *De institutione* for publication in 1996.

3. B. Zimmerman, ed., *Monumenta historica Carmelitana* 1 (Lérins, 1907). See also Marie-Joseph du Sacre-Coeur, "La topographie sacrée du Mont Carmel et la chronologie de l'ordre aux XIIe et XIIIe siècles," *Etudes Carmélitaines* 3 (1913), 139–54.

4. William of Sandwich is named as prior-provincial in a bull of Honorius IV of 1286, *Bullarium Carmelitanum, plures complectens summorum pontificum constitutiones . . . de Monte Carmelo spectantes* (Rome, 1715), 1:35–36. K. J. Egan, "An Essay Toward the Historiography of the Origin of the Carmelite Province in England," *Carmelus* 19 (1972), 80–82, dismisses William's chronicle as spurious.

presented by Ribot must be taken as a composite of possible unknown Orthodox hermits on Mount Carmel.

Any historian dealing with the Carmelite Order must come to terms with the function of Carmelite history-writing. The purpose of Ribot's work was to establish a credible tradition of antiquity for the Order at a time when the Carmelites, having achieved a metamorphosis from hermits to friars, were competing for patronage with the other mendicant Orders across western Europe. Ribot and his contemporaries, notably John Baconthorpe in England,[5] John of Hildesheim in Germany,[6] and Bernard Ollerius in Spain,[7] sought to uphold the claim that the Carmelites had originally been founded by the prophet Elijah, that Elijah's followers had maintained a tradition of unbroken eremitical monasticism on Mount Carmel until the fall of Acre in 1291, and that the sudden transformation of the hermits of Mount Carmel into an international Order of friars was a natural development in keeping with pre-Christian Carmelite origins. The Carmelites were thus not only the oldest of all monastic or mendicant Orders but also older even than the church itself. They were the Christian's link to the oldest expressions of religious faith, the profession of the Old Testament prophet.[8]

5. John Baconthorpe (fl. 1329–47), *Compendium*, in Daniel a Virgine Maria, *Speculum Carmelitanum*, part 2 (*Libri seu opuscula XII de antiquitate . . . de monte Carmelo*), 1:160–66. John was a doctor of theology at Oxford and Paris, prior-provincial of England (1329–33), and author of numerous theological works (C. de Villiers, ed., *Bibliotheca Carmelitana* [Orléans, 1752; new ed. Rome, 1927], 743–53).

6. John of Hildesheim, *Dialogus inter directorem et detractorem de ordine Carmelitanum* (Bodleian Selden Supra MS 41, fols. 92–107); also in Daniel's *Speculum Carmelitanum*, 1:145–56, and Staring, *Medieval Carmelite Heritage*, 326–94.

7. Bernard Ollerius (fl. 1380s), *Informatio circa originem, intitulationem et confirmationem ordinis beate virginis Marie de Monte Carmelo*, in Daniel, *Speculum Carmelitanum*, 1:160–91.

8. The myth of Elianic origins has been a stumbling-block for serious research. Carmelite monks have, in the last twenty years, attempted to clarify the state of knowledge of the early history of the Order. E. Friedman, *The Latin Hermits of Mount Carmel* (Rome, 1979), has used to advantage his location on Mount Carmel itself to reexamine the precise topography of the settlement in the twelfth and thirteenth centuries, but without attempting to discuss the Order in the wider context of the Christian life of the crusader states, or the relations with other Orders in Europe. K. J. Egan has determined to a large degree the pattern of settlement in England, based on a proposed chronology of foundations ("The Establishment and Early Development of the Carmelite Order in England" [Ph.D. thesis, University of Cambridge, 1965]; "Medieval Carmelite Houses: England and Wales," *Carmelus* 16 [1969], 142–226; "An Essay Toward the Historiography of the Origins of the Carmelite Province in England," *Carmelus* 19 [1972], 67–100; "Dating English Carmelite Foundations," *Carmelus* 23 [1976], 96–118). Much more still remains to be done. The transformation from eremitical monasticism to mendicant has been discussed from the starting-point of the Rule itself by C. Cicconetti, *La regola del Carmelo* (Rome, 1973). The reception of the new friars by the

For medieval monks, the choice of Mount Carmel as a suitable location for the service of God was natural. The mountain was preeminent as the site of the greatest achievements of the prophet Elijah. But even this depended on a selective reading of Scripture. In the Old Testament narrative, Elijah's career began not in solitude on Mount Carmel but with his public denunciation of King Ahab, followed by his flight to the brook Charith, east of Jordan, at the limit of Ahab's jurisdiction. It was there, rather than on Mount Carmel, that Elijah was fed by ravens (3 Kings 17:1–7). The prophet subsequently appeared at Zarephath (Sarepta), on the coast of modern Lebanon, where he performed the miracle of the widow's oil-jug and healed her sick son (3 Kings 17:8–24). Only after another personal denunciation of Ahab did Elijah retire to Mount Carmel, where he slew the priests of Baal (3 Kings 18). Elijah then fled to Mount Horeb, on Sinai, in fear of Ahab's queen, Jezebel (3 Kings 19:1–8). After performing further tasks laid on him by God—the anointing of Hazael and Jehu as kings in Aram and Israel, and of Elisha as his own prophetic successor—Elijah clashed with Ahab again over Naboth's vineyard (3 Kings 21:17–29). Ahab's successor Ahaziah, another follower of Baal, sent an army to arrest Elijah in retaliation for the prophet's continued denunciations. Elijah, from the safety of a mountaintop, called down fire from heaven to destroy the soldiers (4 Kings 1:1–18). The mountain where Elijah had taken refuge from Ahaziah is not named, but was assumed by medieval pilgrims and commentators to have been Carmel.

Patristic and medieval commentary celebrated Elijah as the Old Testament "type" of the hermit. Jerome discussed the respective claims of Elijah and John the Baptist to the title "the first monk," alongside the Egyptian desert fathers Anthony and Paul of Thebes.[9] Rupert of Deutz, in the twelfth century, described Elijah as the "author and initiator" of monasticism.[10] To Peter Damian, Elijah was the originator of the eremitical life.[11] Monks themselves, like the Egyptian Onuphrius, were aware of following the example of Elijah; Peter the Venerable, looking back at the generation

---

established Orders and the secular church, and the broader intellectual questions raised by the creation of Carmelite genealogy and the uses of history by the new Order, are areas still in need of study.

9. Jerome, *Vita Sancti Pauli*, *PL* 23:18.

10. Rupert of Deutz, *Commentarium in cantica canticorum* 3, *PL* 168:885. See also his *De Trinitate et operibus*, "In Reg. V, 9–10," *PL* 167:1243–46. For Rupert himself, see J. Van Engen, *Rupert of Deutz* (Berkeley and Los Angeles, 1983).

11. Peter Damian, *De suae congregationis institutis* 15.2, *PL* 145:337.

of Onuphrius as founders, saw Elijah as the ultimate monastic founder-figure.[12] The anonymous twelfth-century *Libellus de diversis ordinibus et professionibus qui sunt in aecclesia* speaks of an eremitical "law" given by God to Elijah, with the result that "many others pleased God through solitude."[13] Gerard of Nazareth, as we have seen, prefaced his biographical collection of hermits by appealing to the example of Elijah.[14]

Elijah's prophetic and eremitical career provided for medieval commentators a catalog of virtues. Bernard of Clairvaux, Hugh of Saint Victor, and Peter Comestor used Elijah's dual role in their exegesis of the Old Testament as an example of spiritual excellence before the revelation of Christ.[15] Philip Ribot, citing the works of John Cassian, Isidore of Seville, and John Chrysostom, found Elijah's special qualities in the linking of prophetic and eremitical roles: in his opposition to godless kings and his zeal for God, but also in his spurning of possessions, his clothing of wild skins, and his dwelling in a cave and on mountaintops.[16] It is not surprising, therefore, to find medieval pilgrims venerating the sites associated with Elijah.

Abbot Daniel worshiped in the cave of Elijah on Mount Carmel in 1107, and the author of the *Work on Geography* (1128–37) mentions Carmel as the place of Elijah's residence with Elisha and of the slaughter of the priests of Baal.[17] The association of Mount Carmel with the career of Elijah was as old as the Christian pilgrimage tradition itself. The account of the pilgrim Egeria (ca. 381–83) speaks of Carmel as "the place where Elijah consecrated an altar to the Lord," while the earlier fourth-century *Itinerarium Burdigalense* mentions the sacrifice Elijah made on the mountain.[18] The Bollandist commentator on Carmelite origins, Father Papenbroek, overlooked this evidence when he denied there was any justifiable claim that

---

12. *Le synaxaire arabe-jacobite (rédaction copte)*, ed. and trans. R. Basset, *PO* 17:567–70; Peter the Venerable, *Letters*, 1:29, Ep.20.

13. *Libellus*, ed. and trans. G. Constable and B. Smith (Oxford, 1972), 12.

14. Quoted by Ribot, *De institutione* 3.8.

15. Bernard of Clairvaux, *Meditatio in passionem et resurrectionem Domini* 14, *PL* 184:763–64; Hugh of St. Victor, *Allegoriae in Vetus Testamentum* 7.11–16, *PL* 175:709–14, *Appendix ad Hugonis opera dogmatica* 108–9, *PL* 177:691–92; Peter Comestor, *Historia scholastica: Liber III regum* 34–36, *PL* 198:1378–81. See also a sermon on Elijah attributed to Augustine, *CCSL* 103:514–18.

16. Ribot, *De institutione* 2.1. (References to Ribot's *De institutione* are to his own divisions of books and chapters, not to Daniel's edition, because the pagination in the *Speculum Carmelitanum* is not continuous.)

17. Wilkinson, *Jerusalem Pilgrimage*, 165, 207–8.

18. *Appendix ad itinerarium Egeriae* 2.5, *CCSL* 175:99; *Itinerarium Burdigalense* 585.1; *CCSL* 175:12.

Elijah was ever believed to have lived on Mount Carmel.[19] Whether or not Elijah lived on Mount Carmel to the exclusion of other sites, Christians from the fourth century on latched on to Carmel as the place, par excellence, of Elijah. Episodes from Elijah's life that were not located specifically on Mount Carmel in the Bible came to be placed there by medieval pilgrims and commentators. Daniel, for example, believed it was on Carmel that Elijah had been fed by the ravens, even though the biblical account says it happened at Charith.[20] In the same way, pilgrims localized a complex of Jewish and Christian traditions around the site of the Holy Sepulcher, even when the episodes to which they referred happened elsewhere in Jerusalem.

As early as the second century, Mount Carmel was known as a place of religious importance in the Jewish tradition. Ribot cited a letter Balbinus wrote to the Emperor Antoninus Pius, in which the importance of Carmel to the Jews was explained. Elijah's sacrifice to God of the priests of Baal made the mountain holy for eternity, as the remains of an ancient altar on the site of the sacrifice showed.[21] According to E. Friedman, Jewish traditions regarding Elijah's activities on Mount Carmel focused on the eastern slopes of the mountain, where Elijah was thought to have performed his sacrifice to God, rather than on the Christian-dominated western slopes and escarpment facing the coast.[22] If there was competition between Jewish and Christian pilgrims for the "correct" site of Elijah's activities on Carmel, or if such an issue found its way into Jewish-Christian polemic, this would in large part explain the insistence of Ribot and later Carmelites on the continuity of the Elianic tradition of eremitism down to their own day. If the Carmelites could be accused of occupying the wrong part of the mountain, their claims to genuine antiquity could be disregarded.

Archaeological survey reports made in 1920–21 by the Department of the Antiquities of Palestine (now under the auspices of the Israel Antiquities Authority) show that a series of rock-tomb complexes was discovered on the northern slopes of Mount Carmel, dating from the early Iron Age. In general, the report did not make much of the discoveries on Carmel:

19. *AASS*, April I, 776.

20. Wilkinson, *Jerusalem Pilgrimage*, 152.

21. Ribot, *De institutione* 3.5. "Mons est nomine Carmelus, in quo vetus Religio, & sanctitatis antiqua est. Elias illic sacrificia semper Deo offerebat. Apparent etiam & nunc vestigia de ara sacrificiorum." For Balbinus, see *AASS*, Jan. I, 237, in the entry for Saint Telephorus.

22. Friedman, *The Latin Hermits*, 98.

The ruined sites are few and far between and do not appear to be of great importance. Carmel has always been the resort of wild characters, and this, together with the scarcity of water in the winter, probably accounts for the lack of important buildings.[23]

In the context of the rock tombs in the Valley of Jehosaphat, however, the tombs on the slopes of Mount Carmel become highly suggestive. If such complexes were used as eremitical dwellings just outside Jerusalem, why not elsewhere? Christian hermits may have been living in the tomb chambers on Carmel as early as the fourth century, when Egeria's tour of the Holy Land based on biblical associations clearly specified the mountain as Elijah's dwelling. The survey concluded that the burials had been disturbed at an early date, but a Jewish cemetery at the foot of Mount Carmel was known to Jewish communities in the Middle Ages, which suggests that the mountain remained important as a holy place for the Jews of the Levant.[24]

The weight of evidence indicates that Carmel was a cult site not only for Jews but also for Christians and pagans in the Roman period. Suetonius describes the visit of Vespasian to Mount Carmel,[25] and in the third century Iamblichus believed that Pythagoras had used the mountain for meditation.[26] The ruins described by Balbinus may indeed have been manmade, but they do not necessarily prove the existence of an altar. Friedman has suggested that the cave at the foot of the northern promontory, known as the "Cave of Elijah" and venerated by Jews, Christians, and Muslims alike, is also of human construction.[27] The walls of the cave are adorned with graffiti but bear no recognizable Christian or Jewish symbols.[28]

In the second half of the fourth century, the hermit Martinian abandoned

---

23. PAM, *Mar Elias II* 148.248 ATQ 259, 22.2.1921. These tombs took the form of square chambers with three arms protruding on each side except the entrance side. Access to the chamber was by a sunken courtyard, approximately 2.5 by 2.4 m. The entrance to the tombs was about 1.6 m high.

24. J. Prawer, *The History of the Jews in the Latin Kingdom of Jerusalem* (Oxford, 1988), 83. Radi, a Jew from an Egyptian family, died in Acre in 1195 and was buried at the foot of Mount Carmel at his own request. This may reflect the Jewish tradition that Acre lay outside the boundaries of Israel, but Haifa, a less important town in the Middle Ages, lay inside.

25. Suetonius, *De vita Caesarum* 5, ed. M. Ihm (Stuttgart, 1967), 298.

26. *De vita Pythagorica* 3, ed. L. Deubner, new ed. V. Klein (Stuttgart, 1975), 11.

27. Friedman, *The Latin Hermits*, 145–46, argues that the location of the cave—exactly on a line with the crest of the mountain and midway in a cross-section of the headland as it juts into the sea—was carefully chosen.

28. A. Quadriah, "Inscriptions in the Cave of Elijah," *Quarterly for the Antiquities of Eretz-Israel and the Bible Lands* 2 (1969), 99–101.

his native city of Caesarea to live in solitude on a mountain site known as the "Place of the Arches," probably on the southern slopes of Mount Carmel.[29] He was often tempted by demons, on the most famous occasion in the guise of a girl who came to him one stormy evening begging for shelter. Martinian gave her food and offered the use of his spare room, while he locked himself in his cell. But she contrived to get into his presence and tempt him with her sexual charms, to which Martinian responded by building a fire and walking into it barefoot, suggesting she join him there. The girl was converted and later joined the convent at Bethlehem founded by Paula and Jerome. Martinian was sufficiently influential in the East to feature in a panegyric by Niketas Choniates; in the Orthodox Church his feast day is February 13. Another early Christian hermit who lived nearby, though not on Carmel itself, was Saint James of Porphyria.[30] James spent fifteen years living in a grotto near Porphyria (modern Haifa), practicing continual asceticism and combating demons who disguised themselves as Samaritans.[31] Both Martinian and James were ignored by the Carmelites. This seems surprising, for one would expect Ribot and his fellow apologists in the later Middle Ages to have exploited the potential of such known eremitical predecessors on Mount Carmel, but fourteenth-century friars did not have ready access to Greek hagiographical works. The Carmelite past thus had to be reinvented. Although insisting on the continuity of eremitical life on Carmel throughout the early Christian and Byzantine periods, Ribot was unable to give names to the hermits. Only with the voracious reading and magpie collecting instincts of John Bale in the 1520s were known monastic figures from the fourth to the seventh centuries appropriated for the Order.[32]

29. *Bibliotheca Sanctorum* 8:1226. Martinian is the same as the Marcian described in *Le synaxaire arabe-jacobite*, PO 16 (1922), fasc. 2, 402–5. On the map printed by R. Röhricht, *Zeitschrift des deutschen Palästina Vareins* 18 (1895), table 6, dating from ca. 1235, the place is called "Foresta des Arches."

30. *Bibliotheca Sanctorum* 6:414–18. There is a partial life of James in Bib. Nat., Paris, MS Grec. 1217, which is perhaps the work of Symeon Metaphrastes.

31. In the *Menologion* of Basil II (Rome, Cod. Vat. Gr. 1613, fol.105) James is shown praying on his knees in a pagan sarcophagus decorated with columns and statuary. This seems to indicate a tradition that James lived in a tomb, probably one of the burial chambers described in the PAM survey of 1921. The presence of the Samaritans in James's hagiography suggests a date in the middle of the sixth century, when there was bitter conflict between Christians and Samaritans in the region of Haifa. This piece of historical realism is unfortunately counterbalanced by the mention of a Bishop Alexander, whose existence cannot be traced.

32. John Bale, *Cronica*, Bodleian Selden Supra 41, fols.127r–141r.

A little later, in 570, the pilgrim known as Antoninus Placentius describes the "monastery of Elisha," half a mile above the "hamlets of the Samaritans," which are themselves a mile from Sykanios.[33] The exact location of this monastery is problematic. Friedman rejected Haifa (suggested by a reading of Eusebius) and opted instead for the wadi 'Ain as-siah, 4 kilometers due south of the cave of Elijah. The cave is located in the cliffs of the northern promontory of Mount Carmel, while the wadi 'Ain as-siah cuts into the slopes of the mountain to the south.[34] This would place the "monastery of Elisha" almost exactly where the thirteenth-century Latin Carmelite hermits settled and built their house, by the "spring of Elijah." In addition, there was a monastery of Saint Margaret on the northern promontory of the mountain overlooking the sea and directly above the cave of Elijah. This site is now occupied, somewhat confusingly, by the Stella Maris Carmelite monastery.[35] There was also a Byzantine laura at the village of Saint John of Tyre (now Tirat ha-Karmel), by the gorge of the wadi al-'Ain. The laura has not been excavated, but the location is suggestively close to Martinian's residence at the Place of the Arches. A further complication is introduced by the figure of Denis of Francheville, a hermit whose cult was preserved by the local Orthodox population. The site of Francheville is now uncertain, though the name seems to refer to a Frankish "new town" of the twelfth or thirteenth century.[36]

33. *Antonini Placentini itinerarium* 3, CCSL 175:130: "A Ptolemaida per mare incontra in civitatem Sucemina Iudeorum est miliario semis per directo, littore maris milia sex. Castra Samaritanorum a Sucamina miliario subtus monte Carmelo. Super ista castra miliario semis monasterium sancti Helisaei, ubi ei occurrit mulier, cuius filium suscitavit."

34. Friedman, *The Latin Hermits*, 61–62. C. Kopp, *Elias und Christendum auf dem Karmel* (Paderborn, 1929), 88, following Eusebius, identified Sykanios as Haifa. Granite columns found on the site were assumed by the Carmelite archaeologist Florian du Carmel to be from the "monastery of Elisha" ("Fouilles operées au Mont Carmel en Palestine," *Etudes Carmélitaines* 4 [1914], 113). This seems to be speculative, but a revised dating has not yet been proposed.

35. Friedman, *The Latin Hermits*, 70, 84, 87–88; idem, "The Medieval Abbey of St. Margaret of Mount Carmel," *Ephemerides Carmeliticae* 22 (1971), 295–348. The construction of two Byzantine monasteries on Mount Carmel, that of Elisha in the wadi 'Ain es-siah, and Saint Margaret's on the terrace above the cave of Elijah, may attest to the strength of the pagan cult on Mount Carmel. The cult was probably that of Helios, for whom Elijah was the ideal replacement not only because of the similarity of the names in Greek (Elias-Helios) but also because of Elijah's defeat of the priests of Baal, the Canaanite predecessor of Helios, and perhaps also his ascension into heaven on a fiery chariot.

36. J. Richard, *Le royaume latin de Jérusalem* (Paris, 1953), 113–21, for "villes franches," new towns with franchises. J. Prawer, *Histoire du royaume latin de Jérusalem*, 2 vols. (Paris, 1969–70), 1:205–6, wrongly identified Denis with Saint Denis, the patron saint of France,

A further survey of Mount Carmel by the Department of the Antiquities of Palestine in 1928 found traces of Byzantine-era buildings in various locations. A Druze village, Daliet al-Karmel, yielded some roughly molded Byzantine stonework, the shaft of a column with a rough capital, a good deal of pottery, some mosaic fragments, and coins of the fourth and sixth centuries. More Byzantine ruins, including some walling, pottery, mosaic, glass, and coins of the reigns of Justinian (527–65) and Phocas (602–10) were found at Khirbet al-Kerak, a one-and-a-half-hour walk southwest of Daliet, and yet more wall remains at Khirbet al-Duweiba.[37] The archaeological evidence, such as it is, indicates substantial occupation of the general area of Mount Carmel in the early Byzantine period, but it does not help to establish more precisely the nature of the monastic settlements. It is tempting to suggest that the wall remains pertained to monasteries or protected laurae rather than to forts, as the survey suggests, but this must remain speculation.

Establishing the complex topography of Mount Carmel and the sites of the various Byzantine monastic foundations is important for a thorough evaluation of the Carmelites' own account of the Order in the twelfth century. As will be seen, Ribot smoothed over the geography of Mount Carmel so as to "telescope" all monastic and eremitical activity on the mountain, an area covering about 12.5 by 7 miles, into an area of unspecified dimensions in which groups of hermits might reasonably be expected to be living in close proximity.

Ribot was less concerned with establishing links between the medieval Carmelite Order and specific eremitical figures on Mount Carmel from the Byzantine period than with making a typological connection between Elijah and the monks of his Order. Elijah was, for Ribot, the first hermit of Mount Carmel, but he was also a monastic founder. After his return to the land of Israel, he established a community of like-minded hermits. "He taught them to observe the monastic life, . . . ordaining that they should praise God devotedly with the singing of psalms and the playing of cithara and cymbals."[38] The *Libellus de ordinibus* had already conceived

---

and Francheville with the village of Palmaria. The topography of the two places differs widely, however. Palmaria was a palm-grove in irrigated land, while Francheville was on a hilltop. For Denis's cult, see H. Michelant and G. Raynaud, *Itinéraires à Jérusalem et descriptions de la Terre-Sainte rédigés en français aux XIe–XIIe et XIIIe siècles* (Geneva, 1882), 89, 104, 179, 189.

37. PAM, *Mar Elias II* 23.8–12.9.1928.

38. Ribot, *De institutione* 1.3.

of Elijah as the recipient of a set of divine precepts or laws, and the raw material of the biblical narrative of Elijah's life provided Ribot with a suitable constituency from which the prophet could form a "monastic" community. Elisha, God's choice as Elijah's successor, was an obvious start (3 Kings 19:19–21).

The "sons of the prophets" Jonah, Micah, and Obadiah and the other minor prophets were added as heirs to the initial foundation.[39] Jonah was linked to Elijah in patristic tradition by Jerome's identification of him as the son of the widow whose life Elijah restored.[40] The minor prophets ensured, according to Ribot, the continuity of eremitical life on Mount Carmel until the time of Christ. Elisha, for example, converted Jonadab son of Rechab to his way of life, and Jonadab's sons continued the tradition.[41] This Ribot understood from Scripture:

> Thus we have obeyed the voice of Jonadab, . . . to drink no wine in all our days, we, our wives, our sons and our daughters; nor to build houses for us to dwell in: neither have we vineyard, nor field, nor seed; but we have dwelt in tents. (Jeremiah 35:8–10)[42]

The Carmelites of the Old Law remained miraculously safe from the attacks of the Assyrians that resulted in the Babylonian Captivity, fulfilling the prophecy of Isaiah, misconstrued by Ribot as "Justice will live in solitude, and righteousness sit on Carmel." Ribot contrasts the safety of the hermits living in the open on the mountain with the fate suffered by the town-dwellers who were carried off into slavery by the Assyrians—again a point that had not been missed by Jerome.[43] For those who cared to see it, this was a rich exegetical jewel. Because the hermits of Mount Carmel, the precursors of Ribot's contemporaries, followed the perfect life, the principles of which had been laid down by Elijah, they were permitted by God to remain in the paradise of their dwelling while the rest of the nation was

39. Ibid., 2.3.

40. Jerome, *Prologum super Ionam*, CCSL 76:378. Peter Comestor, in the twelfth century, repeats the tradition but attributes to it a Jewish origin (*Historia scholastica: Liber III regum* 34, PL 198:1579).

41. Ribot, *De institutione* 4.5.

42. That the minor prophets were proto-monks or hermits had long been part of mainstream Catholic tradition. Ribot quotes Jerome's letter to Paulinus, where Jerome calls himself a follower of Anthony and Paul of Thebes but also of Elijah, Elisha, and the sons of the Prophets (Jerome, *Epistolae* 58, PL 22:583).

43. Ribot, *De institutione* 4.7, quoting Isaiah 32:16; Jerome, *Epistolae* 58, PL 22:583.

led away, into captivity—figuratively, shut out of Eden, like Adam and Eve. Ribot did not, in fact, stress this point as far as he might. He was writing, after all, less than a hundred years after the Carmelites had been expelled from the Holy Land by the new Assyrians, the Muslims.

Ribot overcame the potentially thorny problem of bridging the Old Law and the New Law with considerable ingenuity. Although "cities seemed like prisons, and solitude like Paradise," the Jewish hermits of Mount Carmel, as heirs to Elijah's dual role, did frequent towns and rural communities to work miracles, prophesy, and preach.[44] Every year, in addition, they would go to Jerusalem for the feasts of the Jewish year. Although reformers, they were part of mainstream Jewish religious life and therefore in a similar position to John the Baptist, or those among the Jews whom Jesus converted. "For the monks of this mountain in antiquity, though not in name, were true Christians, upright in faith, as are today's monks."[45] Ribot marshals impressive evidence to show that John the Baptist was likewise a representative of the tradition of the eremitical life of Mount Carmel, even though his activities centered on the Jordan.[46] Soon after Jesus' Ascension, all the Carmelites were gathered in Jerusalem, "in order to celebrate the feast of Pentecost," as Ribot explains.[47] Since they were on Mount Zion, not far from where Peter and the apostles were gathered in the "upper room," they were able to hear the commotion created by the descent of the Holy Spirit and to hear the apostles speaking in tongues. Peter, recognizing the Carmelites as Elijah's followers, preached the gospel and baptized them. The hermits who had missed the event had their opportunity a few days later in the Temple, where they too were baptized by Peter and the apostles.[48] Ribot's rather facile account of the Carmelites' conversion underlines the medieval assumption that Jews who understood the Old Law in its true, allegorical sense would easily see the veracity of the Gospels.

Ribot cites two pieces of evidence to show that the Carmelite settlement extended beyond the original location in the years after the Resurrection. The *Cronica Romana* reports that a group of Carmelite hermits settled near

---

44. Ribot, *De institutione* 3.7.

45. Ibid., 5.1. "Antiqui namque huius montis monachi, etsi non nomine, tamen recta fide fuerunt christiani veri, sicut sunt monachi moderni."

46. Ibid., 5.2. In particular, John Chrysostom's *Commentarium super Matthaeum homilia* 10, and Ambrose's *Epistola ad Vercellenses* 14, the latter of which Daniel (*Speculum*, 1:49) discredits as a later forgery. Bale, *Cronica*, Bodleian Selden Supra MS 41, fol.115r, lists the Baptist as a hermit of Mount Carmel.

47. Ribot, *De institutione* 5.5.

48. Ibid., 5.6–7.

the Golden Gate in Jerusalem in the reigns of Vespasian and Titus, and indeed "spread the Catholic faith in different places in each neighboring region."[49] He then quotes from Josephus Antiochenus, glossed by Daniel as a writer who lived in the age after the apostles, around A.D. 130, to argue that already at this date the Carmelites were paying particular devotion to the Blessed Virgin, building an oratory dedicated to her on Mount Carmel.[50] This Marian connection had become, by Ribot's day, one of the characteristic features of the Carmelite Order. Ribot devoted an entire book to the history of the Blessed Virgin's special patronage of the Order, which began with a vision granted to Elijah of the Mother of God. After his slaughter of the priests of Baal, Elijah prayed for rain and was answered by the appearance of a small cloud hovering over the sea to the west. Although the biblical passage does not elaborate on the cloud, Ribot's Carmelite tradition used it to represent the fourfold vision granted to Elijah. He saw the birth of a sinless child and the time when it would take place, the child's perpetual virginity, and that the child would be God incarnate.[51] The link between Elijah and Mary is further established, Ribot explains, by Elijah's chastity, because he was the first person in history to attain such a state of his own volition throughout his lifetime.

This passage in Ribot's treatise appears to be an explanation, or rationalization, of the Carmelite dedication of the Order to the Blessed Virgin in the thirteenth century.[52] From the very earliest days the sons of the Prophets were able to choose Mary as their patroness because of the special revelation to Elijah, even if the fulfillment and true significance of the vision was not to be understood until a later generation of Carmelites. "You should not think it absurd," Ribot warns, "that the monks now living on Mount Carmel have the same religion as those who lived on the said

49. Ibid., 5.8. "Et tempore Beati Petri Antiochae cathedrati, ipsi in circumquaque regione adjacente diversis locis catholicae fidei insistebant." Daniel (*Speculum*, 1:53) describes the *Cronica Romana* as having lain hidden for many years but deserving of recovery. He gives no clues as to authorship or date.

50. Ribot, *De institutione* 5.8.

51. Ribot, *De institutione* 6.1.

52. This was a standard feature of Carmelite apologetic in the fourteenth century. John of Hildesheim, *Defensorium* 13 (Daniel, *Speculum* 2:152–53), traces the Carmelite connection to the Blessed Virgin in written sources back to Isaiah, who, he argues, was referring to her with the phrase "decor Carmeli" (Isaiah 35:2). John adds that the first Carmelite house after the convent on Carmel itself was built in Jerusalem, on the site of the birth of the Blessed Virgin. In his own day, moreover, the Roman cardinals visited the Carmelite convent on the Feast of the Immaculate Conception, just as they visited the Dominican convent on the Feast of Saint Dominic; this proved that the Blessed Virgin was the true patron of the Order.

mountain before the Incarnation of the Savior."[53] The construction of a chapel on the mountain by the "spring of Elijah," the spot where the water miraculously appeared after his prayer for rain, Ribot dates to A.D. 83. This chapel, dedicated to the Blessed Virgin, marked the point at which the Carmelites became known, says Ribot, as the "Brothers of the Blessed Virgin of Mount Carmel."[54] The spring was well-known as a topographical marker by the sixth century (when Antoninus Placentius referred to it, mistakenly, as the *fons Elisaei*). Ribot was thus establishing architectural evidence for the first conventual buildings of the Carmelite Order in the place that was unarguably the location of the monastery of the thirteenth century.

The history of the Carmelites between the construction of the first chapel to Mary and the arrival of the Franks in the Holy Land with the First Crusade is scantily treated by Ribot. The reader is left to conclude from incidental evidence that the hermits maintained a precarious existence after the Arab invasion of the Holy Land in 638. In a chapter devoted to the habit customarily worn by Carmelites, Ribot explains how the Order abandoned its simple white habit for the *pallium barratum*, the striped habit worn until late in the thirteenth century. This part of the *De institutione* purports to be an extract from the "letter of Cyril of Constantinople" to Eusebius, "prior of the Black Mountain." Cyril attributes the change in dress to a decree of the Khalif 'Umar promulgated after the Muslim occupation of Syria and Palestine. The Muslims were shocked to find the hermits wearing pure white, a color they associated with high officials of state, such as governors of cities, and forbade their further use.[55]

The Muslims appear to have left the hermits on Mount Carmel alone, for their continued presence there is assumed by Ribot without further evidence. In general, Muslim rulers in the Near East did not prevent Christians from continuing to worship as they had before the conquest, although

53. Ribot, *De institutione* 6.5. "Nec ergo debes absurdam reputare, monachos nunc montem Carmeli inhabitantes eiusdem esse religionis cum illis, qui in dicto monte conversabantur ante incarnationem Salvatoris."

54. Ibid., 6.5. The site of the chapel is described simply as being next to the spring of Elijah, in the place where Elijah saw the little cloud climbing from the sea over Mount Carmel.

55. Ibid., 7.6. Under the terms of the "Pact of 'Umar," Christian citizens of lands in Syria that had come under Arab control agreed not to dress like Muslims: "We shall not attempt to resemble the Muslims in any way with regard to their dress, as, for example, with the 'qalansuna,' the turban, sandals, or parting the hair" (trans. N. Stillman, *The Jews of Arab Lands* [Philadelphia, 1979], 157). The historicity of the "Pact of 'Umar" is, however, highly contentious.

the building of new churches was restricted.[56] If groups of hermits did indeed continue to inhabit Mount Carmel during the Muslim occupation, there is little reason to suppose they would have found life more difficult than under Byzantine rule.

The Byzantine period, according to Ribot, saw the adoption of a written Rule provided for the Carmelites by John, bishop of Jerusalem, in the reign of the emperor Arcadius (395–408). Once again, Ribot presents his material as an extended quotation from Cyril of Constantinople. The Rule took the form of an address to John's disciple Caprasius written in Greek, a language, Cyril explains (thus betraying the fourteenth-century provenance of the text), "used greatly at that time in the Holy Land."[57] Cyril is at pains to point out that John's "Rule" was no innovation, because it only confirmed in writing what had been the practice of the Carmelites since the days of Elijah and Elisha. The alleged work of John of Jerusalem presents something of a problem. The style of the material quoted by "Cyril," and thus ultimately by Ribot, as John's, does not differ significantly from Ribot's own Latin. Father Papenbroek, the Bollandist commentator on Saint Albert of Vercelli, suggested that the portions in Ribot's work attributed to John should be treated in the same way as the "Augustinian" writings on the eremitical life, attributed dubiously to Augustine.[58]

John was bishop of Jerusalem between 386 and 417. Nothing attributable to him survives in Greek, but he is believed to have been responsible for drafting the Creed at the synod of Diospolis in 415, a version of which exists in Syriac, and for a fragment of a Florilegium later translated into Arabic.[59] In later Carmelite tradition, these survivals may have been convoluted into the earliest written Carmelite Rule, but it is difficult to see how fourteenth-century Western authors like Ribot could have known enough about early Christian writings in Syriac to have made even such a tentative connection.

John appears in a less than favorable light in an entry from the synaxarion of the Ethiopian church. From his youth he had lived in the monastery of Saint Hilarion the Great, practicing an extreme asceticism,[60] but after his

56. C. E. Bosworth, "The 'Protected Peoples' (Christians and Jews) in Medieval Egypt and Syria," *Bulletin of the John Rylands University Library of Manchester* 62 (1979), 11–36.

57. Ribot, *De institutione* 8.1.

58. *AASS*, April I, 776.

59. G. Graf, *Geschichte der christlichen arabischen Literatur*, vol. 1, Studi e Testi 118 (Vatican City, 1944), 337.

60. *Le synaxaire éthiopien*, ed. and trans. R. Basset et al., *PO* 1 (1907), fasc. 5, 603.

consecration as bishop of Jerusalem he "fell under the spell of Satan" and became greedy for material wealth. He stopped giving alms altogether. An old friend, Epiphanius, went to Jerusalem in person to reprimand him, on the pretext of making a pilgrimage. John welcomed him with a magnificent banquet, which gave Epiphanius an idea for punishing him. He took lodgings in a convent and asked to borrow the bishop's silverware in order to entertain certain visiting elders from Cyprus in proper style. When the silverware arrived, he promptly sold it and gave the money to the poor. When John asked for its return and received no reply, he dragged Epiphanius into the Church of the Holy Sepulcher and swore not to let go of him until the silverware was returned. But he had gone too far. God struck him suddenly with blindness, and did not restore his sight (in one eye only) until Epiphanius interceded on his behalf. The other eye was left blind as a reminder to his soul. John "awoke from the sleep of his negligence as if it had been a dream" and never from that time on kept back a penny for himself.

There is no mention of Mount Carmel, or even of the eremitical life, as opposed to general monastic asceticism. How, then, did Bishop John come to be associated with the Carmelite Order? Because mention of him in this context does not occur elsewhere, it can be assumed either that Ribot himself, or an unknown source of Ribot's, simply picked his name as a likely invented source, to help make the succession of the Carmelite Order seem more convincing, or that John did indeed have some involvement with hermits that was later conflated with the belief that the medieval Order of Mount Carmel had continued uninterrupted since at least the fourth century. The problem still remains, however, of Ribot's access to early Christian writers in Palestine whose work was not translated into Latin.

5

The Early Carmelites

Concrete external evidence for the existence of hermits on Mount Carmel appears for the first time in the twelfth century. Benjamin of Tudela, a Jewish pilgrim who passed near Carmel in the late 1160s, described it thus:

> On the other side [of Haifa] is Mount Carmel, at the foot of which there are many Jewish graves. On the mountain is the cave of Elijah, where the Christians have erected a structure called Saint Elias [Elijah]. On the top of the mountain can be recognized the overthrown altar which Elijah repaired in the days of Ahab.[1]

1. *The Itinerary of Benjamin of Tudela*, ed. and trans. M. N. Adler (London, 1907), 19. The older edition of A. Asher (London 1840), 1:64, has a reading that specifies two Christians but in other points is the same. Benjamin's journey took place between 1166 and 1171 (Adler, 1, n. 2).

Two topographical features on Mount Carmel could be associated with Elijah: the cave on the northern promontory where, Abbot Daniel supposed, Elijah was fed by the raven, and the spring that appeared miraculously in the place where Elijah defeated the priests of Baal and was granted the miracle of rain. Benjamin's reference is clearly to the northern site, to a place directly below the abbey of Saint Margaret. It is difficult to know exactly who is meant by "the Christians"—the Orthodox monks of Saint Margaret, Latin monks, or hermits, either Latin or Orthodox, who had established a laura in one of the places identified with Elijah. In the absence of other evidence for a Latin church or monastery on this part of the mountain, it is safest to assume that Saint Elias (Elijah) was built by the monks of Saint Margaret's below the monastery, to commemorate the cave of Elijah. The cave may have been used as a laura of the monastery.

Fifteen years later Mount Carmel was once again—or still—an important habitation for hermits. John Phocas ends his pilgrimage account with a description of an eremitical foundation on the mountain:

> The Mount is a ridge [lit. yoke] which arises in the bay of Haifa, in the lap of Ptolemais, and stretches as far as the mountains of Galilee. At its sharp end of the ridge, by the sea, is the cave of the prophet Elijah, from which that wonderful man was raised up to the angelic kingdom. A long time ago a large monastery stood in such a place, the evidence of which lies in the ruins which can now be seen. But in the course of time, through which everything decays, and after regular attacks by enemies, it has utterly vanished. Some time ago a monk, a priest in rank, grey-haired and who came from Calabria, lived in this place after having a vision of the Prophet. He erected a wall around the conventual ruins, built a tower and a small church, and gathered about ten Brothers. He still lives in that holy place.[2]

It would be a neat solution to assume that the Calabrian was one of the Christians referred to by Benjamin of Tudela. If the Calabrian was not to be identified with Benjamin's Christians, perhaps he had replaced them, thus

---

2. John Phocas, *Descriptio Terrae Sanctae*, *PG* 133:961–62. The translation by Aubrey Stewart, made for *PPTS* 5 (London 1889) and reproduced in Wilkinson, *Jerusalem Pilgrimage*, 335–36, is inexact and slightly misleading, implying that the ruins of the monastery were on the site of the cave of Elijah, although the Greek is less precise.

attesting to the popularity of Mount Carmel for monks and hermits in the Holy Land, and specifically for the importance of Carmel as an eremitical site for Orthodox monks.

The question of topography, however, is once again problematic. There was no ruined monastery by the cave of Elijah. Saint Margaret's, at the top of the northern cliffs, was still standing, as thirteenth-century pilgrimage evidence shows. The only other monastery that could fit the evidence of Phocas is Saint Elisha, known from the sixth-century account of Antoninus Placentius. But Saint Elisha, as Friedman has convincingly shown, was not by the cave of Elijah at all but by the spring, in the wadi 'Ain as-siah. The Calabrian settlement was therefore about 4 kilometers, as the crow flies, from the foundation mentioned by Benjamin, and may have coexisted with a laura by the cave of Elijah. The pattern of the cultivation of the holy sites on Mount Carmel described by the thirteenth-century pilgrimage guides would thus have begun as early as the 1160s, or before.

Topographical precision is important because of the eventual Latin foundation at the spring of Elijah in 'Ain as-siah and because of the later tradition, epitomized by Ribot, that the Latin Carmelites were not a new foundation but simply new recruits grafted on to an existing monastic settlement. According to Ribot, the Rule given to the hermits by John of Jerusalem served its purpose until the beginning of the twelfth century. But the sudden influx of recruits to Mount Carmel from Europe in the aftermath of the First and Second Crusades posed the problem of language: the Westerners could neither read nor understand Greek.[3] One might suppose that language would have been only a symptom of a broader cultural diffusion among the hermits on Mount Carmel, but Ribot saw no intrinsic difficulties in the integration of Orthodox and Latin Christians. In any case, the problem was solved to Ribot's satisfaction by the intervention of Aimery, the patriarch of Antioch and apostolic legate, who had the "Rule of John" translated into Latin: "Turning his attention to the praiseworthy life of the brothers of the Blessed Mary of Mount Carmel, he showed them special patronage in the Lord in his time."[4] Aimery apparently kneaded the hermits into a distinct group by establishing the office of Prior, the first of whom was Berthold, appointed by Aimery of Antioch.

Berthold made his first appearance in Ribot's *De institutione*, but later

3. Ribot, *De institutione* 8.2.
4. Ibid. ". . . Fratrum Beatae Mariae de monte Carmeli laudabilem conversationem attendens, eos multum specialiter suo tempore in Domino enutrivit."

Carmelite authors accepted his existence as proven.[5] According to Ribot, Aimery established the office of Prior on Mount Carmel in 1121,[6] but this date is a bad slip because Aimery did not become patriarch of Antioch until 1140. Since he died only in 1193 he cannot possibly have been in a position to legislate for hermits in 1121. Even medieval Carmelites recognized the mistake, and in some catalogs of priors-general the date 1154 is given instead for the beginning of his rule.[7]

There were, in fact, two Aimerys active in the ecclesiastical hierarchy of the Latin East in the twelfth century: Aimery of Limoges, patriarch of Antioch (1140–93), and Aimery the archbishop of Caesarea (1180–97) and patriarch of Jerusalem (1197–1202). Aimery of Jerusalem does not appear to have had any dealings with hermits or a community on Mount Carmel, but as ultimate ecclesiastical superior in the entire kingdom he might have been a more appropriate legislator for the Order.[8] There is no contemporary evidence to link Aimery of Limoges to Carmel. Ribot must have adopted him as a credible figure in the twelfth-century history of Mount Carmel from his appearance in Gerard of Nazareth's *De conversatione*. Gerard describes him as an "assiduous promotor of the monastic life" and reports his ruling that no hermit was to live alone on the Black Mountain (outside Antioch) without the supervision of a superior (*sine maiore inspectore*).[9] Aimery clearly took an interest in the activities of hermits in his own province, though whether the hermits themselves regarded the interest as benign is questionable. The Black Mountain was well-known as a center for the monastic life, both cenobitic and eremitical, in the Latin and Eastern traditions. Ribot, by using Aimery, was also able to create a link between the Black Mountain and Carmel. Thus Aimery, in Ribot's account, also "led several [hermits] to the solitude of the Black

5. Zimmerman, *Monumenta*, 269–76, and L. J. Lallement (Jean le Solitaire), *Aux sources de la tradition du Carmel* (Paris, 1953), 49–50, accepted in totality Ribot's account of the twelfth-century "history" of the Order. No office for Berthold appears in the Carmelite Ordinary of Sibert de Beka (ca. 1312), *Ordinaire de l'ordre de Notre-Dame du Mont Carmel*, ed. B. Zimmerman (Paris 1910), made from Lambeth Palace Library, London, MS 193.

6. Ribot, *De institutione* 8.2.

7. Thus Bodleian Selden Supra MS 72, fol. 13v. This is one of John Bale's manuscripts, dating from before 1523; by 1527–33, however, when he compiled the *Cronica*, he had reverted to the 1121 of the *De institutione*, Bodleian Selden Supra MS 41, fol. 147r. For the dating of Bale's works, see Fairfield, *John Bale*, 157–64.

8. Hamilton, *The Latin Church in the Crusader States*, 172.

9. *Duodecima centuria*, col. 1373.

Mountain, . . . where, in caves, they led a secret life of service to the Lord."[10]

What possible connection could the patriarch of Antioch have had to Mount Carmel, in the kingdom of Jerusalem? In 1153 Aimery fell foul of the new prince of Antioch, Reynaud de Châtillon, who had acquired the principality by marrying Constance, the daughter of the ruling house. He was horribly tortured and fled his province. In 1155–56 he was in the circle of Queen Melisende in Jerusalem.[11] A settlement was soon reached with Reynaud, but in 1165 Aimery was again forced out of office as part of the humiliating terms imposed on Antioch by the Byzantine Emperor Manuel Comnenus; he returned to Antioch before 1170. There were two occasions on which Aimery almost certainly passed Carmel—on his way to Jerusalem in 1153, and on his way back between 1156 and 1158.[12] Mount Carmel is situated above the coast road from Acre to Caesarea, which was then, as now, the major north-south route from Jerusalem to Tripoli and Antioch. Aimery would probably have stayed at Acre, the major crusader city on the Palestinian coast, but may have made a devotional detour to Carmel, which, whether hermits lived there nor not, was celebrated by pilgrims as the site of Elijah's miracles.

The reason Ribot gives for Aimery's intervention in affairs on Mount Carmel is made to confirm the preexistence of the original community of Carmelites. Aimery had apparently heard of the influx of hermits from the West, which upset the harmony of the eremitical community. Spurning the advice of their elders, the new hermits failed to live up to the standards of the religious life imposed by the ancient Carmelites. Aimery, understanding that this negligence was due merely to a linguistic barrier, thus had John's Rule translated into Latin. Aimery's career marked, for Ribot, a watershed in the Carmelite Order. But his role is only relevant if we accept the assertion that any Orthodox hermits residing on Mount Carmel before the formal recognition of the monastic community by the papacy in 1226 can be called Carmelites. As we have seen, the evidence for such hermits is sparse and begins only in the 1160s, with Benjamin of Tudela's Christians. The verifiable beginnings of the Carmelite Order, as opposed to its prehistory, came about during the patriarchate of Albert of Vercelli (1205–14).

10. Ribot, *De institutione* 9.1.

11. William of Tyre, 18.1 (Huygens, 809).

12. Zimmerman, *Monumenta*, 274, suggests 1155–60 as the time Aimery must have visited Mount Carmel.

The Rule issued by Saint Albert to "B" and his companions by the spring of Elijah in 'Ain as-siah is the central—indeed, the only—document describing the coalescence of the hermits on Carmel at the beginning of the thirteenth century. Its importance is therefore self-evident. Some discussion will be necessary to clarify some of the problems of dating the Rule and to place it in the context of eremitical monasticism in the West.[13]

The dating of the Carmelite Rule contained in Innocent IV's confirmation of the Order has never been satisfactorily resolved. Ribot's date of 1199 is too early for Albert's involvement,[14] and an alternative Carmelite suggestion of 1171 is even wilder.[15] Of the modern Carmelites, Zimmerman chooses 1210 *ob rationes intrinsecas*,[16] and Marie-Joseph du Sacre Coeur chooses 1207, on the grounds that the date of 1199 given by the "letter of Cyril of Constantinople" must be recalculated to allow for the different Greek dating of the Incarnation.[17] Because the "letter of Cyril" cannot be established as authentic evidence, the date of 1199 would be questionable even if it fell within the period of Albert's patriarchate.

Assuming that the Rule can be ascribed to Albert, it cannot be dated more precisely than 1205–14. Technically some uncertainty about Albert's role remains in the legislation for the Carmelites, since there is no evidence from his patriarchate that might link him to Mount Carmel. The Rule is not found attached to any of the earliest Lives of Albert, and may have been associated with him, or drawn from precepts ascribed to him, after his death.[18] From the 1220s onward, however, he was regarded as the legislator of the Order in papal bulls, so there is no cause to assume that the use of his name was anything other than sincere.

The preface to the Rule gives clear indications of the topography and the nature of the community: "Albert, by the grace of God patriarch of the Church of Jerusalem, sends to his dear sons in Christ B. and the other hermits who live under his obedience on Mount Carmel, near the spring, greetings in the Lord and the blessing of the Holy Spirit."[19] There can be

---

13. Cicconetti, *La regola del Carmelo*, esp. 120–23, concentrates on the legislative content of the Rule in terms of semantic meaning, emphasizing the distinctions between *regula* and *modus vivendi*, and placing the Rule of Saint Albert in the latter category.

14. Ribot, *De institutione* 8.3.

15. *AASS*, April I, 782.

16. Zimmerman, *Monumenta*, 278; G. Wessels, ed., "Regula primitiva ordinis nostrae et mutationes Innocenti IV," *Analecta Ordinis Carmelitarum* 3 (1910), 212.

17. Marie-Joseph, "La topographie sacrée," 47.

18. *AASS*, April I, 773.

19. *La règle de l'Ordre de la Bienheureuse Vierge Marie du Mont Carmel*, ed. and trans. M.

no doubt that the hermits for whom Albert was legislating had already occupied the site in 'Ain as-siah, where the ruins of the later thirteenth-century monastery can still be seen[20] and where Phocas's Calabrian built a church in the ruins of Saint Elisha, rather than the cave of Elijah.

Who were Albert's hermits, and what relationship, *pace* Ribot, did they have to the Orthodox eremitical ventures on Mount Carmel? It is clear that Albert did not institute eremitical life in the way Ribot envisaged for Aimery. The preface says that his Rule was written in response to a direct request for a Rule from the hermits themselves, even though plenty of such Rules already existed.[21] A request for a Rule presupposes a community that has reached the point of maturation where written instructions were deemed necessary. As has been shown, this point varied from one community to the next. At Obazine, Stephen was content to rely on oral direction until it was too late to join the Order of his choice, but the Rule adopted from the beginning by Bernard of Blois and his companions for Jubin proved to be its downfall. The eremitical community on Mount Carmel might have existed without a formal Rule for a number of years before Albert answered their request.

The Rule itself is short and simple, containing nothing of great originality. The preface aside, it might serve as the code of living for any community of hermits. The very simplicity and familiarity of the Rule was, to later Carmelites, an indication that Albert was doing no more than confirming the precepts laid down by John of Jerusalem. According to the Rule, the prior is to be one of the brethren, elected by unanimous vote or at least by the greater part; all the brethren are to promise obedience to him and to exercise it by their deeds, by chastity, and by the renunciation of all property.[22] The hermits are to live in the wilderness, *in heremis*.[23] No

---

Battmann (Paris, 1982), 16. All references to the Rule will be to this edition, which was prepared from the oldest manuscript, the letter of Innocent IV to the Carmelites of 1247 confirming the old Rule and adding subsequent modifications. The letter of Innocent was published by M. H. Laurent in "La lettre 'Quae honorem conditoris,'" *Ephemerides Carmeliticae* 2 (1946), 10–16.

20. The site at 'Ain as-siah was excavated by B. Bagatti, "Relatio de excavationibus archeologicis in Monte Carmelo," *Acta Ordinis Carmelitarum Discalceatorum* 3 (1958), 277–88; 6 (1961), 66–70; 7 (1962), 127–30.

21. *La règle du Mont Carmel*, 16.

22. Ibid., 18.

23. Ibid., 20. The modification of Innocent IV in 1247 (Laurent, "La lettre 'Quae honorem conditoris,'" 12) added the clause "or wherever [places] are given to you," permitting the Carmelites to move away, individually or as a group, from Mount Carmel.

Figs. 6, 7, and 8. ʿAin as-siah on Mount Carmel, site of the Carmelite monastery after 1204. *Upper:* "Spring of Elijah," where, according to medieval tradition, God made water from the rock for Elijah. *Lower:* Ruins of the thirteenth-century Carmelite church. *Facing page:* ʿAin as-siah looking toward the Mediterranean. The spring runs into the ravine, and the church is to the left.

brother may change the *locus* assigned him, or exchange places with another, without the permission of the prior.[24] The hermits are thus both
collectively and individually fixed in locations decided for them. Even the
prior may not choose his cell, but must live at the entrance to the "locus" so
he will be the first to greet any new arrivals to the community.[25]

In the midst of the cells there was to be an oratory for the daily celebration of Mass. Otherwise, the brothers were to stay inside or near their cells,
meditating on the "law of the Lord" and praying.[26] The hermits who knew
the proper canonical offices were to recite them at the proper times, but
those who did not could make do by saying, at Matins, twenty-five Paternosters, except on Sundays and feast days, when they were to say fifty; at
Lauds and all the hours until Vespers they were to say seven Paternosters,

24. Ibid., 26. Ribot, *De institutione* 3.6, discusses the distinctions between various types of
cells: "antrum," located by a river or in a forest; "spelunca," a natural cave; "caverna," a
man-made cell; "tabernaculum," a cell made of wood; "casa," a hut; "casula," its diminutive,
a little hut; "cella," a hidden cell. He quotes from a treatise attributed to Bernard of Clairvaux,
De vita solitaria ad fratres de Monte Dei, on the etymology of "cella," linking it both to "celare,"
to conceal, and "caelum," heaven. Daniel, *Speculum*, 1:35, comments that this work, though
found with Bernard's papers, is ascribed by some to William of Saint Thierry.

25. *La règle du Mont Carmel*, 28.

26. Ibid., 30, 38.

and at Vespers, fifteen.[27] The clear implication is that not all recruits to the community were ordained priests, or even literate, and that it was not necessary to learn the offices. Albert was willing to accept an illiterate like Gerard of Nazareth's Dominic or, presumably, a converted knight like Valerius.[28]

As in a cenobitic community, one day in the week was set aside for a chapter dealing with matters relating to the Order—in particular, correction of the faults of any erring brothers.[29] The rules for fasting and abstinence are also familiar. The brethren were to eat in a common refectory while listening to a passage read from Scripture. They were not to eat meat except for medicinal purposes. There is, however, provision for the possibility that the hermits might have to earn their food by begging.[30] Presumably the hermits grew vegetables or cereals, for they were encouraged to occupy themselves with some kind of work lest leisure afford the devil access to the idle soul.[31] Every day save Sunday between the Exaltation of the Cross (September 14) and Easter was a fast day, except for the old, the weak, and the sick.[32] No hermit was to own property, but everything essential was to be held in common. Asses or mules, and fodder to feed them, were permitted; these might have been needed for work or transportation.[33] Hermits were encouraged to keep silence at all times, and especially between the hours of Compline and Prime, following Isaiah: "In returning and in rest you shall be saved; in quietness and trust shall be your strength." Finally, two clauses establish the proper relationship between the prior and the brethren: the responsibility of the prior for the spiritual welfare of the community, and the obedience owed the prior by the brethren, for "in obedience to a superior eternal life will be found."[34] This final clause makes the later Carmelite identification of the Rule with Patriarch Aimery comprehensible.

Properly speaking, Saint Albert's legislation is not a Rule written for an Order but, in the language of Orthodox monasticism, a *typikon* or formula drawn up for a particular community, like the one Neophytus wrote for his

27. Ibid., 32.
28. *Duodecima centuria*, cols. 1604, 1607.
29. *La règle du Mont Carmel*, 40.
30. Ibid., 24, 44. Again, the provision for begging suggests the possibility of moving away from the wilderness to populated areas.
31. Ibid., 48.
32. Ibid., 42.
33. Ibid., 34, 36.
34. Ibid., 50; Isaiah 30:15, 32:17, ibid., 52, 54.

monks. But despite Ribot's insistence that Albert was merely reimposing the Rule of John of Jerusalem, there is no trace of any specifically Orthodox or Eastern trait in the Rule. If similarities of practice can be found with the activities and ideals of Eastern hermits, this argues only for the homogeneity of eremitical culture throughout the Mediterranean. The legislation in the Rule for the liturgical observation of the hermits, sparse though it is, conforms exactly to that of the canons of the Holy Sepulcher. The offices are thus those of the Augustinian canons throughout western Europe. There is nothing foreign to the customs of European eremitical communities.

Albert's Rule is concise to the point of terseness. He refers to none of the available Rules for established houses or Orders, but his sixteen short paragraphs contain forty Scripture quotations. The contrast with Guy's Customary for Chartreuse (1121–28) is obvious and striking. Prior Guy's prologue claims as sources for his Customary the letters of Jerome, the Rule of Saint Benedict, and other patristic texts.[35] He is anxious to include nothing that might be construed as innovative. The Customary consists of eighty chapters, the last of which is a eulogy on the solitary life and is based on the biblical examples of Isaac and Jacob (both of whom received important revelations while in solitude), Moses, Elijah and Elisha, Jeremiah, John the Baptist, and Jesus.[36]

Despite the comparative prolixity of Guy's Customary, Chartreuse and Mount Carmel must have been remarkably similar foundations in their early years. Both insisted on the segregation of monks in their cells. As Guy says, the longer a monk lives in his cell, the longer he will continue to live there willingly, but if he once goes out he will soon be unable to stay in his cell.[37] Grouped around the oratory, the Carmelites' cells were not strictly neighboring, but set apart from each other. A Carmelite was forbidden to leave his cell. Just as the Carmelites renounced private property, the Carthusians were not allowed to keep gifts sent to them from outside: a gift sent to a monk was to be given by him to another, lest it appear that any monk had possessions of his own.[38] The Carmelite strictures on silence and fasting, and above all the chief principle of an eremitical community presided over by an elected prior, regulated by communal worship and eating,

35. Guiges I, *Coutumes de Chartreuse*, 156 (1984 ed.).
36. Ibid., 80 (288–294).
37. Ibid., 32 (232).
38. Ibid., 59 (268–70).

had already formed the backbone of Carthusian monasticism for ninety years by the time Albert wrote his Rule. Given Albert's experience as a monk and bishop in Italy, it is impossible to believe that his legislation for the hermits of Mount Carmel was not influenced by the success and prestige of the Carthusians, even if, as the Carmelites later claimed, the Rule was merely confirming the best practices of hermits who had already been living on Carmel.

The earliest evidence of the Rule comes from a bull of Pope Honorius III issued in January 1226 to "the hermits of Mount Carmel" and referring to the Rule written by "the patriarch of Jerusalem of blessed memory Albert."[39] A piece of evidence from an unlikely source suggests, however, that recognizable monastic communities were in existence before Albert took office, at any rate as early as 1204. The Cistercian monk Gunther of Pairis wrote an account of his abbot Martin's exploits on the Fourth Crusade. In order to fulfill his crusade vow after the debacle at Constantinople, Martin traveled to the Holy Land. In Acre, the capital of the crusader kingdom since 1191, he was befriended by a native baron of German origin, Bernherus (or Werner). Bernherus tried to persuade Martin to stay behind in the Holy Land, where, he argued, any monk ought to want to live. He assured Martin that, should he choose to stay he could procure for him, through his influence with the king, any bishopric or other ecclesiastical office he might desire.

> For there is in those parts a place known both in modern usage and by the ancient authors as Mount Carmel: a place abundant with every good thing, fertile in fruits of the earth, dressed handsomely with vines and olive groves and generally speaking well endowed with trees, and also rich in pasture-land. On this mountain there are three monasteries, set apart from each other and owning extensive properties. These monasteries could either be run separately, or joined as one with himself [Martin] as abbot and lord presiding over them. But if he preferred rather to preside over monks of his own Order, those communities could be easily transferred to other places.[40]

39. *Bullarium Carmelitanum* (Rome, 1715), 1:1; A. Potthast, *Regesta Pontificum Romanorum* 1.7524.
40. Gunther of Pairis, *Historia Constantinopolitanae*, PL 212: col. 250.

This text is remarkable in many ways: as a statement of the lay control of religious houses (at least as perceived by Bernherus), as an indication of the lengths the barons of the kingdom would go to encourage immigration, and for what it tells us about the situation on Mount Carmel just before Albert organized the hermits into a coherent community. The central question in relation to the early development of the Carmelite hermits is of course what the three monasteries known to Bernherus were. They are "set apart from each other" (*distincta ab invicem*), so Bernherus might have had in mind a settlement anywhere on the mountain. They are functioning and property-owning, so he cannot have been referring merely to the ruins of, say, Saint Elisha, as Phocas apparently was.

If we accept that between 1205 and 1214 Patriarch Albert was legislating for a community that had already been in existence for some years, then we know of three separate foundations on Mount Carmel between around 1170 and 1204: Benjamin's Christians, Phocas's Calabrian foundation, and Albert's Frankish hermits. But this is to assume that Benjamin was talking about a permanent community. The sense of his words indicates merely that a church dedicated to Elias had been built on the mountain, but no more. Presumably such a church, or monastic chapel, would be staffed by a priest or monk, and Saint Margaret's was the likeliest source for priests. If the arrangement had continued until 1204, Bernherus may have been misled into supposing that the church of Saint Elias was a full-fledged community. But, particularly if Saint Elias had been founded as a laura of Saint Margaret's, Bernherus may have been right—the church could have become the focal point of a new foundation.

In any case, Bernherus's evidence argues for the continued existence of the Calabrian community by the spring of Elijah, the site of the Carmelite hermits after 1204. Bernherus must also have meant to include Saint Margaret's, the Orthodox abbey on the northern promontory of Mount Carmel, and Saint John of Tyre, about 6 kilometers to the south of 'Ain as-siah. The sense of the passage certainly suggests that he has in mind established and wealthy monasteries rather than hermitages.

Whether Saint Margaret's was meant as among the foundations on Mount Carmel or not, Bernherus's evidence forces us to consider in a more sympathetic light the claim of Ribot and the later Carmelites that the hermits for whom the Rule of Saint Albert was written were joining an existing community that included Orthodox hermits. Given all the evidence for Orthodox eremitical and monastic activity on Carmel between around 1160 and 1204, it seems unlikely that three Latin foundations unattested elsewhere would suddenly have appeared in their place. Bernherus told Martin he could have his pick of monastic offices: he could take over all three monasteries in a joint foundation, or a single one. Of course, he might have greatly exaggerated his own influence with the ecclesiastical authorities, but his description of Mount Carmel gives the impression that it was a fluid situation in which young communities had not yet coalesced, had perhaps not yet adopted a Rule, and needed the firm hand of an experienced abbot. Such a situation fits well with what we know of eremitical foundations from Gerard of Nazareth. Bernherus may have been to Mount Carmel what Gormundus was to Palmaria, during Elias of Narbonne's tenure.[41]

The weight of evidence suggests that Mount Carmel suddenly became a popular resort of hermits toward the end of the twelfth century. Both the cave and the spring of Elijah became the focal points of new, informal communities of Orthodox and Latin hermits. A later Carmelite tradition indicates why this happened in the last years of the twelfth century. John Bale's *Anglorum Heliades* cites a passage from a fourteenth-century Carmelite author, Walter of Coventry, arguing that the diaspora of the Carmelites to the West began not in 1238, as is generally believed, but as early as 1187, at the time of Saladin's invasion of the crusader kingdom.[42] This is credible only if one accepts the existence of a coherent Carmelite Order before Saint Albert's Rule—in other words, if, like Bale, one labels any hermits active in the Holy Land Carmelites.

But the objection to Walter's thesis is really one of terminology. Saladin's conquests in 1187 made the Galilee dangerous for monks. Indeed, in 1183, the Orthodox monastery on Mount Tabor had been sacked by a Muslim raiding-party.[43] Among the towns to fall to Saladin in autumn 1187 was Haifa. According to Ralph of Coggeshall, the whole region of Mount Carmel was laid to waste. Ralph mentions the existence of a church dedicated to Saint Elijah "over the high bank that overlooks Ptolemais, against the sea, a useful signal for sailors," but does not mention the habitation of Mount Carmel by hermits or monks. In fact, from Carmel to Jaffa and Ramla, the Muslims killed Christians indiscriminately.[44]

41. The name "Bernherus" does not appear in John d'Ibelin's *Lignaces d'Outremer, RHC Lois* 2:470, for the lordship of Haifa.

42. John Bale, *Anglorum Heliades*, British Library, Harleian MS 3838, fol. 9v; Staring, *Medieval Carmelite Heritage*, 279.

43. William of Tyre 22.27 (Huygens, 1052).

44. Ralph of Coggeshall, *De expugnatione Terrae Sanctae per Saladinum*, ed. J. Stevenson, Rolls Series (London, 1875), 230–31.

Ralph's purpose was not to record monastic sites, so his silence cannot be taken as proof that monks on Mount Carmel were massacred by Saladin. But toward the end of the siege of Acre, in July 1191, Saladin again attacked Haifa, destroying its defenses. The Muslims were ejected by Richard I later that summer after the fall of Acre, and a year later, just before his departure for Europe, Richard again visited Haifa.[45] The situation around Mount Carmel was, to say the least, volatile between 1187 and 1192. In such circumstances it is impossible to guess at the fate of nascent eremitical foundations. Perhaps the monks were left alone and the Calabrian community, for example, survived the war intact. More likely, Mount Carmel may have attracted refugee monks from Galilee, either cloistered monks in monasteries like Palmaria, or anchorites who feared for their safety. From such turmoil the Carmelite Order seems to have had its beginnings.

By the time Gunther of Pairis was writing, Mount Carmel, in the military orbit of Acre, was quite safe and apparently prospering. But it is still far from clear what the composition of the eremitical community legislated for by Saint Albert might have been. If taken at face value, Gunther's evidence suggests that, even without the Muslim threat, the eremitical communities were not safe from outside interference. The suggestion that Martin should import monks of his own Order — Cistercians — to populate Mount Carmel is an ironic repetition of the unfulfilled interest shown in the Cistercians by Elias of Narbonne before 1140. By 1204, of course, the Order had established monasteries in the Holy Land[46] and would soon acquire Bernard of Blois's old house at Jubin. In 1209 Peter, bishop of Ivrea and formerly a monk at the Cistercian monastery of La Ferté, was appointed patriarch of Antioch. He had already tried to resign his episcopal office at Ivrea to adopt the eremitical life but had been forbidden to do so by Innocent III.[47] As compensation, perhaps, for this personal disappointment, he campaigned as patriarch of Antioch for incorporating into the Cistercian Order any foundation on the Black Mountain that so wished. After an initial dispute within the Order, Jubin became a daughter-house of La Ferté in March 1214.[48]

Peter was of course acting in the tradition of his predecessor Aimery and

45. Roger of Howden, *Chronica* 3, ed. G. Stubbs, Rolls Series (London, 1870), 119, 185; Matthew Paris, *Chronica Maiora* 2, ed. H. Luard, Rolls Series (London, 1874), 376.

46. L. Janauschek, *Originum Cisterciensum*, vol. 1 (Vienna, 1877), 139, no. 354; 144, no. 365.

47. Hamilton, "Cistercians in the Crusader States," 408.

48. *Les registres de Grégoire IX*, ed. L. Auvray, Bibl. des écoles françaises d'Athènes et de

must have known this from the records of his see. What probably lay behind the rather grandiose plans of Bernherus (which had to be presented in such a way as to make them appear as attractive to Abbot Martin as possible) was the same concern that Aimery of Antioch had expressed for the hermits on the Black Mountain. If the Muslim conquests of 1187 and the war of 1190–92 had added significantly to the eremitical population on Carmel, the ecclesiastical—or secular—authorities in nearby Acre may have believed it necessary to establish firm controls, in the form of a Rule, for the monks. Thus Martin was offered a free hand in bringing about a transformation from unregulated to regulated eremitism.

The hermits under the leadership of "B" at the spring of Elijah were probably only one of the groups of monks on Mount Carmel. What distinguished them from the others was their readiness to accept a Rule and their request for a special Rule from Patriarch Albert. In Carmelite tradition, as transmitted by Ribot but probably established before him, "B" was the second prior-general of the Carmelite Order, Brocardus, who succeeded Berthold in 1199.[49] Historians have, to the present day, accepted Brocardus's existence as genuine,[50] and there is nothing to deny it save the general doubt that must linger over Ribot's presentation of the version of events. Ribot made Brocardus appear genuine by introducing him through the "letter of Cyril of Constantinople." An anonymous Carmelite "Life of Brocardus" does not have any doubt about the functioning of monastic foundations on Carmel during the war with Saladin. Brocardus is made to visit the crusader army besieging Acre in 1190 and 1191 to deliver rousing sermons.[51]

The most intriguing aspect of Brocardus's legendary career was a mission to Damascus entrusted to him by Albert, during which he cured a mamluk

---

Rome (Paris, 1896–1910), 3 vols., vol. 1, no. 3468; Canivez, *Statuta*, 2:172, no. 18; Hamilton, "The Cistercians," 410.

49. Ribot, *De institutione* 8.2. Bale's notebooks have two different dates for Brocardus's career, depending on the dates for Berthold. One tradition, represented in the *Cronica*, Bodleian Selden Supra MS 41, fol. 149v, has Brocardus instituted as "vicarius" on Mount Carmel by the Patriarch Heraclius in 1174, accepting Albert's Rule in 1199 and dying in 1207. The list of prior-generals in Bodleian Selden Supra MS 72, fol. 12r–20v gives Brocardus's dates as 1166–99.

50. E.g., Hamilton, *The Latin Church in the Crusader States*, 252; Zimmerman, *Monumenta*, 276. The church in the Stella Maris monastery on Carmel has three brass floor-slabs with the names of Brocardus (d. 1221), Berthold (d. 1188), and Cyril (d. 1224) in the pavement.

51. *Vita Sancti Brocardi*, AASS, Sept. I, 578.

who had contracted leprosy by making him bathe in the Jordan.[52] The author was reminding his readers of the healing miracle performed on Naaman by the famous Carmelite Elisha (2 Kings 5:9–15). The story has a kernel of fact: in 1213 Innocent III corresponded with "Salphidinus" (Sauf ad-Din), the sultan of Damascus, to arrange a truce between Muslims and Christians and to request the return of Christian prisoners. He charged Patriarch Albert with arranging to have the letter delivered to the sultan, and asked him to report back at the Lateran Council he was then planning.[53] It is not impossible that Albert should have chosen for the mission the prior of the Carmelite foundation, to which, as legislator, he presumably felt a continuing attachment.[54] The Brocardus of Carmelite tradition (including even the name itself) is undoubtedly an unreliable figure, but clearly there did exist someone on whom the cloak of legend was later hung.

Brocardus may even have been an Orthodox monk—perhaps the very Calabrian described by John Phocas, if he had lived that long. The implication of the supposition that after 1187 Mount Carmel became the resort of refugee hermits is that a mixed Orthodox and Latin population of monks was created, just as on the Black Mountain and in the Valley of Jehosaphat. An Orthodox monk from Calabria would have had experience of dealing with Franks, and such dealings may not have been hostile. The claims of Ribot that the Latin Carmelites were grafted on to the existing Orthodox branch of the Order were designed to prove the legitimacy and antiquity of the Order, but whatever Ribot's loose interpretation of history, the basis for such claims was valid. Orthodox hermits had lived by the spring of Elijah not long before Albert's Rule and were probably occupying places on the mountain during the years of the burgeoning Latin monastery.

This is best exemplified by the troublesome figure of "Cyril of Constantinople," whose alleged letter to "Eusebius, prior of the Black Mountain" Ribot quotes extensively.[55] Daniel a Virgine Maria's introduction to Ribot's *De institutione* gives a few sketchy details of Cyril's life. He was born and

52. Ibid., 577.

53. *Regesta Innocenti III* 16.36, *PL* 216:830–31.

54. Zimmerman, *Monumenta*, 278, discounted the possibility that Brocardus could have been the envoy, on the grounds that he was a hermit. R. Röhricht, ed., *Regesta regni Hierosolymitani, 1099–1291* (Berlin, 1892), no. 864, named John, archbishop of Cefalu as the envoy.

55. A version of the letter is printed independently by Daniel a Virgine Maria in *Vinea Carmeli* (Antwerp, 1662), 1.5.21–23. See also G. Wessels, "Epistola S. Cyrilli III prioris generalis et historia antiqua Ordinis nostri," *Analecta Ordinis Carmelitarum* 3 (1914), 267–86, which accepts the existence of Cyril and his authorship of the letter as fact.

educated in Constantinople, and his choice of a monastic career was inspired by the examples of John the Baptist and Samuel. Apparently quite independently, he became convinced of the error of the Orthodox position on the procession of the Holy Spirit and disputed to this effect with the patriarch of Constantinople. In a dream the Blessed Virgin then told him to leave Constantinople for the Order on Mount Carmel, where he would presumably be among like minds.[56] Eventually he became the third prior-general of the Order, ruling between 1231 and 1234.[57]

By the time Bale was collecting his Carmelite material, Cyril's history had expanded. First, he was moved back in time, to correspond with the earlier dates for Berthold, Brocardus, and Albert's Rule. According to the *Cronica* he ruled as prior-general for twenty-seven years, between 1208 and 1234. The Cyril of the *Cronica* not only converted the sultan of Iconium to Christianity but was sent by Manuel Comnenus to the papal court of Alexander III as a legate. In 1165 he had his vision of the Blessed Virgin, then preached in Armenia for an additional ten years, baptizing the king of Armenia as a Catholic. Only then did he retire to Mount Carmel.[58] Although Bale does not exploit it, the additional episode of the mission to Rome presents an opportunity to explain this Byzantine monk's conversion to Roman theology. The preaching mission to Armenia is presumably an appropriation of the agreement between Rome and the Armenian Church under Catholicos Nerses.[59] Bale's printed work, the *Scriptorum maioris Britanniae catalogus* of 1544–47, influenced the Centuriators to include Cyril "Carmelitus" with their list of Gerard of Nazareth's hermits.[60]

The full tradition of Cyril's career before Mount Carmel seems to conflict, by implication, with Ribot, who saw the differences between Orthodox and Latin as essentially linguistic problems easily solved by the translation of an older Greek Rule into Latin. On Mount Carmel, at least in the

---

56. Daniel, *Speculum*, part 1, 1:4. Zimmerman, *Monumenta*, 295, accepted Cyril's existence as genuine, but not his Byzantine origins. Wessels, "Epistola S. Cyrilli," 267–86, is too credulous, following Ribot's chronology uncritically.

57. *AASS*, March I, 497.

58. John Bale, *Cronica*, fol. 150r.

59. Hamilton, "The Armenian Church and the Papacy at the Time of the Crusades," *Eastern Churches Review* 10 (1978), 61–87.

60. *Duodecima centuria*, col. 1610. The Centuriators took most of their Carmelite material from Bale's *Catalogus*, in ibid., col. 945. For correspondence between Matthias Flacius and other Centuriators and Bale, see H. McCusker, *John Bale: Dramatist and Antiquary* (Bryn Mawr, 1942), 67–70.

Carmelite version of events, there was no doctrinal disagreement. Problems caused by the mixing of Franks and indigenous or Greek hermits were blamed by Ribot on the Franks, and Aimery's actions were deemed necessary to "curb the audacity" of the incoming Franks and to safeguard "the safe innocence of the older hermits on that mountain."[61] Either Ribot was untroubled by the complexities of Latin-Orthodox polemics on the papal primacy, the procession of the Holy Spirit, the marriage of clergy, the use of leavened bread in the Eucharist, and so on, or he was prepared to defy his own church's general principles in the cause of furthering his Order. The transition from the purely Orthodox monasticism of the precrusader era to the Latin refoundation gave him no more trouble than that from the "sons of the prophets" following the Jewish Law to the early Christian hermits after the resurrection.

Ribot, of course, greatly modified what must have been the true picture, subordinating Albert of Vercelli to a supporting role and unaccountably attributing the real foundation of a community to Aimery of Antioch. In so doing he extended the foundation process back at least to the 1150s, thus dragging it out over the course of about fifty years. In reality it is impossible to know how long any process of assimilation between Orthodox and Latin monks may have taken. Albert's Rule, however, marks a clear divide. Before the legislation of 1205–14, the refugee hermits of Mount Carmel must have lived without overall supervision, perhaps following oral customs or their own individual practices. If a group or groups of monks had fled from a convent threatened or destroyed by the Muslims (as the Georgian Gabriel fled from Saint Euthymius's in Judaea), they presumably continued to observe the Rules of their houses as best as they could.

Albert's Rule appeared to change the situation on Mount Carmel by determining the precise conditions under which hermits were to live. He accomplished, in effect, what Ribot claimed Aimery had done in the twelfth century. But he regulated sparingly, almost reluctantly. In the preface he is almost apologetic for adding to the proliferation of new Rules for the Christian life.[62] There were plenty of Rules and customs already available from which to choose, but none of them apparently satisfied the hermits. Yet Albert's adds very little to the body of monastic regulation; it contains

---

61. Ribot, *De institutione* 8.2.

62. *La règle du Mont Carmel*, 18. The Fourth Lateran Council in 1215 was to restrict severely the perpetuation of new Orders.

no original thoughts, no rulings that would have been unfamiliar to a Frankish monk, and little that could have been alien to an Orthodox. This is indeed the purpose of the Rule. It is a careful, bland, and inoffensive synthesis of the customs that must already have been practiced by most of the monks on Carmel. It was designed not to create but to give recognition to an existing foundation.

6

The Development of the Carmelite Order in the Latin East

The relationship between Orthodox hermits, such as Cyril and Phocas's Calabrian, and the Latin hermits can probably never be determined precisely. The evidence for the composition of the foundation in the period after the Rule of Albert is hardly less scanty than for the twelfth century. Pilgrims' accounts, however, give some valuable independent testimony. Willebrand of Oldenburgh simply says that on Mount Carmel (which lies directly above Haifa), in the house of Elijah (*mansio Eliae*), Mass is celebrated every day.[1] This gives no indication of the breakdown of monastic communities on Carmel. The account by the pilgrim Thietmar (ca. 1217) is similarly unhelpful. He mentions the cave of Elijah on Mount Carmel, with its chapel, presumably the one referred to by Ralph of Coggeshall, and

1. *Peregrinatores medii aevi quatuor*, 183.

goes on to say: "On the summit of Mount Carmel there is a certain monastery, where Greek and Syrian monks still live."[2] Thietmar must be referring here to Saint Margaret's. The "Syrian" monks were presumably Melkites, Arabic-speaking Orthodox. Neither guide, therefore, gives any indication of the fate of the Orthodox hermits on Carmel, either by the cave or by the spring of Elijah, after the Rule of Saint Albert.

French pilgrimage guides are more explicit. *Les pèlerinages por aler en Jherusalem*, of around 1231, confirms that the monastery of Saint Margaret, "one-and-a-half leagues" distant from the Latin hermits, was still Orthodox, but it also describes the Latin hermits:

> On this same mountain is Saint Margaret's, a convent of Greek monks, also occupying a beautiful place. The convent has some good relics and overlooks the place where Saint Elijah lived, a chapel cut into the rock. Beyond the convent of Saint Margaret, on the ridge of the same mountain, is a very lovely and delightful place where the Latin hermits live who are called brothers of Mount Carmel; there is a little church to Our Lady, and all around the place many springs issuing from the rock of the mountain. It is one-and-a-half leagues from the convent of the Greek monks to the place of the Latin hermits.[3]

The guide known as *Les chemins et les pèlerinages de la Terre Sainte* (1230s) adds nothing substantial to this but confirms that there were two chapels to Elijah—the one by the cave mentioned by Thietmar, and one by the spring where the Latin hermits lived: "Going down from this convent [Saint Margaret's] is a chapel in the rock to the holy prophet Elijah; this is where he performed many miracles, and in the chapel is a good spring of cold water which he found, and indeed made."[4]

Another pilgrims' guide, known as *Les sains pèlerinages*, which cannot be dated precisely but which seems to be a manuscript variant of *Les pèlerinages*, probably also from the 1230s, lists four different foundations: the monastery of Saint Margaret, a community called "hermits of Carmel" by the cave of Elijah, the Latin hermits by the spring of Elijah, and the Orthodox monastery of Saint John of Tyre, in the extreme south of Mount Carmel:

2. Ibid., 21.
3. Michelant and Raynaud, *Itinéraires à Jérusalem*, 89–90.
4. Ibid., 189.

On this same mountain is the convent of Saint Margaret, which is a monastery of black [Greek] monks. It is a beautiful place, and the convent has fine chapels. Below this convent is the place where Saint Elijah lived. In this place is a fine little chapel in the rock where the hermits of Carmel live. Beyond the convent of Saint Margaret, on the ridge of the same mountain, is a beautiful and delightful place where the Latin hermits live who are called brothers of Carmel. There is a very fine little church to Our Lady, and all around that place there are many springs, which issue from the very rock of the mountain. It is one league from their valley to the sea. . . . On the ridge toward Château Pèlerin [Athlit] is a place called Saint John of Tyre; there is a Greek monastery with many good chapels.[5]

This guide provides the closest parallel for the situation on Mount Carmel suggested by Gunther of Pairis. It also indicates that the enterprise begun with the foundation of the church of Saint Elias had proved sufficiently resilient to last until at least around 1231 at the cave of Elijah, and that the Rule of Saint Albert did not manage to absorb all Orthodox and Latin hermits into a single foundation. We are left, then, with only the possibility of Phocas's Calabrian community by the ruins of Saint Elisha becoming part of the Carmelite Order.

A mixed community of Orthodox and Latin hermits on Mount Carmel may appear at first sight bizarre. Mixed cenobitic communities, however, were not unknown before the twelfth century, particularly in Italy—a region, like the Holy Land, of uncertain religious frontiers. In 977 the monastery of Saint Bonifacio in Rome was granted to Sergius, archbishop of Damascus, who became abbot of a dual community of Greek and Latin monks that flourished for twenty years.[6]

Admittedly, there was less doctrinal and political disagreement between Orthodox and Latins in the tenth century than in the twelfth, but the Latin Church in the kingdom of Jerusalem offered considerable freedom of existence and expression for the Orthodox, particularly at the level of the parish and in monastic organization. Moreover, it was among hermits—however one defines them—that the greatest degree of theological or doctrinal

---

5. "Les sains pèlerinages que l'on doit requere en la Terre Sainte" (ibid., 104).

6. B. Hamilton, "The Monastery of S. Alessio and the Religious and Intellectual Renaissance in Tenth-Century Rome," *Studies in Medieval and Renaissance History* 2 (1965), 265–310.

freedom was to be found. The reason such monastic leaders as Aimery, or Peter the Venerable in the West, were so concerned to ensure that hermits lived under a Rule was because no one could assess the liturgical and doctrinal orthodoxy of hermits who lived alone and unsupervised. Yet Albert was evasive about the liturgical practices he wanted his monks to follow. They were to say the canonical hours by themselves if they knew them, but if not they could instead simply say twenty-five Paternosters at Matins and fifty on Sundays, fifteen at Vespers, and seven at Lauds and at the other hours. This rule may well have been aimed at hermits who were not ordained priests and had never received any monastic training, but it may equally have been designed to welcome into the foundation Orthodox hermits whose offices would not have corresponded with those of the Franks. In any case, even the prior presumably could not tell whether an Orthodox monk were saying an office from his own rite privately in his cell. The Rule of Saint Albert is so concise and generic that it is difficult to believe Orthodox hermits could have found much in it to dispute, particularly if they were allowed to follow their own rite.

Later Carmelites assumed that the Rule of Saint Albert was taken from Basil's writings.[7] This claim was refuted by the Bollandist Father Papenbroek, whose detailed analysis showed that the Rule owed nothing to any Greek influence.[8] The point, however, is surely that the practices Albert recommended were, by nature rather than by design, almost identical to those of Neophytes on Cyprus and would have been equally approved by Elias of Narbonne or Bernard of Blois. There is a fundamental unity of monastic custom that bridges doctrinal or theological divides. At this level, it is difficult to see how Saint Albert's Rule changed the way of life of the hermits on Mount Carmel, wherever they had practiced their monasticism before. Ribot's account is flawed in many points of detail, but at the deepest level he understood the legacy the Carmelites of the thirteenth century had received from their monastic and eremitical predecessors on Carmel.

In one important respect the Rule of Saint Albert transformed monasticism on Carmel. Hermits living without a Rule, unless already ordained priests (which, as the Rule of Saint Albert confirms, was not the case for all Carmelites), would have no ecclesiastical status in terms of canon law. They might be considered "conversi" or lay brothers—even (if not native to

---

7. As summed up from Bale, by the Centuriators (*Duodecima centuria*, col. 944); see Staring, *Medieval Carmelite Heritage*, 74–76.

8. *AASS*, April I, 785.

the kingdom of Jerusalem) "peregrini"—but only after the papal confirmation of the Rule could they be considered a "collegium" or "domus religiosa." The first confirmation of the Order dates from the pontificate of Honorius III, but it is likely that it had already been recognized in some form by Innocent III before Albert's death in 1214, since the Fourth Lateran Council a year later sought to limit the proliferation of new Orders.[9] Albert was sufficiently experienced as an ecclesiastical administrator, and in close enough touch with the papacy, to have had his Rule approved without delay.

Honorius III's confirmation, dated 1226, addresses the Carmelites as "Brother hermits of Mount Carmel."[10] In Innocent IV's bull *Quae honorem conditoris*, of 1247, they are called "hermits of Saint Mary of Mount Carmel."[11] In 1256, however, Alexander IV omitted "hermits" from the title, referring only to "his dear sons, the provincial, prior, and other brothers of the Order of the Blessed Mary of Mount Carmel in the Holy Land."[12] The change in titles implies a change in the structure and conception of the Order. Innocent's bull of 1247, *Quae honorem conditoris*, modified the Rule of Saint Albert superficially but in so doing caused a revolution within the Order.[13] The Carmelites were permitted to settle in places other than their hermitage on Mount Carmel, but they were still prohibited from owning property and thus had to beg. They became, in effect, mendicants rather than hermits, and expanded with remarkable rapidity throughout Europe. The circumstances of this sea change and the

9. Mansi, *Sacrorum conciliorum*, 22:1002–3. "Ne nimia religionum diversitas gravem in ecclesia Dei confusionem inducat, firmiter prohibemus, ne quis de cetero novam religionem inveniat: sed quicumque voluerit ad religionem converti, unam de approbatis assumat. Similiter qui voluerit religiosam domum fundare de novo, regulam et institutionem accipiat de religionibus approbatis." Innocent III, however, may himself have composed a Rule for the Order of Saint Spiritus de Saxia: *Regula ordinis S. Spiritus de Saxia*, PL 217:1129–58. Ribot, *De institutione* 7.5, quotes Sibert de Beka's *Tractatus de consideratis super Carmelitarum Regula*, to the effect that the Carmelites were forced to petition Innocent in 1215, through the offices of Albert's successor as patriarch, Ralph, to recognize them as an Order.

10. *Bullarium Carmelitanum*, 1:1.

11. For the text of the bull, see M.-H. Laurent, ed., "La lettre 'Quae honorem conditoris,'" *Ephemerides Carmeliticae* 2 (1946), 10–16; A. Staring, ed., "Four Bulls of Innocent IV: A Critical Edition," *Carmelus* 27 (1980), 273–85.

12. *Bullarium Carmelitanum*, 1:15.

13. The bull of 1247 marks the culmination of a period of papal concern for the constitution of the Order. In 1245 Innocent IV had first (on June 8) confirmed the rulings that the Carmelites were not to own property; then, on July 27, he permitted them to leave Mount Carmel and found priories overseas because of the Muslim threat. *Registres d'Innocent IV*, ed. E. Berger, 4 vols. (Paris, 1884–1921), 1: no. 1311; *Bullarium Carmelitanum*, 1:8.

subsequent development of the Carmelites as friars lie outside the range of this book,[14] but in the context of monasticism in the Latin East we must consider the growth and ordering of the Carmelite Order in the crusader states.

Carmelite historians have assumed that the initial dispersal of the Carmelites occurred in 1238, with the threat of Muslim invasion.[15] This is somewhat puzzling, for in 1238–39 the situation of the Franks in the crusader states was quite stable. When the treaty Frederick II had made with al-Kamil for the return of Jerusalem to Christian hands expired in 1239, Theobald IV of Champagne was on hand to drive out the Muslims who tried to reoccupy the city. Al-Kamil had been defeated by the Seljuks of Rum, and then became embroiled in a civil war with his brother al-Ashraf until 1237. In 1238 al-Kamil died and the Ayubid empire fragmented as al-Salih and al-Adil II struggled for power. While these events were distracting the Muslim Near East, Theobald recaptured Ascalon in 1239, and in 1241 al-Salih was forced to make a treaty with Richard of Cornwall that confirmed the concessions made by al-Kamil in 1229 and added to Christian possessions the eastern Galilee and Tiberias, Jaffa, Ascalon, and Sidon. In Galilee the frontier was once again the Jordan, as it had been before 1187. The Carmelites had more reason to be concerned for their future after the sack of Jerusalem by the Kharasmians in 1244 and the ravaging of the Holy Land. Innocent IV's bulls of 1245, 1247, and 1248 were responses to Carmelite fears for their safety, but there was no bull between 1238 and 1245.

Innocent reconfirmed the Rule of Saint Albert for the benefit of the two Carmelite brothers, Reginald and Peter, who had gone to Rome to ask for a modification of the Rule on the question of the ownership of property. In the late 1220s mild dissension had arisen in the Order over how strictly Albert's prohibition of property should be interpreted. Gregory IX's bull of 1229, *Ex officio nostro*, confirming Albert's Rule, explicitly forbad the Order to own any property.[16] Gregory allowed the hermits to own only asses and the food necessary to keep them. This ruling was the origin of the transformation of the hermits into friars, for it put the Carmelites on the same level as the new mendicant Orders. But Innocent IV went further than had been

---

14. Cicconetti, *La Regola del Carmelo*, 189–297.

15. Ribot, *De institutione* 9.3; Bale, *Anglorum Heliades*, London, British Library, Harleian MS 3838, fol. 12r; L. J. Lallement, *Aux sources de la tradition du Carmel* (Paris, 1953), 95, following Vincent of Beauvais, *Speculum historiale* 30, ed. B. Beller (1624; repr., Graz, 1965), 1274–75.

16. *Bullarium Carmelitanum*, 1:522, for Innocent's bull of 1247; 1:4–5, for Gregory IX's bull. See also Ribot, *De institutione* 9.4.

expected. He declared the Rule "doubtful" and appointed two commissioners, Hugh, cardinal priest of Saint Sabina, and William, bishop of Tortosa, both Dominicans, to reform the Rule of Saint Albert.[17] Innocent's "confirmation" of 1247 thus represents a watershed that was no less significant in its effects than Albert's legislation. On the question of property, Innocent repeated Gregory IX's ruling of 1229, specifying that all belongings should be held in common and shared out by the prior himself, and that no property should be owned by the Order.[18] The schism that had disrupted Jubin under Bernard of Blois, and the disciplinary problems Elias of Narbonne had faced concerning standards of asceticism at Palmaria in the 1130s, were not permitted to occur on Mount Carmel in the thirteenth century. The difference lay in the strict papal control exercised over the hermitage on Carmel since 1226. Like Francis and Dominic, Patriarch Albert had understood the need to involve the papal curia intimately with the development of specific communities.[19]

The effect of the modifications made at the recommendation of the two Dominican commissioners was, in the view of Ribot, simply to liberate the Carmelites from the restrictions imposed on them by the Rule of Saint Albert. That Rule, which he treated simply as a legislative restatement of the measures taken by Aimery of Antioch, had been necessary in the conditions of the twelfth century, when the original hermits were swamped by newcomers and the truly Carmelite way of life was threatened by diffusion. Now Innocent was releasing the Carmelites to follow the true vocation of Elijah,[20] by permitting them to live elsewhere than in the cells assigned to them on Mount Carmel, to which they had been restricted by Albert's Rule. The Dominican commissioners' modification of the Rule to allow mobility was a response to the pressing need, after 1244, for the hermits to leave Carmel for safer places for long periods. Naturally, the Dominicans used the model of their own Rule, with the result that the Carmelites after 1247, while preserving the text of their primitive Rule, imitated the Dominicans in the internal organization of their Order. But Ribot saw the Innocentian modification not as bringing the Carmelites into conformity with mendicants rather than monks, but as acknowledging the original vocation of the Order to preach, teach, and prophesy, as Elijah and

---

17. Laurent, "La lettre 'Quae honorem conditoris,'" 11.

18. Ibid., 13.

19. For papal relations with Francis and Dominic, see R. B. Brooke, *The Coming of the Friars* (London, 1975), 32–33, 91–93.

20. Ribot, *De institutione* 8.6.

the sons of the prophets had done in Israel. Ribot viewed the changes of 1247 as a development fully in line with the early history of the Carmelites, not as a betrayal or revision of the principles of the Order. The imposition and confirmation of Albert's Rule, by contrast, represented an interlude of considerable poverty and inactivity for the Order. This interpretation was to be the Carmelites' constant refrain in defense of their Order's antiquity from the later thirteenth century onward.

In a map of about 1235, probably drawn to accompany a pilgrims' guide to the Holy Land, the Carmelite settlement is described as an "heremitarium."[21] In 1263, however, Urban IV referred to the undertaking of a monastic building on Mount Carmel as an *opus sumptuosum* and granted an indulgence to all Christians who contributed to the work.[22] Twenty years later the monastery of the Carmelites on the summit of Mount Carmel was mentioned in the terms of a treaty between the kingdom of Jerusalem and al-Mansur, sultan of Egypt.[23] By now there were two distinct monastic foundations on Carmel: Saint Margaret's for Orthodox monks, and the Latin Carmelites at the spring of Elijah:

> At the second mile from there is the monastery of Saint Mary of Carmel, a beautiful and agreeable place, situated between mountains, where the Latin brothers live doing penance. Thereafter, at a mile's distance, is the monastery of the Blessed Virgin Margaret. On Mount Carmel, in that part overlooking the city of Porphyria, which is today called Cayphas, pilgrims lead the solitary life after the example and manner of that holy man and hermit the prophet Elijah, next to the fountain called the spring of Elijah, not far from the monastery.[24]

The ambitious building program to establish a permanent physical presence for the Order was no more than the restitution of what, according to Ribot, had historically been the nature of the Carmelite Order. Purporting

21. Röhricht, *Zeitschrift des deutschen Palästina Vareins* 18 (1895), table 6. A charter of 1250 (idem, *Regesta regni Hierosolymitana*, no. 1189) mentions the "vinea domus S. Eliae de Carmelo."

22. *Bullarium Carmelitanum*, 1:28.

23. Röhricht, *Regesta*, no. 1450.

24. "Philippi descriptio Terrae Sanctae," 86.7, ed. W. Neumann, *Österreicher Vierteljahresschrift für Katholische Theologie* 2 (1872), 76–77. Philip goes on to describe the monastery of Saint John of Tyre. See also Burchard of Mount Zion's description (*Peregrinatores medii aevi peregrinatores*, 83).

to quote William of Sandwich, Ribot recalled the houses maintained by the Carmelites in cities in Roman and Byzantine Palestine before they were lost in the Arab invasion of 638–39.[25] Only after the Frankish occupation of the Holy Land did the Carmelites once more have the opportunity to build. "In various deserts and cities alike in Syria they built monasteries of their Order, fitting and convenient for the solitary life to be observed in them, according to the Rule commemorated among them."[26] According to Ribot, the Carmelites built houses in Acre, Tyre, Sarepta (south of Sidon, where Elijah had performed the miracle of the oil jug), Tripoli, and Jerusalem. All these were urban foundations, but they also settled in the wilderness on Mount Lebanon, on the Black Mountain, on Mount Quarantana and in a deserted place twelve miles east of Mount Carmel called Valim.[27] The Black Mountain was an obvious place for Ribot to claim for the Carmelites, given its venerable eremitical tradition. Mount Quarantana seems to have been an appropriation from Jacques de Vitry, who described hermits living there in imitation of Jesus in the same passage in which he mentioned Carmel.[28]

Ribot's statement of Carmelite prosperity is based on a grain of truth. Pilgrimage literature indicates that the Carmelites had extensive properties in the kingdom of Jerusalem and in Antioch. Ludulph of Suchem, who visited the Holy Land in about 1350, was familiar with the Carmelites in Europe, but he went to Mount Carmel to see the place of their origin: "On this mount [Carmel] a very beautiful monastery built in honor of Holy Mary can be seen to have stood. The friars who derive their origin from there are called Carmelites to this day. They are begging friars, and one may see that they once had fifteen fair convents in the Holy Land."[29]

How far can Ludulph's number of fifteen be justified? The Chapter-General of the Order in 1259, held in Messina, mentions the presence of "several brothers from the Holy Land, particularly from the convent at Acre and the convent at Mount Carmel."[30] In a bequest of 1264, a citizen of Acre, Saliba, left five bezants to the Carmelites, presumably of that town,

25. Ribot, *De institutione* 9.1.

26. Ibid., 9.2. Ribot attributes this expansion to the activities of Aimery of Antioch, thus projecting it back into the twelfth century.

27. Ibid. No place called "Valim" seems to have existed, although Röhricht, *Regesta*, no. 973, mentions an individual by the name of Valinus: "Pandulfus, sener domini Valini."

28. Ibid., 9.1; Jacques de Vitry, *Historia Hierosolymitana*, 52 (Bongars, 1075).

29. *Ludolphi de itinere Terrae Sanctae* 28, ed. F. Deycks (Stuttgart, 1851), 49. Ludulph does not mention the locations of the other houses, nor does it appear that he visited their ruins.

30. Zimmerman, *Monumenta*, 203.

while in 1273 two Carmelites of Acre, James and Dominic, were witnesses to a transaction between Thomas, treasurer of the Hospital, and a towns-man called Richard.[31] Acre, of course, was the capital city of the second kingdom of Jerusalem. Given its commercial and political importance and its geographical proximity to Mount Carmel, it would be surprising not to find Carmelites there once the campaign of expansion had begun. The only other Carmelite house in the Holy Land for which documentary evidence can be supplied is the convent at Tyre, which is mentioned in a bull of Urban IV.[32]

The only reason for connecting the hermits on Mount Quarantana with the Carmelites is that in Jacques de Vitry's text it precedes a short passage on the hermits who followed the example of Elijah by living on Mount Carmel. Presumably Ribot knew that a Latin monastic foundation had flourished on Mount Quarantana in the twelfth century. But the topo-graphical exactitude of Jacques in describing the location of the hermits on Carmel makes it unlikely that he could have intended both sets of hermits to be Carmelites. Moreover, Jacques was active in the Holy Land between 1216, when he became bishop of Acre, and 1227, when he left for France. His appointment as patriarch of Jerusalem in 1240 came just before his death, before he could embark for Outremer. He could only have known of the hermitage on Mount Carmel before the building program of the 1260s and 1270s, and before the expansion of the Order in the Holy Land and beyond.

The transplanting of the Order into western Europe, approved by Inno-cent IV, had been predicted, according to Daniel a Virgine Maria, by "Cyril of Constantinople," who had died in 1234. It was important that the Order be spread "among men of different nations," so that when the "persecution, because of which they had to leave the Holy Land" came, the Order might not be eradicated.[33] With hindsight, this seems logical enough. But Ribot, speaking through William of Sandwich, provincial of the Order in 1291, attributed the collapse of the Carmelites in the Holy Land to this very policy of transplantation: "When this holy Order began to transplant itself away from the Holy Land and go across the seas, then it began to be eradicated in Palestine."[34] Vocations and funds, Ribot explains, were

---

31. Röhricht, *Regesta*, nos. 1334, 1389–91.
32. *Bullarium Carmelitanum*, 1:523.
33. Daniel, *Speculum Carmelitanum*, 1:98.
34. Ribot, *De institutione* 9.8. "Quando autem haec sacra Religio incoepit de Terra Sancta ad cismarinas partes per modum praedictam transplantari, tunc etiam coepit ipsa in Terra Sancta de Palestina eradicari."

drained from the Carmelite projects in Palestine to the safer European foundations. This change merely reflected a general tendency in the direction of popular piety: "In those days no one dared to make the pilgrimage of the Christians to the tomb of our Lord. Because of this the Brothers of this Order, who used to be sustained in their monastery in Jerusalem by the alms of pilgrims, were in danger of starving."[35]

But even if Christians were no longer making the pilgrimage to Jerusalem because the tolls demanded by the Muslims made access too difficult and expensive, the function of the Carmelites in the Holy Land need not have been jeopardized. After all, they had started in the difficult conditions of 1187–1204, in a state of chronic warfare. They were supposed to be poor hermits, owning no property. But the papal bulls of the 1250s–60s show how radically the Order had changed. The bull of Alexander IV, *Vitae perennis gloria* (1261), tried to encourage pilgrims by granting an indulgence to everyone who visited a Carmelite church in Syria or Cyprus.[36] In another bull of the same year, *Speciali gratia*, he confirmed the Order's status under the protection of the Holy See. The Carmelites, by becoming friars, had also become dependent on Christian society for their upkeep.

Four years later, in 1265, the incursions of Sultan Baibars scattered the Carmelites from Mount Carmel itself, and Clement IV was forced to make a special appeal to European bishops to welcome fleeing Carmelites.[37] The state of crisis was ended by the treaty of 1268, which restored Carmel to the Latin kingdom, but perhaps too much damage had already been done to Christian confidence. Paradoxically, it is at this time—when with hindsight it is easy to absolve Europeans of any further interest in the Holy Land— that the Carmelite campaign of expansion was at its greatest extent. Ribot's disappointment in the failure of alms does not tell the whole story. What he found most irksome was not that Christians ignored the Carmelites in general, but the diversion of alms from the foundation on Mount Carmel to

---

35. Ibid. "In diebus autem illis nulla audebat fieri peregrinatio Christianorum ad sepulchrum Domini: propter quod Fratres huius Religionis, qui in Monasterio Ierosolymitano solebant de eleemosinis peregrinorum sustentari, tunc fame periclitabantur." William refers only to the poverty of the monastery at Jerusalem, to which access became increasingly difficult after 1244, when the city was recaptured by the Turks. There were long stretches when the papacy forbade pilgrims to visit Jerusalem because it was in the hands of infidels.

36. *Bullarium Carmelitanum*, 1:21.

37. Ibid., 32.

Carmelite houses in Europe. Indeed, during the period 1258 to 1291 the Carmelites achieved their most rapid expansion in England.[38]

Ludulph von Suchem spoke, in the 1350s, of an Order of "begging friars," a term that makes them indistinguishable from the Franciscans, Dominicans, and Augustinians. About 150 years after Albert's Rule, the Order had changed almost beyond recognition. The reasons for these changes, the ways in which they were achieved, and the reception of the Carmelites as friars in Europe lie at the heart of Ribot's *De institutione* and subsequent Carmelite historiography. The history of the Carmelites is the history of ecclesiastical change, and even of the decline of monasticism as the preeminent spiritual force of the church. The fluidity that must have characterized the original foundation hardened in the first quarter of the thirteenth century. The Rule of Albert brought the hermits under the supervision not only of the local ecclesiastical authorities but of the papacy as well. Subsequent developments lay in the hands of popes and were dictated by papal politics as much as by local conditions. The transformation of the hermits of Carmel into begging friars with priories across Europe, from Cyprus to Britain, by the end of the century, shows a new direction of spirituality. It may be, as Ribot lamented, that pilgrims lost interest in Mount Carmel as the fortunes of the kingdom waned, but in a broader perspective the church's needs had simply outgrown the type of eremitical monastic foundation that the Carmelites represented. There were many new foundations in the West in the thirteenth century, but most of them were, or became, like the Carmelites, Orders of friars.

Such considerations, however, belong properly to another book. The origins of the Carmelite foundation show us the problems and the nature of Latin monasticism in the Latin East. From the tangled and contradictory evidence of Ribot and the pilgrimage literature, a picture emerges of an ancient holy site with a sufficient spiritual charge from its biblical associations with Elijah to attract hermits. It may have been the fall of the kingdom of Jerusalem in 1187 that made Carmel particularly attractive as a sanctuary for monks and hermits, but there can be no doubt that Elijah was recognized in both Eastern and Western traditions as the originator of the eremitical life, and that this reputation explains the original impetus to settle on the mountain.

In the last years of the twelfth century and the early years of the thirteenth, a number of vibrant communities of Orthodox and Frankish monks

---

38. K. J. Egan, "Dating English Carmelite Foundations," *Carmelus* 23 (1976), 96–118.

flourished in close neighborhood on Mount Carmel. The extent to which these communities overlapped is uncertain, but that the conditions for a mixed foundation existed is indisputable. The revival of some of the most traditional features of Orthodox monasticism in Palestine in the twelfth century has already been demonstrated. The enterprise of the anonymous Calabrian in restoring the ruins of the early Christian monastery of Saint Elijah in the wadi 'Ain as-siah, and of the monks of Saint Margaret's in establishing a laura in the Cave of Elijah, are further manifestations of this tendency. The arrival of the Latin hermits who petitioned Patriarch Albert for a Rule turned Carmel into a monastic center of the same nature as the Black Mountain. The extent of contact between Latin and Orthodox monks on Mount Carmel can never be proven, but at least one lay lord, Bernherus, saw little to obstruct the joining of communities in the interests of good ecclesiastical government. In the uncertain times created by Saladin's invasion of 1187, the war of 1190–92 and the succession crises of the 1190s, it is reasonable to suppose that communities of hermits did much as they pleased, free from consistent external control. The fate of many Latin monasteries during this period can only be inferred, and for this reason the early history of the Carmelite hermitage is a vital, if obscure, chapter in the history of monasticism in the Latin East.

7

The Geography of Holiness

Underlying the phenomenon of eremitical or any kind of settlement in the Holy Land is the assumption that one place may be holier than another. The first Christians had proclaimed the irrelevance of special places for worshiping God—Jerusalem was no holier than Rome, for the whole world had been equally redeemed. The early Christians revolutionized mainstream Judaism precisely by making the whole of the created world neutral and uncharged. In a celebrated letter to Paulinus of Nola, Jerome questioned the importance of Jerusalem as a pilgrimage destination,[1] while at about the same time Gregory of Nyssa argued that the churches and altars of his native Cappadocia could not be less efficacious than those of the Holy

---

1. Jerome, *Epistolae* 63, *PL* 22:579–86.

Land.[2] In a sermon, Jerome explained the universality of Christ's redemption: "When I speak of the cross, I mean not the wood but the Passion. That cross is in Britain, in India, in the whole world. . . . Happy is he who carries in his own heart the cross, the resurrection, the place of the Nativity of Christ and of his Ascension."[3]

These were essentially the same arguments that were later used by Bernard and Peter the Venerable to discourage monastic pilgrimages and settlements in the Holy Land, with which we introduced this book. The evidence of Gerard of Nazareth, Jacques de Vitry, Godric of Finchale, and of the pilgrimage accounts shows that Franks were drawn to settle in the Holy Land as monks or hermits despite such doubts. As we have seen, they were able not only to follow the pattern of reform monasticism widespread in the West from the last quarter of the eleventh century, but also to learn from the native Orthodox monks devotion to particular sites. It is now time to examine more closely the nature of the attractions and compulsions at work in the lives of individual hermits.

Jerome had rationalized his own emigration to the Holy Land by explaining his need to be physically close to the biblical sites for a proper understanding of Scripture. Early Christian pilgrimages, such as that by Egeria in the 380s, are rooted in and assume a deep familiarity with the Scriptures. Egeria's geography was determined by the specific geography of the Bible: wherever the children of Israel had wandered on their way to Canaan, she too would go, even if it added unnecessary complications to her itinerary.[4] Egeria had little time for the new churches built to commemorate events in the Bible. She could relive the events themselves, with an appropriate liturgical celebration to accompany each site. For Jews, however, certain sites, notably the city of Jerusalem itself, had always been sacred, not so much because of what had happened there but because they had been set apart by God. This is enshrined in Scripture itself: "His foundation is in the holy mountains. The Lord loveth the gates of Zion above all the tabernacles of Jacob."[5] The course of Jewish history had maintained the sacred quality of the city of Jerusalem even while the Jewish people were in

---

2. Gregory of Nyssa, *Epistolae* 2.8–9, *PG* 46:1012.

3. Jerome, *Tractatus de Psalmo XCV*, ed. G. Morin, *CCSL* 78, 154.

4. *Itinerarium Egeriae* 9.6, *CCSL* 175:49–50. "And although, as I have said, I had already seen these places, . . . yet I wanted to learn fully all about the places the children of Israel had traversed as they marched from Rameses to Sinai; therefore it was necessary to return again to the land of Goshen."

5. Psalm 86:1–2.

exile. It was during the Babylonian Captivity that much of the Jewish Law was compiled, if not codified, and during the Roman diaspora that the necessity for an official codification of the Law became urgent, in order to preserve the integrity of rites that could no longer be performed in Jerusalem.

A Christian "holy place" was not the same as a "sacred place"—be that a city, like Jerusalem, or a pagan oracle.[6] Such a "sacred place" differs from all other places by virtue of God's choosing it—which gives the spiritual charge to events subsequently taking place there. Christians saw places in another way, for the lives of Christ and the apostles endowed places that had never before been "sacred" with the quality of "holiness"—Bethlehem, Nazareth, the Jordan, and so on—and resanctified Jerusalem by adding a fresh layer of charged sites, particularly Golgotha and the Sepulcher. Jerusalem was thus freed from its "sacredness," its having been marked out for the Jews by God, and was instead made "holy" by virtue of the act of redemption performed there. The Emperor Constantine's construction of churches on the sites of the birth, crucifixion, and resurrection of Jesus gave concrete shape to the idea of a Christian holy place. Writing to Macarius, bishop of Jerusalem, he referred to the discovery of the Sepulcher as a metaphor for his own discovery of Christianity.[7]

Eusebius, the emperor's biographer and panegyrist, was uncertain about this. The veneration of the Sepulcher, although in itself praiseworthy, should not be allowed to obscure the message of the Gospels. Had the Sepulcher never been discovered, the Gospels would not have been less convincing. Christians should not base their faith on the discovery of the tomb. Eusebius preferred to see the Anastasis church as symbolic of the power of salvation, as a harbinger of the final age, when the physical form of Jerusalem will be transformed: "So on the monument of salvation itself was the new Jerusalem built. . . . Perhaps this was that strange and new Jerusalem, proclaimed in the oracle of the prophets."[8]

Constantine's Christian rebuilding of Jerusalem renewed the city, and the renewal was a clear pointer to the New Jerusalem that was to come. The same deliberate playing on the theme of the heavenly city is found in the

---

6. The distinction here between "holy" and "sacred" is not intended to be philologically accurate, but rather to offer an interpretation of the way these sites were described. Latin pilgrimage accounts use "sanctus" universally, e.g., "sancta loca," *Antonini Placentini itinerarium*, ed. P. Geyer, CCSL 175:159; "sancta mons Syna," *Itinerarium Egeriae*, 37.

7. Eusebius, *Vita Constantini* 2.28, PG 20:1088–89.

8. Ibid., 2.33, PG 20:1093.

monastic chroniclers who tried to make the First Crusade comprehensible within the scheme of human salvation. Baldric of Dol, reflecting on the moment at which the crusaders first caught sight of Jerusalem, cannot resist the parallel between the walled Judaean town and the heavenly city:

> This city which you see is the cause of all our labor. This Jerusalem is the likeness of the heavenly Jerusalem; this city is the form of that to which we aspire. . . . Surely, if you consider well and properly, this Jerusalem which you see, to which you have come and before which you now stand, prefigures and portends that heavenly city.[9]

The preaching and reportage of the First Crusade explored the idea of the holiness of the Holy Land for the first time since the patristic age:

> This land we have deservedly called holy in which there is not even a footstep that the body or spirit of the Savior did not render glorious and sanctify, which embraced the holy presence of the mother of God, and the meetings of the Apostles, and drank up the blood of the martyrs shed there.[10]

The Holy Land was the theater of man's redemption: the place in which the history of salvation could be seen firsthand. In rationalizing the course of the crusade, the clerical chroniclers wrote of the Holy Land as though it were the rightful property of Christendom, and its seizure from the Muslims thus a redress of natural justice.[11]

This kind of assumption corresponds to what the American historical geographer J. K. Wright called "geopiety." Geographical understanding, as manifested in the writings of Americans until the "mid-third of the eighteenth century, . . . absorbed piety from the surrounding intellectual atmosphere as a towel does moisture from a down-East fog."[12] Wright's discussion was based on the treatment of physical topography according to a general "geopietic awareness," rather than on the understanding of cer-

---

9. Baldric of Dol, *Historia Jerosolimitana* 4.13, *RHC Occ.* 4:100–101.

10. Ibid. 1.4, *RHC Occ.* 4:14.

11. On this general theme, see J. Prawer, "Jerusalem in the Jewish and Christian Perspectives of the Early Middle Ages," *Gli Ebrei nell'alto medioevo*, Settimane di studi 26 (Spoleto, 1980), 739–95.

12. J. K. Wright, "Notes on Early American Geopiety," in his *Human Nature in Geography* (Cambridge, Mass., 1966), 253.

tain areas of the world in the light of religious history, but his terminology provides a useful formula for viewing the settlement of the Holy Land by the Franks in the twelfth and thirteenth centuries. A student of Wright, Yi-Fu Tuan, further explored the implications of the term "geopiety" as expressing a reciprocal relationship between humankind and the earth in specified locations.[13] The Holy Land might be said to have enjoyed such a relationship in the crusader period. The country itself was a relic, a spring of holiness, according to one report of Urban II's crusading sermon at Clermont in 1095: "If you aspire to the source of that holiness and glory, if you cherish these [places] which are the marks of his foot-prints on earth. . . ."[14] The land had been made holy by Christ's being born, living and dying there, and as a result it had the power to confer holiness on those who chose to live there.

The implication of Baldric of Dol's words as the crusaders stood in front of Jerusalem in 1099 is that the possession of the earthly city would make inevitable admission into the heavenly city. Thus also Eusebius had drawn the parallel between new Christian Jerusalem built by Constantine and the heavenly city. It is this parallel that lies at the heart of the monastic and eremitical settlement of the Holy Land.

Hermits and anchorites had always been a public feature of the Christian life of the Holy Land. The first and most celebrated followers of the exemplars Elijah and John the Baptist were attracted by the complete solitude of the Egyptian desert, but by the fourth century the more-fertile Palestine and Syria had the same appeal.[15] Hilarion, the Byzantine hermits of the Carmel region, and the fourth-century hermits described in Theodoret of Cyrrhus's *Religiosa historia* appear on the surface to have followed similar ascetic regimes to the masters of the *De vitis patrum*, and to have understood the same things of the monastic life.

These early Christian monks, however, cannot be seen as the true predecessors of the Frankish monks of the crusader states, such as Gerard of Nazareth's subjects or the Latin hermits of Mount Carmel. The purposes and expectations of the eremitical life may have remained remarkably

---

13. Yi-Fu Tuan, "Geopiety: A Theme in Man's Attachment to Nature and to Place," in D. Lowenthal and M. J. Bowden, eds., *Geographies of the Mind* (Oxford, 1976), 21.

14. Guibert de Nogent, *Gesta Dei per Francos* 2.4, *RHC Occ.* 4:138.

15. P. R. L. Brown, "The Rise and Function of the Holy Man in Late Antiquity," in his *Society and the Holy in Late Antiquity* (London, 1982), 109: "It was in Egypt that the theory and practice of the ascetic life reached its highest pitch of articulateness and sophistication. Yet the holy men who minted the ideal of the saint in society came from Syria, and later from Asia Minor and Palestine—not from Egypt."

uniform across eight centuries, but a new element had been introduced into the practice of the medieval hermits: the importance of geographical location. Emigrés from France, Italy, Spain, or the Low Countries who came to the Holy Land on pilgrimage or crusade but stayed behind as monks found something in the quality of the place itself that caused a spiritual charge they had not experienced in Europe. There was a new compulsion at work in the twelfth- and thirteenth-century hermits. They were choosing not just the eremitical life, but the eremitical life in the Holy Land rather than in a forest, village, or mountain glade close at hand.

Theodoret's monks—to focus on a single group of early Christian examples—were all natives of northern Syria, the region with which Theodoret himself was most familiar. Peter Brown has pointed to the felicity of the semi-desert of Syria as a place for hermits. It was less awesome, the solitude less total, than that of the Egyptian desert, and the Syrian hermit could not stay so far out of the reach of human society.[16] P. Canivet, from a different angle, argues that the solitary holy man became the main branch of Syrian monasticism because the monastic life of that region was itself not well defined. In the two cultural worlds of Syria, the Hellenistic and the Syriac, neither the Pachomian nor the Basilian models of monasticism could claim primacy.[17] Theodoret's hermits came from both worlds (of his eighty-seven examples, twenty-three have Semitic names, thirty-seven Greek, seventeen Latin, and 1 a Persian name), but they were all essentially indigenous. There is no indication that their impulse toward eremitism— or, more generally, monasticism—owed anything to the idea of the holy quality of a particular region.[18]

This is not to say that in the traditions of Eastern monasticism Jerusalem was not regarded as exercising or possessing holy qualities that might affect those who chose to live there. Thomas of Marga, compiling his *Book of the Governors* to present a Persian rival to the catalog of Egyptian ascetics, made use of the work of a contemporary from the monastery of Mount Izla who had copied Palladius's *Paradise* and visited the celebrated Egyptian eremitical site at Scete, and Jerusalem, to look for firsthand materials.[19]

---

16. Ibid., 110–12.

17. Theodoret of Cyrrhus, *Historie des moines de Syrie*, ed. and trans. P. Canivet and A. Levoy-Molinghen (Paris, 1977), 11–12.

18. Julian and his companions did make a pilgrimage—but to Sinai, because of its associations with Moses, rather than to Jerusalem (ibid. 2.13 [Canivet, 222–23]).

19. *The Book of Governors: The Historia Monastica of Thomas Bishop of Marga, A.D. 840*, ed. and trans. E. A. Wallis Budge, 2 vols. (London, 1893), 1:175.

One of Thomas's own subjects had done the very same: Mar Cyprian visited and worshiped in all the holy places in Jerusalem, as well as Mount Sinai, en route to the tombs of Anthony and Pachomius in Egypt.[20] Everywhere he went, Cyprian observed the customs of the monks:

> And just as the bee that is skillful in her handicraft formeth and buildeth up the honeycomb in her dwelling from herbs and grasses, so also did this holy man gather together habits of the monastic life from each of the holy men and did perfect them in himself; and having endued himself with the venerable garb of the monks in one of the monasteries of the orthodox which were there, . . . the chosen vessel deemed that henceforth he might become an anchorite.[21]

The impulse to the eremitical life, in Cyprian's case, sprang from the double source of the proven holiness of the Egyptian monks and the holy places themselves. A similar fusion can be seen in the story from the synaxarion of the Armenian Church of the Antiochene couple Andronicus and Athanasia. Having separated in order to live monastic lives in Egypt, they decided independently to make the pilgrimage to Jerusalem. On the way they met, by coincidence. Athanasia recognized her husband but did not reveal her identity to him, and they traveled together in mutual silence. Convinced that Athanasia was a monk of exceptional holiness, Andronicus proposed that they settle in a hermitage together on their return to Egypt. Athanasia agreed, but still did not tell her husband who she was, so they lived together in chaste and virtuous contemplation for a number of years until, on his wife's death, Andronicus laid out her body for burial and discovered her true identity.[22] In this story Jerusalem acts as a focus for the "spiritual marriage" of the couple, perfecting the earthly marriage they had abandoned. As with most synaxarion examples, the story represents an ideal of holy behavior rather than providing an inherently factual biography. The most significant aspect of the story in this context is the role of Jerusalem as a physical place which, through the attraction it exerts on monks, enables Andronicus and Athanasia to be reunited. Jerusalem is both the accepted place for the expression of monastic devotion and, figuratively,

---

20. Ibid., 2:585.

21. Ibid., 586–87.

22. *Le synaxaire arménien de Ter Israel*, ed. and trans. G. Bayan, *PO* 19 (1926), fasc. 1, 79–84.

the means by which the couple's perfection is achieved. Like Mar Cyprian, Andronicus and Athanasia know that Egypt is the unquestioned site of monastic "practical holiness," but the pilgrimage to Jerusalem is the pivot on which their fulfillment as Religious rests.

Another example from the Armenian synaxarion shows Jerusalem attracting the vocations of a whole family. The Byzantine merchant Xenophon sent his sons John and Arcadius to Beirut for their higher education. Their ship was wrecked and they were assumed dead, although they had managed to escape and reach land, whereupon they both became monks, one in Jerusalem and the other in an unspecified monastery. Later, Xenophon and his wife went on pilgrimage to Jerusalem, and heard from an elderly hermit that their sons were alive and well and living a life of holiness. In thanksgiving, Xenophon and his wife decided to stay in the Holy Land too, Xenophon becoming an anchorite and his wife entering a convent.[23] The Holy Land thus transformed the lives of a Christian family, enabling them separately to follow monastic careers that would have been impossible under normal circumstances.

Xenophon and his family, unlike Andronicus and Athanasia, remained behind in the Holy Land. Pilgrimage could in some cases attain a permanent hold over an individual's life, changing its direction irrevocably. Another Armenian example, John, bishop of Colonia, resigned his office, unable to cope with the demands it entailed. He went to Jerusalem on pilgrimage and, concealing his true identity, entered the monastery of Saint Sabas, where he worked as a porter, then kitchen boy, and finally guest-master. The abbot was so impressed with him that he insisted on having him ordained by the patriarch of Jerusalem. The secret came out, and John confessed that he was already a bishop but that he preferred an anonymous monastic life.[24]

The pilgrimage, and the adoption of the monastic life in Jerusalem, freed John from the spiritual despair that had beset him as bishop and thus enabled him to fulfill his vocation on earth. This radical break with his past was crowned with triumph when, during a raid by Persians, John's prayers for the safety of the monastery were answered by lions appearing to stand guard at the gate.

An example from the Jacobite synaxarion shows Jerusalem exercising the same compelling attraction to a royal princess who gave up an earthly

23. Ibid., 94–97.
24. Ibid., *PO* 21 (1930), fasc. 6, 458–62.

kingdom for its sake. Princess Matrona went to Jerusalem on pilgrimage accompanied by a bodyguard and attendants provided by her father. She was struck by the sudden desire to enter a convent but prevented from so doing by the bodyguard. She eluded her guards by writing a letter in which she explained that she was about to die but that her body would not be found anywhere after her death. In disguise, she gave her guard the slip and escaped to Jericho, where she found an old hermit who invested her with a monastic habit. She lived in the desert for twenty-eight years, until discovered by another hermit.[25] This fictional account (which seems to foretell the story of Christina of Markyate in the twelfth century) was popular enough to be included, with scarcely a change, in the synaxarion of the Ethiopian Church too.[26]

These stories, of varying degrees of fantasy, might be discarded as simple repetitions of common hagiographical *topoi* were it not for genuine examples of individuals from the tenth to the thirteenth centuries in whose lives the presence of Jerusalem or the Holy Land in general exercised a similar compulsion. Certain *topoi* continued to be used in formulaic stories because they were so compelling that they could be given verisimilitude by the lives of real hermits and monks. Jacques de Vitry observed the attraction for hermits of certain topographical features of the Holy Land. Some hermits chose to follow the example of the Savior, living on Mount Quarantana, where Jesus was traditionally supposed to have spent forty days in seclusion after his baptism. Other hermits, Jacques noted, preferred the example of Elijah and settled on Mount Carmel above Haifa, where they "led the solitary life in modest cells like beehives, abundant with spiritual sweetness."[27]

The hermits mentioned by Jacques de Vitry, the hermits of Mount Carmel and those who comprise what is left of Gerard of Nazareth's *De conversatione servorum Dei*, with a few other scattered references, are the fullest representations for the crusader period of the tradition glimpsed in the synaxarion stories. Gerard's work in particular should be seen as part of

---

25. *Le synaxaire arabe-jacobite (rédaction copte)*, ed. and trans. R. Basset, *PO* 3 (1909), fasc. 3, 290.

26. *Le synaxaire éthiopien*, *PO* 15 (1927), fasc. 5, 716, where the princess is said to be from Constantinople.

27. Jacques de Vitry, *Historia Hierosolymitana* 52 (Bongars, 1075). "Alii ad exemplum et imitationem sancti viri et solitarii Eliae Prophetae in monte Carmelo . . . non longe a monasterio beatae virginis Margaretae, vitam solitariam agebant in alvearibus modicarum cellularum, tamquam apes Domini, dulcedinem spiritualem mellificantes."

a broader trend in the Latin colonization of the Near East, which exempli-
fies the themes of devotion to the holy places and the claims that could be
made on them by Christendom.

Of Gerard's twenty-two hermits, eight were certainly born and raised in
Latin Europe and came to the Near East in adult life, only one is described
as a native of the Holy Land,[28] and the origins of the others are unknown,
though all have Frankish names and were of Frankish descent.[29] Gerard's
work is based largely on personal knowledge of the individuals discussed.
This is particularly the case with the two fullest accounts, those of Bernard
of Blois and Elias of Narbonne. Because Elias died in 1140 (by which time
Gerard was bishop of Laodicea), Gerard must have known him before he
himself began to climb the church hierarchy, possibly when a monk in
Nazareth.[30] The careers of Bernard and Elias can be placed in a reasonably
firm chronological context. Bernard visited Baldwin II in prison in 1123,
while Elias came to Jerusalem while Fulk was king (1131–43).[31] The
Hungarian hermit Cosmas, with unspecified companions, appears in a
charter of the Holy Sepulcher dated to 1135.[32] Most of the other hermits
were probably also active between the reigns of Baldwin I and Baldwin III
(1100–1162), but those before, say, the succession of Baldwin II (1118)
Gerard is unlikely to have known personally. Even those who are not
categorized as native to Latin Europe must have been first-generation
"pullani," whose parents had been among the first Frankish settlers, unless
they were born in the West and brought as young children to Outremer.

The career of Elias of Narbonne has already been outlined. Elias represents to an extreme degree the phenomenon of the unsettled individual
seeking in the Holy Land a resolution to professional or personal despair.
Gerard's account suggests that his initial intent was simply to perform the
traditional pilgrimage to the Holy Places: "On the advice of certain members of his family, he went to Jerusalem in the reign of King Fulk, there to

28. Rainaldus is described as "natione Galileus" (*Duodecima centuria*, col. 1604). Bernard
of Blois is not said definitely to have been born in Blois, but it must at any rate have been the
region from which his family came (col. 1605).

29. The apparent exception, Cyril "Carmelitus" (ibid., col. 1610), was not taken from the
De conversatione of Gerard but from John Bale.

30. Ibid., cols. 1379–80. Gerard is described briefly by the Centuriators as "patria Gali-
laeus, ordinis S. Benedicti monachus primum prope Nazareth, deinde apud Antiochiam
Carmelitanae sectae eremita." This, of course, is impossible, because the Carmelites did not
reach Antioch until the middle of the thirteenth century.

31. Ibid., cols. 1608, 910.

32. *Le cartulaire du Saint-Sépulcre*, 219–220.

make the round of the places of the birth, passion, and resurrection of the Lord."[33] Nothing is said of Elias's spiritual or emotional state of mind. There is no explicit statement (as will be seen, for example, with Guy of Pomposa or John of Parma) that the pilgrimage gave Elias an escape from the cares of everyday life or represented a natural progression in fulfilling his vocation. He did not, however, simply "go to" Jerusalem, but "sought" it (*petiit*). Although it is part of the standard vocabulary of pilgrimage, the word *petiit* suggests that the journey offered a challenge that Elias expected might change—or even better—his life. A little later, Gerard explains that while still in France Elias had determined to go to Spain to preach the Christian faith to the Muslims. He does not say whether the project was ever realized, but the fact that Elias was thinking in such terms reveals the channels along which his mind was working. Perhaps his family had vetoed the dangerous preaching trip in Spain in favor of the more conventional pilgrimage—but if that were the case it is noteworthy that he decided for the greater physical, and perhaps psychological, hardships of Jerusalem rather than Santiago de Compostela, nearer at hand. Elias's proposed evangelization of Spain indicates that he was seeking a spiritual and physical challenge that would enable him to break the routine of his life. Clearly he expected to find it in the pilgrimage to Jerusalem.

In the Holy Land, Elias became a "new man." At some point on his pilgrimage (Gerard says merely *in itinere*) he turned aside and took holy orders at a hermitage. The passage seems to suggest that he became a priest before reaching Jerusalem, completed his pilgrimage, and then retired to a large cave with some of the brethren from the hermitage.[34] In any case, his decision to embark on an eremitical life was simultaneous with his experiencing the Holy Land, whether it is attributed to the emotional charge of the places of Christ's birth, death, and resurrection or to the larger experience of peregrination.

Other hermits known to Gerard had also come to Jerusalem as pilgrims. Bartholomew, evidently of noble birth, abandoned his virtuous and beautiful wife and his homeland to make the pilgrimage, and there became a knight of the Temple. Later he retired to the Black Mountain to live a

---

33. *Duodecima centuria*, col. 1608. ". . . quorundam suorum familiarum consilio Hierosolymam petiit sub Fulcone rege, ut ibi loca nativitatis, passionis et resurrectionis Domini lustraret." The verb *lustraret*, here translated figuratively "made the round of," has a literal meaning of "purify" or "cleanse." Gerard may, in this context, want to suggest the effect of the pilgrimage on Elias with the same word that describes the activity of making the pilgrimage.

34. Ibid., col. 1608.

monastic life.[35] Hugo, described as *transalpinus*, came to the Holy Land as a crusader in the reign of Baldwin I but became a monk, first at Jubin, then at Machanath, doubtless following Bernard of Blois.[36] Valerius, a Burgundian knight, left his homeland to make the pilgrimage to Jerusalem but entered the cloister at Jubin instead. Later he chose to leave the monastery for a harsher life of total solitude and lived as a hermit for twelve years.[37] Ralph also came to Jerusalem on pilgrimage and intended to return to his homeland, but when he fell into the hands of pirates and was robbed he gave up and became a shepherd in the Holy Land. He would erect wooden crosses wherever his sheep grazed, establishing makeshift places of personal prayer and meditation. Eventually he entered the cloister at Carraria, but he evidently preferred the solitary life and fled to the wilderness again.[38] In the cases of Bartholomew, Hugo, and Valerius, all from the knightly class, the pilgrimage (or in Hugo's case, crusade) was to be in a sense perpetual: having seen the holy places and fulfilled their pilgrims' vows, they were unable to return to normal society. Ralph attempted to return, but gave up after a single try, which suggests that he was not convinced of the greater merit of going home.

Bartholomew, Hugo, and Valerius, and another hermit and monk of Machanath, William, also a knight, fall into a recognizable category of aristocrats who followed an extreme path of world-denial, giving up their wealth, status, and profession of arms for a life of anonymous humility.[39] Bernard and his companions who founded Clairvaux were all from the knightly class, and the Cistercian Order continued to rely on converted knights for membership.[40] What distinguished Gerard's knightly hermits was that in their case the Holy Land, rather than the cloister, exerted an irresistible force of attraction.

35. Ibid., col. 1605.

36. Ibid., col. 1606.

37. Ibid., col. 1607. Even as a hermit in the wilderness Valerius maintained a precarious contact with his cloister. Twice or three times a priest came from Jubin to celebrate Mass especially for him, and to give him Communion.

38. Ibid., col. 1608. Ralph died in Tripoli in 1142, having fled Antioch during the siege of John Comnenus in 1138. According to Gerard, his tomb in Tripoli became the center of a cult, where many were healed (ibid., col. 1753).

39. The model of the soldier-saint for the tenth to twelfth centuries is often taken to be Gerard of Aurillac, eulogized in Odo of Cluny's biography, *De vita sancti Geraldi Auriliacensis comitis*, *PL* 133:639–709. Gerard, however, retained his status in the aristocratic hierarchy even after embracing his "monastic life in the world," continuing to act as feudal lord to his vassals.

40. Bouchard, *Sword, Miter, and Cloister*, 46–64.

A further example of the denial of the secular aristocratic life for the eremitical, either unknown to Gerard or not included in the Centuriators' selection, is the career of William of Maraval, a French knight who abandoned his military past after an interview with Pope Eugenius III and went on pilgrimage to Jerusalem on the pope's instructions.[41] The pope commended him to the care and authority of Fulcher, patriarch of Jerusalem, to whom William duly reported after completing his pilgrims' vows. Fulcher offered to accommodate him in his entourage, presumably so that William might have the proper supervision for embarking on a holy, if still lay, life. The patriarch's words suggest the reformation of William's life, but only in the broadest terms. William rejected the offer, preferring a life of greater solitude. He asked to have built for him a little hut in the atrium of the patriarch's house, *instar umbraculi in vineis et turgurii leprosarum*, in which he lived for nine years.[42] He was in many ways a typical hermit, despite the unconventional habitat, displaying qualities that would have been universally recognizable as evidence of monastic conversion. "He sat in solitude, and kept silent, knowing that silence is the cult of justice. . . . He lived a pauper in his cell, but rich in his conscience, storing up treasure in heaven, but possessing nothing in the world."[43]

The decision to live in a cell within the patriarch's house corresponds to the tradition of anchorites living in cells adjoining parish churches followed by Wulfric of Haselbury in England, and in the Holy Land by another of Gerard's examples, Dominic.[44] Presumably William remained, though a layman, under the jurisdiction of the patriarch, and perhaps even followed a rudimentary Rule. Because William's meeting with Eugenius seems essentially to have been a confession, in which he was instructed to place himself under the authority of the patriarch of Jerusalem, the period of seclusion that followed may have taken the form of a penance.

William's seclusion was interrupted by a visit from friends who had heard rumors of his new life and had come from Europe to find and rescue him. Persuaded, by a rather rhetorical account of the abuses and horrors suffered by his homeland, that his duty lay elsewhere, he accompanied his friends to Italy, intending to live as a virtuous knight. But after being severely wounded in battle he realized his error and decided to return to Jerusalem.

41. *Theobaldi vita S. Guilelmi eremitae*, AASS, Feb. II, 459.
42. Ibid., 460.
43. Ibid., 459.
44. *Duodecima centuria*, col. 1604.

On the return journey he was captured by pirates, but released when it became apparent that he was a man of God. He lived another two years in solitude, but this time—to escape the pestering of former friends—in an unspecified wilderness, characterized as both physical and psychological.[45] He left the Holy Land to visit the shrine of Saint James at Compostela, returned to Italy, where he embarked on an unhappy career as superior of a monastery near Pisa, and eventually settled, in eremitical solitude once again, at Maraval, near Siena, where he died in 1157.[46]

The greater part of William's career was spent in France and Italy, but the interrupted interlude in Jerusalem was of greater importance. The pilgrimage to Jerusalem presented William with an opportunity to reshape his life. The stage of repentance had already been reached in the interview with the pope. The standard penance of making the pilgrimage to Jerusalem was then extended by the period of incarceration. The attempt to return to his previous life, albeit with a change of heart, was punished by his severe wound, making necessary a further and more rarefied eremitical existence. The second, shorter stage of eremitism in the Holy Land perfected his reform. Says William's biographer: "Christ has many soldiers who began strongly, stood firm, and conquered. But there are few who turned back from flight and reimmersed themselves once more in the danger from which they had escaped."[47] Like Ralph the shepherd, William was to find it impossible to leave the Holy Land so easily. The second stage may be seen as the necessary preparation for beginning a monastic life elsewhere, but the influence of Jerusalem was to be constant. Even after the Holy Land had been left behind, its psychological geography continued to pervade his actions. During his abortive return to the knightly life, and in his later career as a monk, his biographer uses the imagery and examples of the Old Testament to describe the events of his life—he is Saul, or Elijah, or Israel in Egypt.

William's experiences might be categorized as an extreme example of the penitential pilgrimage, but his story echoes even more the career of one of the most popular hermit-saints of the early church, Mary the Egyptian. A prostitute from Alexandria, Mary tried to enter the Church of the Anastasis in Jerusalem on the feast of the Invention of the Cross, but a heavenly force prevented her from passing through the door. Realizing that the obstruc-

45. *Theobaldi vita S. Guilelmi eremitae*, 462–63.
46. Ibid., 463–93.
47. Ibid., 462.

tion, which she alone felt, was caused by her sinful life, she repented on the spot and, guided by the Blessed Virgin, walked to the Jordan, where she lived as a hermit for the rest of her life.[48] Mary's initial impulse for going to Jerusalem was not penitential. She had accompanied a group of Alexandrian pilgrims in order to ply her trade, and only curiosity led her to the Anastasis. Once convinced of her sinfulness, however, there was no question of returning to Alexandria. The Holy Land—in Mary's case, the Jordan, where Christ was baptized—became the geographical as well as psychological expression of the new direction of her life.

This simple story, which had an understandable appeal for the medieval pilgrim to the Holy Land, is the pattern on which subsequent examples of the eremitical life in the Holy Land are based. This is not to say that Gerard of Nazareth, for example, necessarily relied on texts of Sophronius or Hildebert of Le Mans. Mary the Egyptian is an apocryphal example of a phenomenon illustrative of a strand of medieval piety. Long before the crusade and the Latin settlement, the Holy Land had provided a focus for the redirection of individual lives, as in the synaxarion examples already discussed.

One of the most adventurous of all Holy Land hermits was Symeon of Trier. Born in Syracuse of Greek parentage in the last quarter of the tenth century, Symeon was educated in Constantinople, but as soon as he was able he "ran to the tomb of the Lord."[49] His pilgrimage lasted seven years, for he stayed behind to work as a pilgrim guide—"a pauper wishing to follow the pauper Christ"—before moving to the banks of the Jordan, where he lived as companion to a hermit in a ruined tower. He entered monasteries, first in Bethlehem, then on Mount Zion, but he was always restless in a community and preferred to live for long periods as an anchorite, on one occasion attracting such attention that boatloads of tourists came to find him in his cave by the Red Sea. This disillusioned him sufficiently to try the cenobitic life again, but eventually he left the monastery for a series of travels that took him to the court of Duke Richard of Normandy and finally to Trier, where he ended his life living in a cell built into the Roman wall.[50]

Symeon's career is fascinating as an example of the breadth of monastic

---

48. The two fullest accounts of Mary's life are Sophronius, *Vita Sanctae Mariae Aegypticae, PL* 73:673–90, and Hildebert of Le Mans, *Vita Beatae Mariae Aegypticae, PL* 171:1321–40. See also Honorius of Autun, *Speculum Ecclesiae, PL* 172:906.

49. *Vita S. Symeoni, AASS,* June I, 87.

50. Ibid., 88–91.

experience that could be attained by an individual at the beginning of the eleventh century, but in this context what is of greatest importance is the initial location of his monastic career. Symeon chose to live in the Holy Land—rather than return to Constantinople or even to Syracuse—after his pilgrimage because he was unable to leave the places charged with the presence of Christ. When he did eventually leave, it was at the prompting of fellow monks rather than his own decision.[51]

The attraction of Jerusalem was also felt by Latin monks. John of Parma, born in 984, was given to the cathedral of Parma as an oblate and later became a canon. But "like Abraham, he left his country and family, and sought the holy places to be able to pray there, and went to Jerusalem, to the very sight of the tomb of the Lord."[52] He stayed behind in Jerusalem and took the habit of a monk, only returning to Italy because Sigifred, bishop of Parma, could find no one but John with sufficient qualities to be abbot of his new monastery. His stay in Jerusalem appears to have been brief and in his biography acts only as a prelude to the greater glories of his career as abbot of Parma. Nevertheless, it marked the beginning of his monastic vocation and may be seen as determining his future achievements. Like John of Colonia, he abandoned his previous niche, using Jerusalem as a way out from a life that had presumably lost its appeal. Being a monk in Jerusalem confirmed and recharged his spiritual life.

An almost identical contemporary example is Guy of Pomposa (d. 1046), a young Ravennese who escaped the marriage his father had arranged to go on pilgrimage to Rome, where he became a priest. From Rome Guy went to Jerusalem, intending, if Christ gave his approval, to remain there. In a dream, however, Christ summoned him back to Ravenna, where he was to fulfill his vocation for the solitary life under the guidance of an elderly hermit.[53] Although he never lived there, Guy's case gives Jerusalem an even more central place than John of Parma's. Guy's career was one of gradual progression to the eremitical life, from aristocratic youth to pilgrim, priest, and finally hermit. The theme of spiritual progression is emphasized by his

51. Ibid., 88. Symeon was chosen by the brethren of Mount Zion to go to Normandy to collect the donation promised by Duke Richard. He refused to go at first, until told that his obedience to the abbot required it. It is not difficult to believe that his brethren had lost patience with him and seized the opportunity to be rid of such a troublesome monk.

52. *Vita S. Iohannis, AASS*, May V, 180.

53. *Vita S. Guidonis abbatis Pomposiani, AASS*, March III, 910. Another anonymous life of Guy, *AASS*, March III, 918, does not mention the pilgrimage to Jerusalem at all.

two pilgrimages, the more familiar and less demanding journey to Rome, then the road to Jerusalem, the culmination of a pilgrim's aspirations. Even priesthood was for Guy a step on the spiritual ladder, but at the top was the eremitical life. Guy, like John, thought of Jerusalem as his destiny. But though he was called to live elsewhere, the pilgrimage to the holy city was the springboard for his future career, and sanctity, as a hermit.

Pilgrimage to Jerusalem continued to function as a watershed in the life of the penitent, the dissatisfied, or the bored, even when not followed by a lifetime of monasticism in the Holy Land. Rayner of Pisa, born to a prosperous bourgeois family in about 1115, was converted to the ideal of the monastic life by Albert of Corsica and began a lengthy period of voluntary seclusion and fasting in his parents' home. He went to Jerusalem around 1140, fasting for forty days on the ship (with the result that his uneaten food rotted, causing a stench that pervaded the entire ship).[54] After fulfilling his pilgrims' vows, Rayner lived as a wandering hermit in the Holy Land for a further thirteen years, in Nazareth, on Mount Tabor, on Mount Quarantana, and finally in Jerusalem. Although he was to return to Italy and end his life there, the intensity of his initial vocation could be fulfilled only in the Holy Land.

For two twelfth-century English hermits, as for Guy of Pomposa, Jerusalem was one stage on the road to the eremitical life. As a young merchant, Godric of Finchale made the pilgrimage in utter poverty and barefoot.[55] On a second visit some years later, he did not change his clothing until he reached the Holy Sepulcher, and wore rope-soled shoes that caused terrible blisters.[56] Between his two pilgrimages the course of his life had changed utterly. He gave up the life of commerce to become a hermit, living in the wilderness of northeastern England. Although Godric chose the eremitical life in his native land, Jerusalem continued to figure in his career. On one occasion a pilgrim who had just returned from the Holy Sepulcher made him a gift of some relics, which prompted a panegyric from Godric on the city of Jerusalem: "This city . . . is the type of supernal happiness, for which I have always sighed in my breast."[57] According to an anonymous

54. Benincasa, *De S. Rainerio Pisano*, *AASS*, June IV, 351. For a modern treatment of Rayner, see N. Caturegli, *Raineri Scacceri: Il santo di Pisa* (Pisa, 1961).

55. William of Newburgh, *De rebus Anglicis* 2.20, ed. R. Howlett, Rolls Series (London, 1884), 149.

56. Reginald of Durham, *Libellus S. Godrici*, 54.

57. Ibid., 301.

redaction of Godric's life, he visited Jerusalem on one occasion in spirit and reported back his experiences to his friends.[58]

Like Godric, the English hermit Roger, the companion of Christina of Markyate between 1118 and 1122, adopted the life of a solitary after a pilgrimage to Jerusalem.[59] As in the synaxarion legends, the city of Jerusalem itself exercised an appeal as a distant vision, powerful enough to draw individuals to itself and thereby change their lives. It was not necessary to live there permanently, like Gerard of Nazareth's hermits, but even those who returned home brought away with them something of the quality of the holiness they had seen or felt. Thus the detail of Roger's having been a pilgrim makes sense in the context of his patronage of the young anchoress Christina; he becomes her means of access to the holy city, just as Godric is for his friends. If the hermit who stays in the Holy Land is a perpetual pilgrim, the pilgrim who is converted to the eremitical life but returns afterward to a "normal" land forms a channel through which the deposits of holiness in Jerusalem may reach others.

Few of the scattered references to hermits in the kingdom of Jerusalem give much indication of the content of their lives, or of how their practice of eremitism might differ from that of hermits living in any other Christian society. Often we know their habitat: the rock tombs in the Valley of Jehosaphat, the Black Mountain, Mount Quarantana, a wadi on Mount Carmel. In general, hermits lived as they imagined their exemplars— Christ, Moses, Elijah, or John the Baptist—had done. This meant, of course, living in the actual spot where the exemplar had lived and accomplished the feats that made the land itself powerful. It could also entail following a certain occupation. Some hermits in Jerusalem, for example, were especially attracted to the care of lepers. Godric himself stayed in the Hospital of Saint John for several months helping with the care of the sick,[60] while two of Gerard's hermits—Ralph and Alberic—worked at a lazarhouse just outside the city. Ralph, although of noble birth, gave up everything to serve the lepers.[61] Alberic ate the scraps left by the lepers, kissed each of them daily at Mass, and washed and dried their feet. When he

---

58. Ibid., 131 n. 3.

59. *The Life of Christina of Markyate*, ed. and trans. C. H. Talbot (Oxford, 1959), 80–82.

60. Reginald of Durham, *Libellus S. Godrici*, 57.

61. *Duodecima centuria*, col. 1603. See above, Chapter 1. This is not the same Ralph who became a shepherd after being waylaid by bandits.

found himself disgusted by the blood and secretion from their sores mixed in the water, he immersed his face in the bucket and drank from it.[62]

Until the councils of Paris in 1212 and Rouen in 1214, lepers were not required to live in specially designated houses, but even before this they were customarily regarded as Christians who had been set apart from the rest of society for a unique kind of suffering. The terrible effects of the disease emphasized the "otherness" of the leper. The misfortune of leprosy could be explained only by the sin of the sufferer, which might provoke horror or pity from the unafflicted but might also give rise to the notion that the leper, by being chosen to suffer in a special way, was uniquely privileged in a similar fashion to those who voluntarily abdicated their position in the world: monks or hermits.[63] Lepers would eventually be set aside to the extent of living under a quasi-monastic Rule, with vows of poverty, chastity, and obedience. They came to be regarded as an Order within Christian society, ordained by God.[64] Their confinement to lazar-houses—as monks were confined to a cloister—was both protective and oppressive, with the effect of removing a dangerous element from healthy society. It was peculiarly fitting that hermits, who were voluntary outcasts from society, should be found caring for lepers, and even more so in Jerusalem, where Christ had performed his miracles of healing on lepers. Caring for lepers in Jerusalem was one way in which a hermit emphasized his separateness from the rest of society, by imitating the activities of Christ on earth.

The career of Rayner of Pisa in the Holy Land provides a further example of the same emulatory behavior. Rayner had been attracted by the forty-day fast before arriving in Jerusalem, but once there he repeated it on Mount Quarantana, in the very place where Christ had been tempted.[65] Rayner's progress is characterized by intense charges of spiritual power while imitating Christ's actions or following in his footsteps. In the Church of the Holy Sepulcher, where in full view of the public he stripped off his clothes and asked a priest to invest him with a pilgrim's robe, he had a vision of the Holy

62. Ibid.

63. L. Le Grand, *Statuts d'hôtels-Dieu et de léproseries* (Paris, 1901), xxvi–xxvii. For the subtle and sinister shift in attitudes to and treatment of lepers, see R. I. Moore, *The Formation of a Persecuting Society* (Oxford, 1987), 45–60.

64. As early as 1145, Louis VII referred to the lepers of Saint Lazare's, near Paris, as ensuring the salvation of their souls while living under bodily infirmity (Le Grand, *Statuts d'hôtels-Dieu*, xxvii).

65. *Vita S. Raynerii Pisani*, 354–55.

Spirit descending like a dove.[66] On Mount Tabor, where he spent forty days, he had a vision of the Transfiguration as if it were actually happening as he stood watching.[67] When he invited a beggar to share his food, the bread remained whole no matter how much was eaten, a miracle that happened ten times over. God told him later, "Today I have made you like me."[68]

On another occasion, after Rayner had been whisked miraculously from Jerusalem to Bethlehem, God used the same words:

> I have made you in the likeness of myself: for as I made myself the son of my people for the salvation of the human race, assuming flesh from my handmaid, and as I took that flesh up to heaven, where it is with me now, so now I am made the son of my Christian people, for their salvation, by putting on your flesh.[69]

This astonishing passage shows how far a hermit could go. From merely imitating the behavior of Christ, in the place where Christ lived, Rayner has been made into Christ on earth in his own day. In Christian teaching this was the expected fulfillment of all people's lives throughout the world, but the continued appeal of the Holy Land as a place for hermits to live reflects the assurance that it could best be accomplished in places that still contained in themselves a residue of holiness from the events that had taken place there.

"Geopiety," according to Yi-Fu Tuan, was expressed in ancient societies by love of a particular country, or patriotism.[70] This is understood to have changed with the spread of Christianity and the "neutralisation of the sacred," and the consequent process of sanctifying places through associations with individual acts of religious heroism. "The long-term effect of the Christian doctrine was to denude nature of its spirits and its mystery."[71] It is true that patriotism means very little in a medieval context when placed alongside literary examples from the ancient world. But the association of

---

66. Ibid., 352–53.
67. Ibid., 356.
68. Ibid.
69. Ibid., 357.
70. Yi-Fu Tuan, "Geopiety," 24: "The piety of the ancient Greeks and Romans was the love of country," citing Pericles's funeral oration from Thucydides, *History of the Peloponnesian War* 2.36, trans. C. F. Smith, Loeb Classical Library (London, 1951), 321.
71. Yi-Fu Tuan, "Geopiety," 26.

places with the lives of individuals did not necessarily remove "mystery" from a particular land. Fulcher of Chartres, looking back on the first generation of crusader settlement in the Holy Land, was not surprised that one day the sun appeared in the sky in the shape of a hyacinth bloom. Natural marvels were to be expected in the land where God worked daily wonders for his people.[72] Such blessings did not come only from the sky. In 1119 the tombs of the patriarchs Abraham, Isaac, and Jacob were miraculously discovered in a hidden cavern under the church at Hebron.[73] The appearance of new relics reinforced the perception of the Holy Land as a specially sanctified place. Such discoveries were not unique to the Latin East, but they had a special poignancy in the kingdom of Jerusalem. The canons of Hebron had long suspected the existence of the tombs, but did not know where to look for them until the location was revealed to one of their number. Points of contact with the history of salvation lay all around them; their discovery could be taken as a mark of special favor.

If "patriotism" in the terms that we understand it, as devotion to a sovereign state, is not applicable to medieval society, it may only mean that the word itself has undergone changes of meaning. Raymond d'Aguilers, a participant in the First Crusade, called the Old Testament prophets his *patres,* and the Holy Land the *patria* of Christendom.[74] Rayner of Pisa's biographer expresses the same thought when he describes the saint imitating Christ so successfully in the place where he accomplished the salvation of humankind. The language of the clerical chroniclers of the crusade describing the appeal of Jerusalem finds its tangible expression in the lives of those who followed the monastic vocation in the crusader states and by doing so abandoned lands, families, or careers there or in other lands.

A monastic purist like Bernard might see the dangers for monks of too close a mental association between the earthly and the heavenly Jerusalem, but the spare, fragmentary evidence of Gerard of Nazareth, the lives of individuals like William of Maraval, and the anonymous communities of Mount Carmel suggest that his was the minority view. As Burchard, a canon of Mount Zion in the 1280s, observed, "What hour is there of the day or night, all the year round, in which every devout Christian does not, by reading, singing, chanting, preaching or meditating read what has been

---

72. Fulcher of Chartres, *Historia Hierosolymitana* 3.37.3 (Hagenmeyer, 748).

73. *Canonici Hebronensis tractatus de inventione sanctorum patriarchum* 1–2, *RHC Occ.* 5:305–13.

74. Raymond d'Aguilers, *Historia Francorum qui ceperunt Iherusalem* 20, *RHC Occ.* 3:300.

done or written in this land, its cities and holy places?"[75] The weight of the daily liturgy impressed Jerusalem on devout Christians, so that it seemed its spiritual benefits could be enjoyed only by physically being there. "O solitude, in which those stones are born from which the city of the great king of the Apocalypse will be built!" cried Peter the Cantor.[76] The New Jerusalem would arise from the wilderness. To live in the wilderness of eremitism in the Holy Land was surely to prepare for the heavenly city.

75. *Peregrinatores medii aevi quatuor,* 20.
76. Peter the Cantor, *Verbum abbreviatum* 72, *PL* 205:213.

Conclusion

"Exposed to the world as I am, I groan to the very marrow of my being when I call to mind your death to the world and your solitude." Thus Peter the Venerable expressed to Gislebertus his envy of the hermit's way of life.[1] Even a cenobitic monk who, like Peter, doubted that human discipline was sufficient to maintain a truly spiritual life in solitude could recognize the power and long for the challenge of the eremitical ideal. Defenders of the eremitical life argued that solitude was nothing to fear. The hermit was never alone, declared Peter the Cantor, for in Christ's company he could glimpse the glory of God.[2]

In widely diverging traditions, and throughout the medieval period, the

1. Peter the Venerable, *Letters*, 1:28, Ep. 20.
2. Peter the Cantor, *Verbum abbreviatum* 72, *PL* 205:214.

solitary life was proclaimed as the consummation of monasticism, and hermits as the purest interpreters of the tradition established by Moses, Elijah, and John the Baptist. The heights of perfection that could be climbed in solitude were described in similar terms by both Eastern and Western monks. The Persian hermit Nerses was so inflamed by the Holy Spirit that when he attended divine services with other monks he could not concentrate on what was happening at the altar, so unused was he to dividing his mental capacity between the spiritual and the corporeal. Whereas the sacred mysteries raised the consciousness of most monks to God, Nerses had already attained a state of permanent union with God.[3] In twelfth-century England, Christina of Markyate's companion Roger was so absorbed by the Holy Spirit when praying that he did not even notice when the devil set fire to his cowl. "What think you then must have been the fire that burned inwardly in his spirit, when it rendered his body insensible to the material fire that burned without?"[4] The Syrian monk and later Jacobite patriarch of Antioch, Gregory bar Hebraeus, used a variety of images to describe this state of true contemplation, none finer than that of the dove:

> When, by the hard labours of asceticism, the body has been cleansed and the mind purified, the windows of the senses have been shut and the room of the heart is enlightened, then the dove will show herself to the mind: not lastingly, however, but as a flash of lightning which appears and vanishes, she shows her beauty, making sweet her fruit to the palate.[5]

As the broad range of these examples indicates, this state of monastic perfection could in theory be attained anywhere. Solitude, as Peter the Venerable commented in another letter, was internal, not dependent on outside forces.[6] Hermits could be found throughout the Christian world in the Middle Ages, living in woods or mountain glades, in caves overlooking deep gorges, in cells built into city walls or adjoining village churches, on islands or in the desert.

In practice, however, it was impossible to stop even highly sophisticated monks, who knew intellectually that no one place ought to give greater spiritual benefits than another, from aspiring to the Holy Land as

---

3. Thomas of Marga, *Book of the Governors* (1893 ed.), 2:540.

4. *Life of Christina of Markyate* (Talbot ed.), 105.

5. Gregory bar Hebraeus, *Book of the Dove* 3, ed. and trans. A. J. Wensinck (Leiden, 1919), 1.

6. Peter the Venerable, *Letters*, 1:188, Ep. 59.

the ultimate source of monastic perfection. Some Westerners—such as William of Maraval or Godric of Finchale—found that the experience of pilgrimage and penance in the Holy Land changed the direction of their lives. For those who had already decided on a monastic career, like Rayner of Pisa, the *eremum* of the Holy Land refined their vocation and trained them for future achievements. Others, of whom Elias of Narbonne or the converted knights who joined Bernard of Blois's new foundation at Jubin are examples, found this sense of place strong enough to compel them to settle permanently in the Holy Land. This was not a Western phenomenon alone. Neophytus the Cypriot roughly parallels Rayner of Pisa, while the subject of one of his hagiographies, Gabriel, and the Georgian hermits discovered by John Phocas correspond to the Frankish monks described by Gerard of Nazareth.

The qualities of the land itself, sanctified as it was by the footsteps of Jesus, the apostles and the martyrs, attracted Orthodox and Latins alike. The Old Testament prophets who were regarded as proto-hermits had lived in the Judaean desert, or on Mount Carmel, or in Galilee, and a natural and organic line of descent could be traced from them to the early Christian monastic heroes, such as Sabas, Hilarion, and Euthymius. Nowhere else could such intimate contact with the roots of monasticism be found; nowhere else did the monk live so fully in the spiritual past. The other great breeding grounds of early monasticism, Egypt and Syria, had been dislocated from Mediterranean Christianity by a combination of the doctrinal and political struggles of the fifth and sixth centuries and the Arab invasions of the seventh century. Palestine, because of its strong Greek Orthodoxy, remained relatively intact. When the crusaders wrested Palestine and western Syria from the Muslims, they found the strong links of the Christian population to the center of the Greek Orthodox world damaged but not broken. The Crusades exposed early Christian monastic traditions to view once more and made it possible for Westerners to imitate forms of life previously known to them only through literary texts. The Frankish warriors who captured Jerusalem could see themselves as the Israelites smiting the Amalekites; the monks who settled in the Holy Land, as the pioneers who built laurae in the cliff sides of the Judaean desert.

A similarity of purpose and ideal enabled monks from differing doctrinal traditions and who used different liturgies and worshiped in different languages to share the same sites. This was true of established cenobitic sites, such as Mount Tabor with its neighboring houses of Latin and Orthodox monks, of individual hermits in the Valley of Jehosaphat, and especially of the nascent community on Mount Carmel. The significance of this is more difficult to assess than its actual occurrence. Save for the rare case where one can determine the Orthodox origin of a specific eremitical practice, as in Godric's diet, the influence of Orthodox practice on Franks must be inferred rather than demonstrated. Naturally, individuals were susceptible to influence in a way that communities were not; thus Ursus, one of Gerard of Nazareth's hermits, seems to betray some of the traits of Orthodox eremitical monasticism seen in the career of Gabriel the Stylite. But insofar as such influence was important, it seems to have been above all one of attachment to place rather than of example in the organization of communities. Latin hermits needed to learn nothing from the Orthodox about the practice of the eremitical monasticism—they had the examples of dozens of such foundations in the West. The sources give us tantalizing glimpses of potential influences, but rarely show us whether the effects of such potential were realized. But in looking too closely for the influence of Eastern traditions on Western traditions, we may be asking questions that would not have occurred to our subjects themselves. Franks like Gerard of Nazareth or Godric of Finchale may have taken for granted what we find noteworthy: that they shared common assumptions about the virtues of the eremitical life and the spiritual charge to be tapped in certain holy places. Fundamentally, eremitical monasticism was not dependent on doctrine or even on liturgy; its basis was spiritual and historical.

The history of such communities as can be followed in the Latin East suggests that they followed Western practice closely—perhaps too closely. The failure of Latin foundations cannot be attributed solely to the failure of the Franks to retain territory in the thirteenth century; some of them had begun to decline already in the twelfth century. Jubin faltered, and survived only by purging its reforming elements; Palmaria, originally an eremitical community, overthrew its reform-minded abbot. They could be saved only by absorption into the centralized Orders of Cîteaux and Cluny. The best-documented and most intriguing foundation, the Carmelite, adopted the alternative route of establishing independence by obtaining direct papal recognition. But Mount Carmel is an example of the ultimate failure of the Frankish eremitical enterprise. A disparate community of hermits, which may have comprised Latin and Orthodox, requested a Rule in order to maintain their coherence. From the rudimentary guidance they received from Albert of Vercelli, the Carmelites had within a century become a mendicant Order comparable not to the Cistercians or the Cluniacs but to the Franciscans and the Dominicans. The eremitical practices that characterized the foundation in the wadi 'Ain as-siah had been abandoned.[7] Such an expansion indicates some success, but Neophytus probably would not have been impressed.

What can explain the different routes taken by the revived Orthodox monasticism in the twelfth-century Latin East and the new eremitical foundations of Latin monks? External political conditions, to begin with. Manuel Comnenus poured money into specific building and restoration projects as part of imperial policy. Orthodox monks were untroubled by the Latin episcopacy and therefore suffered none of the intervention experienced on the Black Mountain under Aimery of Antioch. The direction taken by monasticism on Mount Carmel owed something to the political instability of Galilee, quite probably after the disaster of Hattin and certainly in the middle of the thirteenth century. But we must look deeper than this. At root, eremitical monasticism in the West was a reforming movement, a new broom to sweep Benedictine cloisters clean. The reform that Henrietta Leyser has characterized as the "new monasticism" met needs and desires that were not adequately met for all monks in established monasteries. This process was at its peak in the years between about 1050 and 1130, but by the time it had begun to be effective in the Latin East, in the 1130s and 1140s, the Western reform movement was already losing much of its eremitical force. The Carmelites may be seen as the last representatives of the "new monasticism." Eremitical foundations of the late eleventh century like Cîteaux had, one hundred years later, become absorbed into the church establishment, and the "new monks" of the early thirteenth century were the mendicant followers of Francis and Dominic. Compared with the followers of Robert of Molesme or Robert of Arbrissel in the West, the monks described by Gerard of Nazareth were latecomers, operating at the tail end of the monastic reform movement.

The direction of change in Latin foundations in the crusader states was part of the natural rhythm of change within the Western Church. By contrast, the Orthodox Church moved to its own rhythm, based less on periodic cycles of reform and entrenchment than on imitation of an invari-

---

7. This was recognized, and lamented, by at least one section of the Carmelite Order in the later thirteenth century. The seventh prior-general, Nicholas Gallicus (1265–70), resigned his office and retired to Mount Carmel, where he wrote the *Ignea sagitta*, an agonized plea for a return to the values and way of life of the first hermits. The *Ignea sagitta* was edited by A. Staring in *Carmelus* 9 (1962), 271–307.

able tradition.[8] The indigenous hermits and monks of the Holy Land were not trying, like Bernard of Blois, to break away from existing conditions, or to found something new, like Elias and his companions in the cave in the Valley of Jehosaphat. They cultivated, instead, the ruins of early Byzantine monasteries, such as Saint Elisha on Mount Carmel or Saint John the Baptist in the Jordan Valley, and appealed for funds in restoring them. They were the direct followers of Elijah, of Sabas, Euthymius, and the monks who had been martyred by the Persians in 614. They had no concept of reform, but rather saw themselves as preserving an organic tradition rooted in the history of the land itself.

For Western monks, the tendency to seek the historical roots of monastic traditions never rose above the level of exegesis. Scholarly monks might, like Peter the Venerable, automatically think of hermits as the imitators of the desert fathers,[9] but they were unwilling or unable to take such imitation as literally as Orthodox monks. The only coherent attempt to identify monastic practice as derived from the unbroken procession of monks or hermits on a particular site was the Carmelites' invention of historical tradition, exemplified in this book by Philip Ribot. By acknowledging the human as well as sacred history of their chosen holy place, the Carmelites were able to present themselves as the heirs of an unbroken lineage of eremitical monasticism. Ironically, they had by this time long ceased even to be hermits, and the Carmelite production of a historical tradition is part of the fraught history of mendicant relations in the thirteenth and fourteenth centuries, rather than of the monastic culture of the Latin East.

---

8. "The characters, the settings, the costumes, are always different; the action does, always, vary; but the essential dynamic behind it does not" (Galatoriotou, *The Making of a Saint* 3, speaking of the process of sanctification in Orthodox culture).

9. Peter the Venerable, *Letters*, 1:29, Ep. 2, quoting the Egyptian abbots Moyses and Arsenius, from *De vitis patrum* 3.109 and 190, *PL* 73:781, 801.

Selected Bibliography

It would be futile to attempt a comprehensive survey of the existing bibliography for all the themes covered in this book. I have therefore restricted myself to the major texts used. More bibliographical information is given in the footnotes.

Primary Sources

al-Harawi, Ali ibn abi Bakr. *Guide des lieux de pèlerinage.* Ed. and trans. J. Sourdel-Thomine. Damascus: Institut Français de Damas, 1953.

"Annales de Terre Sainte." Ed. R. Röhricht and G. Raynaud. *Archives de l'Orient Latin* 2 (1884), 427–61.

Anon. "The First and Second Crusades from an Anonymous Syriac Chronicle." Trans. A. S. Tritton with notes by H.A.R. Gibb. *Journal of the Royal Asiatic Society,* 1933, part 1, 69–101; part 2, 273–305.

Anonymi Gesta Francorum. Ed. H. Hagenmeyer. Heidelberg, 1890.

Antonini Placentini itinerarium. Ed. P. Geyer. *CCSL* 175. Turnhout, 1965.

The Arabic Life of St. Pisentius. Trans. De Lacy O'Leary. *PO* 22, fasc. 3. Paris, 1930.

Bale, John. *Cronica seu fascicula temporum ordinis Carmelitarum.* Oxford, Bodleian Selden Supra MS 41.

Benjamin of Tudela. *Itinerary.* Critical text, translation, and commentary by M. N. Adler. London: H. Froode, 1907.

Bibliotheca Carmelitana, notis criticis et dissertationibus illustratum. Ed. C. de Villiers. Orléans, 1752. New ed. by G. Wessels. Rome: Institutum Carmelitanum 1927.

The Book of Governors: The Historia Monastica of Thomas Bishop of Marga, A.D. 840. Ed. and trans. E. A. Wallis Budge. 2 vols. London, 1893.

Bostius, Arnoldus. *De illustribus viris ordinis fratrum beatissime Virginis Mariae de Monte Carmelo.* Ed. Christine Jackson-Holzberg. *Zwei Literaturgeschichten des Karmelitenordens. Untersuchungen und kritische Edition.* Erlangen: Palm & Enke, 1981.

Bradley, Thomas. *Libellus de institutione fratrum Carmelitanum ordinis.* Cambridge University Library MS Ff 6.11.

Die Briefe des Petrus Damiani. Ed. V. Reindel. 3 vols. *MGH.* Munich, 1983–89.

Bullarium Carmelitanum, plures complectens summorum pontificum constitutiones . . . de Monte Carmelo spectantes. Vol. 1. Rome, 1715.

Le cartulaire du Saint-Sépulcre de Jérusalem. Ed. G. Bresc-Bautier. Paris, 1984.

"Chartes de l'abbaye cistercienne de Saint-Serge de Giblet en Syrie." Ed. E. Petit. *Mémoires de la Société Nationale des Antiquaires de France,* 5th ser., 8 (1887), 20–30.

"Chartes de l'abbaye de Notre-Dame de la Vallée de Josaphat en Terre-Sainte." Ed. Ch. Kohler. *Revue de l'Orient Latin* 7 (1899), 108–222.

"Chartes de l'abbaye du Mont-Sion." Ed. E.-G. Rey. *Mémoires de la Société Nationale des Antiquaires de France,* 5th ser., 8 (1887), 31–56.

Chartes de la Terre-Sainte provenant de l'abbaye de Notre-Dame de Josaphat. Ed. H.-F. Delaborde. Bibliothèque des écoles françaises d'Athènes et de Rome, fasc. 19. Paris, 1880.

Chronique d'Ernoul et de Bernard le Trésorier. Ed. L. de Mas Latrie. Paris, 1871.

"La chronique de Terre-Sainte." Ed. G. Raynaud. *Les gestes des Chiprois.* Société de l'Orient latin, Ser. historique 5. Geneva, 1885.

The Chronography of Gregory Abu'l Faraj, . . . commonly known as Bar Hebraeus. Ed. and trans. E. A. Wallis Budge. London: Oxford University Press, 1932.

Enchiridion locorum sanctorum. Ed. D. Baldi. Jerusalem: Typis P. P. Franciscanorum, 1935.

Fulcher of Chartres. *Historia Hierosolymitana.* Ed. H. Hagenmeyer. Heidelberg: Universitäts-Buchhandlung, 1913.

Gregorii Barhebraei chronicon ecclesiasticum. Ed. and trans. J. B. Abbeloos and T. J. Larry. 3 vols. Paris, 1872–77. (Latin)

Gregory bar Hebraeus. *The Book of the Dove and Ethikon.* Ed. and trans. A. J. Wensinck. Leiden: E. J. Brill, 1919.

Guiges I. *Coutumes de Chartreuse.* Ed. and trans. "un chartreux." Paris: Editions du Cerf, 1984.

Hugh of St. Victor. *Exegetica dubia in Scripturam Sanctam. PL* 175:633–751.

Hugh the Frenchman. "Tractatus de conversione Pontii de Larazio." Ed. Etienne de Baluze. In *Miscellanea.* Lucques, 1761. 1:179–84.

Itinera Hierosolymitana Crucesignatorum. Ed. S. De Sandoli. Vol. 2. Jerusalem: Franciscan Printing Press, 1980.

Itinera Hierosolymitana et descriptiones Terrae Sanctae. Ed. T. Tobler and A. Molinier. 2 vols. Geneva, 1879–95.

Itinéraires à Jérusalem et descriptions de la Terre-Sainte rédigés en français aux XIe–XIIe et XIIIe siècles. Ed. H. Michelant and G. Raynaud. Geneva, 1882.

Itinerarium Egeriae. CCSL 175. Turnhout, 1965.

Jacques de Vitry. *Historia Hierosolymitana.* In J. Bongars, ed., *Gesta Dei per Francos.* Hanau, 1611.

———. *Lettres.* Ed. R.B.C. Huygens. Leiden: E. J. Brill, 1960.

Jerusalem Pilgrimage, 1099–1185. Ed. J. Wilkinson. London: Hakluyt Society, 1988.

John Kinnamos. *The Deeds of John and Manuel Comnenus.* Trans. Charles M. Brand. New York: Columbia University Press, 1976.

John Phocas, *Descriptio Terrae Sanctae. PG* 133:927–63.

Die Kreuzzugsbriefe aus dem Jahren 1085–1100. Ed. H. Hagenmeyer. Innsbruck: Universitäts-Buchhandlung, 1901.

Laurent, M.-H. "La lettre 'Quae honorem conditoris' (1 Octobre 1247)." *Ephemerides Carmeliticae* 2 (1946), 5–16.

The Letters of Lanfranc, Archbishop of Canterbury. Ed. and trans. H. Clover and M. Gibson. Oxford: Clarendon Press, 1979.

Lettres des premiers chartreux, S. Bruno, Guiges, S. Anthelme. Ed. and trans. "un chartreux." Paris: Editions du Cerf, 1962.

Libellus de diversis ordinibus et professionibus qui sunt in aecclesia. Ed. and trans. G. Constable and B. Smith. Oxford: Clarendon Press, 1972.

The Life of Christina of Markyate, a Twelfth-Century Recluse. Ed. and trans. C. H. Talbot. Oxford: Clarendon Press, 1959.

Matthew of Edessa. *Chronique et continuation de Grégoire le prêtre.* Ed. and trans. E. Dulaurier. Paris, 1858.

Matthias Flacius Illyricus et al. *Duodecima centuria.* Vol. 6 of *Ecclesiasticae historiae, integram ecclesiae Christi ideam . . . secunda singulas centurias perspicuo ordine complectens.* 7 vols. Basel, 1562–74.

Michael the Syrian. *Chronique.* Ed. and trans. J.-B. Chabot. 4 vols. New ed. Brussels: Culture et Civilisation, 1963.

Monumenta historica Carmelitana. Ed. B. Zimmerman. Vol. 1. Lérin: Ex typis abbatiae, 1907.

Odo of Deuil. *De profectione Ludovici VII in orientem.* Ed. and trans. V. G. Berry. New York: Columbia University Press, 1948.

Payen Bolotin. *De falsis heremitis qui vagando discurrunt.* Ed. J. Leclercq. "Le poème de Payen Bolotin contre les faux ermites." *Revue Bénédictine* 68 (1958), 77–84.

Peregrinatores medii aevi quatuor: Burchardus de Monte Sion, Odoricus de Foro Julii, Ricoldus de Monte Crucis, Willibrandus de Oldenborg. Ed. J.C.M. Laurent. Leipzig, 1864.

Peter Damian. *Vita sancti Romualdi.* Ed. G. Tabacco. Rome: n.p., 1954.

Peter the Cantor. *Verbum abbreviatum.* PL 205:21–555.

Peter the Venerable. *Letters.* Ed. G. Constable. 2 vols. Cambridge, Mass.: Harvard University Press, 1967.

Philip of Harvengt. *De institutione clericorum.* PL 203:663–1203.

"Philippi descriptio Terrae Sanctae." Ed. W. Neumann. *Österreichische Vierteljahresschrift für katholische Theologie* 11 (1872), 1–78, 165–74.

The Pilgrimage of the Russian Abbot Daniel in the Holy Land. Trans. Col. C. W. Wilson. *PPTS* 4. London, 1895.

Recueil des historiens des croisades. Paris, 1841–1906.

Historiens Occidentaux. Ed. A. Beugnot et al. 5 vols. 1844–95.

Documents Arméniens. Ed. Ch. Kohler. 2 vols. 1869–1906.

Historiens Orientaux. 5 vols. 1872–1906.

Historiens Grecs. 2 vols. 1875–81.

Recueil des plus anciens actes de la Grande Chartreuse 1086–1196. Ed. B. Bligny. Grenoble: CNRS, 1958.

Regesta regni Hierosolymitana, 1097–1291. Ed. R. Röhricht. Berlin, 1892.

Regesten der Kaiserurkunden des Ostromischen Reiches. Ed. F. Dolger. Fasc. 2. Munich, 1925.

Reginald of Durham. *Libellus de vita et miraculis S. Godrici, heremitae de Finchale.* Surtees Society. London, 1847.

La règle de l'Ordre de la Bienheureuse Vierge Marie du Mont Carmel. Ed. and trans. M. Battmann. Paris: Desdée du Brouwer, 1982.

Ribot, Philip. *De institutione et peculiaribus gestis religiosorum Carmelitarum.* London, Lambeth Palace, Ms. 192.

Rorgo Fretellus de Nazareth et sa description de la Terre Sainte. Ed. P. C. Boeren. Amsterdam: North-Holland Publishing Company, 1980.

Rupert of Deutz. *De victoria verbi Dei. PL* 169:1215–1502.

S. Anselmi Cantuarensis Archiepiscopi opera omnia. Ed. F. S. Schmitt. 6 vols. Stuttgart: Frommann, 1968.

S. Bernardi opera. Ed. J. Leclercq, H. Rochais, and C. H. Talbot. 8 vols. Rome: Editiones Cistercienses, 1957– .

"Saints de Chypre." Ed. H. Delehaye. *Analecta Bollandiana* 26 (1907), 161–301.

Sancti Benedicti regula monachorum: Textus ad fidem cod. Sangall. 914. Ed. P. Schmitz. Brussels: Editions de Maredsous, 1949.

Speculum Carmelitanum, sive historia eliani ordinis fratrum beatissime Virginis Mariae de Monte Carmelo. Ed. Daniel a Virgine Maria. 4 parts in 2 vols. Antwerp, 1680.

Staring, A., ed. "Four Bulls of Innocent IV: A Critical Edition." *Carmelus* 27 (1980), 273–85.

———. *Medieval Carmelite Heritage: Reflections on the Early Nature of the Order.* Textus et studia historia Carmelitana 16. Rome: Institutum Carmelitanum, 1989.

Statuta capitulorum generalium ordinis Cisterciensis, 1116–1786. Ed. J.-M. Canivez. 2 vols. Louvain: Bibliothèque de la Revue d'histoire ecclésiastique, 1933–41.

Le synaxaire arabe-jacobite (rédaction copte). Ed. and trans. René Basset. *PO* 1, fasc. 3, Paris, 1907; *PO* 3, fasc. 3, Paris, 1909; *PO* 11, fasc. 5, Paris, 1915; *PO* 16, fasc. 2, Paris, 1922; *PO* 17, fasc. 3, Paris, 1923; *PO* 20, fasc. 5, Paris, 1929.

Le synaxaire arménien de Ter Israel. Ed. and trans. G. Bayan. *PO* 5, fasc. 3, Paris, 1910; *PO* 6, fasc. 2, Paris, 1911; *PO* 15, fasc. 3, Paris, 1927; *PO* 16, fasc. 1, Paris, 1922; *PO* 18, fasc. 1, Paris, 1924; *PO* 19, fasc. 1, Paris, 1926; *PO* 21, fascs. 1–6, Paris, 1930.

Le synaxaire éthiopien. Ed. and trans. René Basset et al. *PO* 1, fasc. 5, Paris, 1907; *PO* 7, fasc. 3, Paris, 1911; *PO* 9, fasc. 4, Paris, 1913; *PO* 15, fasc. 5, Paris, 1927.

Synodicon Orientale, ou recueil de synodes Nestoriens. Ed. J.-B. Chabot. Paris: Bibliothèque Nationale, 1902.

Theoderici libellus de locis sanctis editus circa A.D. 1172. Ed. T. Tobler. Saint Gall, 1865.

Theodoret of Cyrrhus. *Histoire des moines de Syrie.* Ed. and trans. Pierre Canivet and Alice Levoy-Molinghen. Paris: Editions du Cerf, 1977.

———. *Religiosa historia. PG* 82:1279–498.

Vita di Antonio, antico versione anonima latina. Ed. G.J.M. Bartelink. N.p: Fondazione Lorenzo Valla, 1974.

Vita Sancti Gualbert Abbatis. AASS (July) 3:343–453.

Vita Stephani Obazinensis. Ed. and trans. M. Aubrun. Clermont-Ferrand: Institut d'études du Massif Central, 1970.

Voyages faits en Terre-Sainte par Thietmar en 1217 et par Burchard de Strasbourg en 1175, 1189, ou 1225. Ed. J. de St. Genois. Brussels, 1851.

Walter the Chancellor. *Bella Antiochena, 1115–1122.* Ed. H. Hagenmeyer. Heidelberg, 1896.

Wilkinson, J., ed. *Jerusalem Pilgrimage, 1099–1185.* London: Hakluyt Society, 1988.

Willelmi Tyrensis Archiepiscopi Chronicon. Ed. R.B.C. Huygens. *CCCM* 63 and 63A. Turnhout, 1986.

Wulfric of Haselbury by John, Abbot of Ford. Ed. M. Bell. Somerset Record Society 47. London, 1933.

Secondary Sources

Alishan, A. M. *Sissouan ou l'Arméno-Cilicie: Description géographique et historique.* Venice, 1899.

Anastos, M. V. "Some Aspects of Byzantine Influence on Latin Thought." In *Twelfth-Century Europe and the Foundations of Modern Society,* ed. M. Clagett, G. Post, and R. Reynolds. Madison: Wisconsin University Press, 1961.

Atiya, Aziz. *A History of Eastern Christianity.* London: Methuen, 1968.

Auberger, J.-B. *L'unanimité cistercienne primitive: Myth ou realité?* Cîteaux studia et documenta 3. Achel: Admin. de Cîteaux, 1986.

Bagatti, Bellamino. "Relatio de excavationibus archeologicis in Monte Carmelo." *Acta ordinis Carmelitarum Discalceatorum* 3 (1958), 277–88; 6 (1961), 66–70; 7 (1962), 127–30.

Baker, D. "Crossroads and Crises in the Religious Life of the Late Eleventh Century." In *The Church in Town and Countryside,* ed. D. Baker, 137–48, Studies in Church History 16 (Oxford: Blackwell, 1979).

Baker, D., ed. *The Orthodox Churches and the West.* Studies in Church History 13. Oxford: Blackwell, 1976.

Baldwin, M. W. *Raymond III of Tripoli and the Fall of Jerusalem.* Princeton: Princeton University Press, 1936.

Berlière, Ursmer. "Les anciens monastères bénédictins de Terre-Sainte." *Revue Bénédictine* 5 (1888), 437–46, 502–12, 546–62.

Bligny, Bernard. *Saint Bruno.* Rennes: Universitaire Ouest-France, 1984.

Bouchard, Constance. *Holy Entrepreneurs.* Ithaca: Cornell University Press, 1991.

———. *Sword, Miter, and Cloister: Nobility and the Church in Burgundy, 980–1198.* Ithaca: Cornell University Press, 1987.

Burkitt, F. C. "Christian Palestinian Literature." *Journal of Theological Studies* 2 (1901), 174–85.

Cahen, C. *Orient et Occident au temps des croisades.* Paris: Variorum Reprints, 1983.

———. *La Syrie du nord à l'époque des croisades et la principauté franque d'Antioch.* Paris: P. Geunther, 1940.

———. *Turcobyzantia et Oriens christianus.* London: Aubier Montaigne, 1974.

Campbell, Mary B. *The Witness and the Other World.* Ithaca: Cornell University Press, 1988.

Cerulli, E., ed. *Etiopi in Palestina: Storia della comunità etiopica di Gerusalemme.* 2 vols. Rome: Librario dello Stato, 1943–47.

Chalandon, F. *Les Comnènes: Jean II Comnène (1118–43) et Manuel I Comnène (1143–80).* 2 vols. Paris: Alphonse Picard, 1912.

Charon, C. "Le rite byzantin et la liturgie chrysostomiene dans les patriarcats melkites." *Studi e richerche intorno a S. Giovanni Crisostomo.* Rome: n.p., 1907.

Chitty, D. J. "Two Monasteries in the Wilderness of Judaea." *Palestine Exploration Fund Quarterly Statement 1928,* 134–52.

Cicconetti, Carlo. *La regola del Carmelo.* Rome: Institutum Carmelitanum, 1973.

Clark, J.P.H. "Thomas Maldon, O.Carm., a Cambridge Theologian of the Fourteenth Century." *Carmelus* 29 (1982), 193–235.

Classen, P. "Das Conzil von Konstantinopel 1166 und die Lateiner." *Byzantinische Zeitschrift* 48 (1955), 339–68.

Clay, Rotha Mary. *The Hermits and Anchorites of England.* London: Methuen, 1914.

Constable, Giles. *Monks, Hermits, and Crusaders in Medieval Europe*. London: Variorum Reprints, 1988.

Constable, Giles, and J. Kritzeck, eds. *Petrus Venerabilis, 1156–1956: Studies and Texts Commemorating the Eighth Centenary of His Death*. Studia Anselmiana 40. Rome, 1956.

Cottineau, L.-H. *Répértoire topo-bibliographique des abbayes et prieurés*. Mâcon: Protat, 1935–37.

Crowfoot, J. W. "The Churches at Bosra and Samaria-Sebaste." In *British School of Archaeology Supplementary Papers* 4 (London), 1937.

Darrouzès, J. "Les documents byzantins du XIIe siècle sur le primauté romaine." *Revue des Etudes Byzantines* 23 (1965), 42–88.

Dondaine, A. "Hugues Etherien et Léon Toscan." *Archives d'histoire doctrinale et littéraire du Moyen Age* 27 (1952), 67–134.

Dorèsse, J. "Monastères coptes aux environs d'Armant en Thébaide." *Analecta Bollandiana* 67 (1949), 327–60.

———. "Saints coptes de Haute-Egypte." *Journal Asiatique* 236 (1948), 247–70.

Dupront, Alphonse. "La spiritualité des croisés et des pèlerins d'après les sources de la première croisade." *Pellegrinaggi e culto dei santi in Europa fino alla Ia crociata*. Todi: Centro di studi sulla spiritualità medievale, 1963.

Edbury, P. W., ed. *Crusade and Settlement*. Cardiff: Cardiff University Press, 1985.

Egan, K. J. "Dating English Carmelite Foundations." *Carmelus* 23 (1976), 96–118.

———. "An Essay Toward the Historiography of the Origins of the Carmelite Province in England." *Carmelus* 19 (1972), 67–100.

———. "The Establishment and Early Development of the Carmelite Order in England." Ph.D. thesis, Cambridge University, 1965.

———. "Medieval Carmelite Houses: England and Wales." *Carmelus* 16 (1969), 142–226.

Enlart, Camille. *Les monuments des croisés dans le Royaume de Jérusalem: Architecture réligieuse et civile*. 2 vols. Paris: P. Geuthner, 1925–28.

L'eremitismo in Occidente nei secoli XI e XII. Miscellanea del Centro di Studi Medioevali 4. Milan, 1965.

Every, George. "Syrian Christians in Palestine in the Middle Ages." *Eastern Churches Quarterly* 6 (1945–46).

Fairfield, L. P. *John Bale: Mythmaker for the English Reformation*. West Lafayette, Ind.: Purdue University Press, 1976.

Folda, Jaroslav, ed. *Crusader Art in the Twelfth Century*. BAR International Series 152. Oxford: British School of Archaeology in Jerusalem, 1982.

Friedman, Elias. *The Latin Hermits of Mount Carmel: A Study in Carmelite Origins*. Rome: Teresianum, 1979.

———. "The Medieval Abbey of St. Margaret of Mount Carmel." *Ephemerides Carmeliticae* 22 (1971), 295–348.

———. "Nicola Calciuri, O.Carm. (d. 1466), a Genuine Witness to the Carmelite Monastery in Wadi 'Ain as-siah?" *Carmelus* 32 (1985), 60–73.

Galatariotou, Catia. *The Making of a Saint: The Life, Times, and Sanctification of Neophytus the Recluse*. Cambridge: Cambridge University Press, 1991.

Gougaud, Louis. *Ermits et reclus: Etudes sur d'anciennes formes de vie réligieuse*. Vienne: Abbaye Saint-Martin de Liguge, 1928.

Graf, G. *Geschichte der christlichen arabischen Literatur*. Vol. 1. Studi e Testi 118. Vatican City, 1944.

Hamilton, Bernard. "The Armenian Church and the Papacy at the Time of the Crusades." *Eastern Churches Review* 10 (1978), 61–87.

———. "The Cistercians in the Crusader States." In *One yet Two: Monastic Tradition East and West*, ed. M. B. Pennington, 405–22. Cistercian Studies 26. Kalamazoo, Mich., 1976.

———. *The Latin Church in the Crusader States: The Secular Church*. London: Variorum Publications, 1980.

———. "Re-building Zion: The Holy Places of Jerusalem in the Twelfth Century." In *Renaissance and Renewal in Christian History*. Ed. D. Baker, 105–16. Studies in Church History 14 (Oxford: Blackwell, 1977).

Hamilton, Bernard, with P. A. McNulty. "Orientale lumen et magistra latinitatis: Greek Influences on Western Monasticism, 900–1100." *Le millénaire de Mont Athos, 963–1963: Etudes et mélanges* 1 (1963), 181–216.

Hill, Rosalind. "Pure Air and Portentous Heresy." In *The Orthodox Church and the West*. Ed. D. Baker. Studies in Church History 13 (Oxford: Blackwell, 1976), 135–40.

Hirschfeld, Y. *The Judaean Desert Monasteries in the Byzantine Period*. New Haven: Yale University Press, 1992.

Hunt, E. D. *Holy Land Pilgrimage in the Later Roman Empire, 312–460*. Oxford: Clarendon Press, 1982.

Hunt, Lucy-Anne. "Art and Colonialism: The Mosaics of the Church of the Nativity in Bethlehem (1169) and the Problem of Crusader Art." *Dumbarton Oaks Papers* 45 (1991), 69–85.

Hussey, J. M. *The Orthodox Church in the Byzantine Empire*. Oxford: Clarendon Press, 1986.

Janauschek, L. *Originum Cisterciensum*. Vol 1. Vienna, 1877.

Janin, R. *Les églises orientales et les rites orientaux*. New ed. Paris: Letouzey & Are, 1955.

Jotischky, Andrew. "Gerard of Nazareth, John Bale, and the Origins of the Carmelite Order." *Journal of Ecclesiastical History* 46 (1995).

———. "Manuel I Comnenus and the Reunion of the Churches: The Evidence of the Conciliar Mosaics in Bethlehem." *Levant* 26 (1994), 207–23.

Kedar, B. Z. "Gerard of Nazareth, a Neglected Twelfth-Century Writer of the Latin East: A Contribution to the Intellectual History of the Crusader States." *Dumbarton Oaks Papers* 37 (1983), 55–77.

Kedar, B. Z., et al., eds. *Outremer: Studies Presented to Joshua Prawer*. Jerusalem: Yad Izhak Ben-Zvi Institute, 1982.

Knowles, David. *The Religious Houses of Medieval England*. London: Sheed & Ward, 1940.

Knowles, David, and R. Neville Hadcock. *Medieval Religious Houses: England and Wales*. London: Longman, 1971.

Kopp, Clemens. *Elias und Christendum auf dem Karmel*. Collectanea Hierosolymitana 3. Paderborn, 1929.

Labande, E.-R. "Eléments d'une enquète sur les conditions de déplacement du pèlerin aux Xe–XIe siècles." *Pellegrinaggi e culto dei santi in Europa fino alla Ia crociata*. Todi: Centro di studi sulla spiritualità medievale, 1963.

Lackner, Bede. *The Eleventh-Century Background of Cîteaux*. Washington, D.C.: Cistercian Publications, 1972.

Lallement, L. J. (Jean le Solitaire). *Aux sources de la tradition du Carmel*. Paris: Beauchesne, 1953.

La Monte, J. L. "To What Extent Was the Byzantine Empire the Suzerain of the Latin Crusading States?" *Byzantion* 7 (1932), 253–64.

Leclercq, Jean. "La crise du monachisme aux XIe et XIIe siècles." *Bullettino dell' Istituto storico Italiano per il medio evo* 70 (1958), 19–41.

———. *Etudes sur le vocabulaire monastique du moyen âge*. Studia Anselmiana, fasc. 48. Rome, 1961.

———. "Monachisme et pérégrination." *Studia Monastica* 3 (1961), 33–52.

———. "Pierre le Vénerable et l'érétisme clunisien." *Studia Anselmiana* 40 (1956), 99–103.

———. *Saint Pierre Damien: Ermite et homme d'église*. Rome: Edizioni di Storia e Letteratura, 1960.

Lekai, Louis. *The Cistercians*. Kent, Ohio: Kent State University Press, 1977.

Levanon, Yosef. *The Jewish Travellers in the Twelfth Century*. Lanham, Md.: University Press of America, 1980.

Lewis, Bernard, and P. M. Holt, eds. *Historians of the Middle East*. Oxford: Oxford University Press, 1962.

Leyser, Henrietta. *Hermits and the New Monasticism*. New York: St. Martin's Press, 1984.

Magdalino, Paul. *The Empire of Manuel I Komnenos, 1143–1180*. Cambridge: Cambridge University Press, 1993.

Marie-Joseph du Sacre-Coeur. "La topographie sacrée du Mont Carmel en Palestine, et la chronologie de l'Ordre, aux XIIe et XIIIe siècles." *Etudes Carmélitaines* 3 (1913), 139–54.

Martin, J.-P. "Les premiers princes croisés et les Jacobites de Jérusalem." *Journal Asiatique* 12 (1888), 13 (1889).

Mas Latrie, L. de. *Histoire de l'Ile de Chypre sous le règne de la maison de Lusignan*. 3 vols. Paris, 1852–61.

Mayer, H. E. *Bistümer, Kloster, und Stifte in Königsreich Jerusalem*. Schriften der *MGH* 26. Stuttgart, 1977.

———. "Latins, Muslims, and Greeks in the Latin Kingdom of Jerusalem." *History* 63 (1978), 175–92.

Mayr-Harting, H. "Functions of a Twelfth-Century Recluse, Wulfric of Haselbury." *History* 60 (1975), 337–52.

Morin, G. "Rainaud l'ermite et Yves de Chartres: Un épisode de la crise du cénobitisme aux XIe–XIIe siècles." *Revue Bénédictine* 40 (1928), 99–115.

Murphy, Roland. "The Figure of Elias in the Old Testament." *Carmelus* 15 (1968), 230–38.

Nicholson, R. L. *Jocelyn III and the Fall of the Crusader States, 1134–99*. Leiden: E. J. Brill, 1973.

Palmer, A. N. "The History of the Syrian Orthodox in Jerusalem." *Oriens Christianus* 75 (1991), 16–43; and 76 (1992), 74–94.

Pena, I., P. Castellana, and R. Fernandez. *Les reclus Syriens*. Studium Biblicum Franciscanum 23. Milan, 1980.

Petit, François. *Norbert et l'origine des Prémontrés*. Paris: Editions du Cerf, 1984.

Phipps, Colin. "Romuald, Model Hermit: Eremitical Theory in St. Peter Damian's Vita Beati Romualdi, chapters 16–27." In *Hermits, Monks, and the Ascetic Tradition*. Ed. W. J. Shiels. Studies in Church History 22. Oxford: Basil Blackwell, 1985.

Prawer, Joshua. *Crusader Institutions*. Oxford: Oxford University Press, 1980.

———. *Histoire du royaume latin de Jérusalem.* 2 vols. Paris: Editions du CNRS, 1969–70.

———. *The History of the Jews in the Latin Kingdom of Jerusalem.* Oxford: Clarendon Press, 1988.

———. "Jerusalem in the Christian and Jewish Perspectives of the Early Middle Ages." *Gli Ebrei nell'alto medioevo.* Settimane di studi 26. Spoleto: Centro Italiano di Studi Sull'Alto Medioevo, 1980, 739–95.

Rey, E. *Les colonies franques de Syrie aux XIIe et XIIIe siècles.* Paris, 1883.

———. *Les familles d'Outremer de Du Cange.* Paris, 1869.

Riant, P. "Eclaircissements sur quelques points de l'histoire de l'église de Bethléem." *Revue de l'Orient Latin* 1 (1893), 140–60, 381–412, 475–525.

———. *Etudes sur l'histoire de l'église de Bethléem.* 2 vols. Genoa, 1889; Paris, 1896.

Richard, Jean. *Le comté de Tripoli sous la dynastie toulousaine.* Paris: P. Guethner, 1945.

———. *Orient et Occident au Moyen Age: Contacts et Rélations XIIe–XIVe siècles.* London: Variorum Reprints, 1976.

———. *Le royaume latin de Jérusalem.* Paris: Presses Universitaires de France, 1953.

Riley-Smith, J. S. *The Feudal Nobility and the Kingdom of Jerusalem, 1174–1277.* London: Macmillan, 1973.

———. *The Knights of St. John in Jerusalem and Cyprus, c. 1050–1310.* London: Macmillan, 1967.

Röhricht, R. *Geschichte des Königsreichs Jerusalem, 1100–1291.* Innsbruck, 1898.

Rose, R. B. "Church Union Plans in the Crusader Kingdom: An Account of a Visit by the Greek Patriarch Leontius to the Holy Land, A.D. 1177–78." *Catholic Historical Review* 73 (1987), 371–90.

Runciman, Sir Steven. "The Byzantine 'Protectorate' in the Holy Land in the Eleventh Century." *Byzantion* 18 (1948), 207–15.

Sauget, J.-M. *Premières recherches sur l'origine et les charactéristiques des synaxaires melkites.* Brussels: Société des Bollandistes, 1969.

Setton, K., gen. ed. *History of the Crusades.* 2d ed. Madison: University of Wisconsin Press, 1969– .

   M. L. Baldwin, ed., *The First Hundred Years.*
   R. L. Wolff and H. W. Hazard, eds., *The Later Crusades, 1189–1311.*
   H. W. Hazard, ed., *The Art and Architecture of the Crusader States.*
   N. P. Zacour and H. W. Hazard, eds., *The Impact of the Crusades on the Near East.*

Sivan, Emmanuel. "Le caractère sacré de Jérusalem dans l'Islam aux XIIe–XIIIe siècles." *Studia Islamica* 27 (1967), 149–82.

Stern, H. "Les représentations des conciles dans l'église de la Nativité à Bethléem." *Byzantion* 11 (1936), 101–52; *Byzantion* 13 (1938): 415–59.

Sumption, Jonathan. *Pilgrimage: An Image of Medieval Religion.* London: Faber & Faber, 1975.

Tibble, Steven. *Monarchy and Lordships in the Latin Kingdom of Jerusalem.* Oxford: Clarendon Press, 1989.

Tobler, Titus. *Zwei Bucher topographie von Jerusalem und seinem Umgebungen.* 2 vols. Berlin, 1853–54.

Tuan, Yi-Fu. "Geopiety: A Theme in Man's Attachment to Nature and Place." In *Geographies of the Mind,* ed. D. Lowenthal and M. J. Bowden. Oxford: Oxford University Press, 1976, 11–41.

Van Engen, John. "The 'Crisis of Monasticism' Reconsidered: Benedictine Monasticism in the Years 1050–1150." *Speculum* 61 (1986), 269–304.

——. *Rupert of Deutz*. Berkeley and Los Angeles: University of California Press, 1983.

Vincent, H., and F. M. Abel. *Bethléem, le sanctuaire de la Nativité*. Paris: n.p., 1914.

——. *Jérusalem, recherches de topographie, d'archéologie et d'histoire*. 3 vols. Paris: n.p., 1912–26.

Vogel, Cyrille. "Le pèlerinage pénitentiel." *Pellegrinaggi e culto dei santi in Europa fino alla Ia crociata*. Todi: Centro di studi sulla spiritualita medievale, 1963.

Voobus, Arthur. *A History of Asceticism in the Syrian Orient*. CSCO Subsidia 14–15. Louvain, 1958.

Wanroij, M. van. "Elijah, Example of the Solitary and Contemplative Life." *Carmelus* 16 (1969), 251–63.

Weitzmann, Kurt. "Loca Sancta and the Representational Arts of Palestine." *Dumbarton Oaks Papers* 28 (1974), 33–55.

Wessels, G. "Epistola S. Cyrilli III prioris generalis et historia antiqua Ordinis nostri." *Analecta ordinis Carmelitarum* 3 (1914), 267–86.

White, Lynn T., Jr. *Latin Monasticism in Norman Sicily*. Cambridge, Mass.: Medieval Academy of America, 1938.

Wilken, Robert. *The Land Called Holy*. New Haven: Yale University Press, 1992.

Wright, John Kirtland. *The Geographical Lore in the Time of the Crusades*. New York: American Geographical Society, 1925.

——. *Human Nature in Geography*. Cambridge, Mass.: Harvard University Press, 1966.

Index